Daniel Rynhold is Assistant Professor of Modern Jewish Philosophy at Bernard Revel Graduate School of Jewish Studies, Yeshiva University, New York. He has held teaching positions at King's College London and the London School of Jewish Studies, and is the author of a previous book entitled *Two Models of Jewish Philosophy: Justifying One's Practices* (2005).

INTERNATIONAL LIBRARY OF HISTORICAL STUDIES

See www.ibtauris.com/ILHS for a full list of titles

AN INTRODUCTION TO
MEDIEVAL JEWISH PHILOSOPHY

DANIEL RYNHOLD

I.B. TAURIS

LONDON · NEW YORK

Published in 2009 by I.B.Tauris & Co. Ltd
6 Salem Road, London W2 4BU
175 Fifth Avenue, New York NY 10010
www.ibtauris.com

Distributed in the United States and Canada Exclusively by Palgrave Macmillan,
175 Fifth Avenue, New York NY 10010

International Library of Historical Studies, vol. 57

ISBN   978 1 84511 748 1 (Pb)
        978 1 84511 747 4 (Hb)

A full CIP record for this book is available from the British Library
A full CIP record for this book is available from the Library of Congress
Library of Congress catalog card: available

Typeset in Ehrhardt by Dexter Haven Associates Ltd, London
Printed and bound in Great Britain by CPI Antony Rowe, Chippenham

For Sharon

Contents

Preface

I was first taught medieval Jewish philosophy by someone called Avram Stein during a 'gap year' spent in Israel. I was immediately enthralled, and having applied to read Natural Sciences at university, within two weeks of my return to the UK I had changed to a philosophy degree and never – well, rarely – looked back.

Though it informed everything we were being taught, what grabbed my interest back then was not the history of medieval Jewish philosophy or detailed analysis of its sources. It was simply the arguments and concepts, whether valid or not, with which these thinkers dealt, and their daring, as I saw it at the time, in pushing the envelope of what I had thought Jewish thinkers could think. This introduction is similarly intended to draw beginners in through an approach that is more philosophical than historical, initiating readers into the discipline by introducing some of its main thinkers and arguments. It is first and foremost a philosophical introduction to medieval Jewish thought.

As a result, this book is neither original nor an exhaustive scholarly account of all the thinkers, arguments and sources of medieval Jewish philosophy. There are many excellent (and longer) books that cover that material in depth. Instead this is a highly selective work that is entirely parasitic on the detailed historical and philosophical scholarship that it necessarily leaves well in the background in order to engage as wide a readership as possible. But rather than being a parasite that destroys its host, I hope that this book might encourage some of its readers to engage with the texts and scholarship on which it is based. Reading this book is not a substitute for that sort of detailed study, but an entry level work that attempts to explain basic ideas and arguments as straightforwardly as possible, hopefully without overly compromising the integrity of the material. Philosophy is not easy, and even an introductory work requires some concentration from its readers, but the book is intended to be accessible to any reader willing to put in that minimum of effort. It should be suitable for undergraduates taking courses in Religious or Jewish Studies with no philosophical background, or undergraduates in philosophy with no background in Judaism wanting a window onto this particular area of philosophical endeavour. But it is also written for those who simply want to discover the world of medieval Jewish philosophy. For those who never look at another book on the subject, I hope it is genuinely interesting and informative. If it whets the appetite of some for further study, I hope they will look back at it fondly once they have outgrown it. These are its modest ambitions.

The book is progressive, with each chapter assuming that little extra knowledge afforded by previous chapters. Chapters are split into numbered (and titled) sections, which are subsequently referenced in the text in bold type, e.g., **4.2** refers to chapter 4, section 2. For ease of reading, footnotes have been kept to an absolute minimum, but an annotated further reading section at the end of each chapter lists books used in writing the chapter and others that will further develop your study of the topic.

There are, as ever, a host of people to thank. Heartfelt gratitude goes to Professor Menachem Kellner of Haifa University for his encouragement and immense scholarly generosity in reading drafts of every chapter, at times while sheltering from Katyusha rockets in Haifa. Never has the claim that I am fully responsible for any remaining errors been truer. I hope above all else that Menachem can read this final version in peace. Professor David Hillel Ruben has been a fount of advice and support throughout my career so far, from his comments on this manuscript, to his years supervising my doctorate. I always try to tailor my writing to his high standards of philosophical acuity. Again any failure to do so is entirely down to me. I am also very grateful to Alex Wright of I.B. Tauris, whose patience and understanding as I continually pushed back my deadline is much appreciated.

Over the years, this material has been discussed in many different educational settings and I would like to thank all the students who have wittingly or unwittingly contributed to this final formulation. I would, however, like to single out for special mention the students and friends from Borehamwood synagogue that for over two years made up my 'Wednesday night group'. Especial thanks to Sharon and Mark Sacofsky who hosted the group every week, and Jackie and David Graham for helpful comments on some early chapters. The writing of the book itself was started during a sabbatical from the department of Theology and Religious Studies of King's College, London, and completed during my first year in New York at Yeshiva University, where I have enjoyed the tutelage and encouragement of the now retired dean of the Bernard Revel Graduate School, Professor Arthur Hyman.

My greatest debt is always to my family. Firstly to my parents, David and Valerie Rynhold, a constant source of love and inspiration, and I hope that I have kept my promise to dad that he would have an easier time with this introductory book than he had with my first more specialised publication. Also to my parents in law, Betty and Dudley Saul, whose unstinting generosity and support never ceases to amaze me. To my children Zack, Chloe, Aimee and Phoebe, because they are my greatest joy, because they were so excited about being mentioned in my previous book that Chloe asked if they could be mentioned in this one too, and because Phoebe wasn't born last time around. But mostly to Sharon, who is always there for me, even though I have forced her halfway around the world and she has to put up with me locking myself away and dealing with this abstruse material while she keeps the family going. Finally I want to acknowledge and thank Avram Stein, my teacher all those years ago who is ultimately the reason that I am doing this. I dedicate the book to Sharon, though, who would like to have a word with him.

ABBREVIATIONS AND TRANSLATIONS

The following is the list of translations cited frequently in this book, together with the abbreviations used to refer to them in the text:

Aristotle

Translations of Aristotle's works are taken from Jonathan Barnes, *The Complete Works of Aristotle: The Revised Oxford Translation*, 2 vols. References to individual works are by book, chapter and Bekker reference. Bekker references are to page numbers, column letters and line numbers in the standard edition of the Greek text and are used universally by Aristotle scholars. So *Physics*, II. 3, 194b18–19 would refer to Book II, chapter 3, Bekker reference 194b18–19 of Aristotle's *Physics*.

Saadia Gaon

Emunot: Book of Beliefs and Opinions (*Emunot ve-De'ot*), trans. S. Rosenblatt (New Haven, Conn.: Yale University Press, 1948). References are by book, chapter and page number in this translation; e.g. (*Emunot*, III: 7, 158) refers to Book III, chapter 7, page 158.

Moses Maimonides

Guide: The Guide of the Perplexed trans. Shlomo Pines, 2 vols (Chicago: University of Chicago Press, 1963). References are to part, chapter and page number in this translation. Translations from the *Mishneh Torah* are based on *Mishneh Torah: The Book of Knowledge*, trans. Moses Hyamson (Jerusalem: Feldheim, 1974).

Judah Halevi

Kuzari: The Kuzari, trans. H. Hirschfield (New York: Schocken Books, 1964). References are by book, paragraph and page number in this translation.

Levi Gersonides

Wars: The Wars of the Lord (*Milhamot Adonai*), 3 vols, trans. Seymour Feldman (Philadelphia, PA: Jewish Publication Society, 1984, 1987 and 1998). References are by book, chapter and page number in this translation.

Hasdai Crescas

Light: Light of the Lord (*Or Adonai*). There is no complete English translation of this work. Translations have been taken from the following: 1) J. David Bleich (ed.), *With Perfect Faith: The Foundations of Jewish Belief* (New York: Ktav, 1983), abbreviated as Bleich, *WPF*. The Crescas excerpts are translated by Seymour Feldman. 2) Warren Zev Harvey, 'Hasdai Crescas's Critique of the Theory of the Acquired Intellect', PhD dissertation, Columbia University, 1973. Abbreviated as Harvey, *HCC*.

References are by book, part, chapter and page number in the relevant translation; e.g. (*Light*, II: 5, 2, 475) refers to Book II, part 5, chapter 2, page 475.

Preface

NOTE

1   References to the *Babylonian Talmud* and Maimonides' *Mishneh Torah* are to the standard editions. References to the *Babylonian Talmud* take the form *b* followed by name of the tractate and folio number.

Introduction

What is Medieval Jewish Philosophy?

When people ask 'What is philosophy?', as they often do to those who study the subject, it can be embarrassingly difficult to give an answer. A famous twentieth-century British philosopher, G. E. Moore, is said to have replied by gesturing at his bookshelves saying 'It's what all those are about,' which is probably as good a place to start as any. Simply diving in and studying some of the likely occupiers of Moore's shelves – Plato's *Republic*, Descartes' *Meditations* and Hume's *Enquiry Concerning Human Understanding* – is probably far more helpful than immediately embarking on abstract definitions of philosophy.

What then of Jewish philosophy? Given that Jewish philosophy is a subsection of philosophy as whole, and any serious student of the former will eventually need to be at home with much of Western philosophy in order to make head or tail of its Jewish counterpart, it is unlikely to be much easier to define. One could, of course, be a Jewish G. E. Moore and point to another bookshelf containing Saadia Gaon's *Book of Beliefs and Opinions*, Maimonides' *Guide of the Perplexed* and Franz Rosenzweig's *Star of Redemption*. But the question arises as to what grounds one has for putting Maimonides and Rosenzweig on the one shelf and Plato and Descartes on the other (not to mention the argument over where Spinoza should go). So what are the shelving criteria? What distinguishes *Jewish* philosophy from philosophy? It cannot simply be that it is philosophy that is written by Jews, for Moore's 'Plato shelf' would have plenty of books written by philosophers who happen to be Jewish but are not doing Jewish philosophy. Nobody of sound mind and politics would think of calling Einstein's general theory of relativity Jewish science just because Einstein was Jewish. So, it is often argued, there must be something about the content of Jewish philosophy that marks it out as Jewish. The question is – what?

The answer is not as clear as one might imagine. Indeed, there are those who would respond to our question by arguing that there *cannot* be any such thing as Jewish philosophy. Even with regard to a book viewed by many as the most important work in the history of Jewish philosophy, Maimonides' *The Guide of the Perplexed*, Leo Strauss famously writes

> that it is not a philosophic book – a book written by a philosopher for philosophers – but a Jewish book: a book written by a Jew for Jews. *Its first premise is the old Jewish premise that being a Jew and being a philosopher are two incompatible things.*[1] (Emphasis added)

Now this is certainly not an uncontroversial view of the *Guide*. But the fact that a serious Maimonidean scholar can doubt that the *Guide* is a work of Jewish philosophy, and doubt the very possibility of there being such a thing, might lead one to wonder what exactly we take Jewish philosophy to be.

Philosophy, however one eventually defines it, has often been taken to be an enterprise that searches for objective, universal truths that are available in principle to all rational enquirers. Philosophers, on this conception, wish to understand how things really are, independently of how we think they are. I might, for example, believe that God exists or that humans have an immortal soul. But why should I expect the world to match those beliefs? Philosophers would want to show whether or not these beliefs are objectively true; they are looking for objective truths about the universe that are independent of personal opinion. Moreover, if either of those is shown to be objectively true, then they have universal application. They are not just true for certain groups. If we take Judaism, however, we find a particular religion shaped by a particular normative system set out in a book – the Torah – intended for a specific nation. And within this contrast lies the problem.

When talking of Jewish philosophy, the philosophical nature of the project implies a search for universal truths, yet its Jewish subject matter seems to be specific to Jews and thus contrary to this universal nature of philosophy. And that is basically the predicament that has led some thinkers to question whether there can be such a thing as Jewish philosophy any more than there can be Jewish science or Jewish mathematics. If Einstein's theory of general relativity is true, it is part of the corpus of scientific truth. Those Jews who have contributed to science or mathematics have done so to the disciplines as a whole, for these subjects cannot contain laws or concepts that are only applicable to certain ethnic groups and, it is claimed, the same is true of Jewish philosophy. Either, for example, God exists, or God does not. If there were conclusive proof of either, then that would make it a philosophical truth, one that is not limited to a single religious or cultural group. Even if it were conclusively proved by a Jew working in the field, it would not therefore be *Jewish* philosophy. So any Jewish 'content' must either contradict or be incidental to the philosophical nature of the enterprise.

We can see then that questions of definition are themselves complicated philosophical questions that one could spend a whole book discussing (and yes – people have). There are many questions one could level at the assumptions I have made in setting up the above problem, such as questioning the definition of philosophy with which we began. And yet, with regard to Jewish philosophy, the above dilemma is one with which many thinkers continue to grapple, though it is as much an issue for Christian philosophy, Muslim philosophy, or indeed any philosophy that is the province of a particular religious or cultural group. Many definitions have been suggested, from the view that Jewish philosophy is philosophical work created by Jews (and some who suggest this 'bite the bullet' when it comes to general philosophical works by thinkers of Jewish origin), to the view that it is simply philosophy that deals with the Jewish religion. I do not intend to deal further with abstract questions of definition here – interested readers can look to the further reading section. What we *can* do, however, is say something about the characteristics of *medieval* Jewish philosophy. But before so doing, one needs at least some basic acquaintance with the Jewish context in which our medieval thinkers were working.

1. JUDAISM: SOME NECESSARY PRELIMINARIES

The founding moment for the Jewish religion is the revelation of the Torah to Moses at Mount Sinai. Though the term can be used to refer to the whole corpus of Jewish belief and practice, Torah more narrowly defined is made up of the five books of Moses – *Bereshit* (Genesis), *Shemot* (Exodus),

Vayikra (Leviticus), *Bamidbar* (Numbers) and *Devarim* (Deuteronomy) –
and is believed in rabbinic tradition to have been given in its entirety to
Moses at Mount Sinai, probably sometime in the thirteenth century BCE[2]
(very approximately). The Torah is the first section of the Hebrew Bible,
known in Hebrew as the *Tanakh*, an acronym of the three works that make
it up – Torah (lit. instruction), *Nevi'im* (Prophets) and *Ketuvim* (Writings).
Very close to the makeup of what Christians call the Old Testament, though
not identical to it in every detail, the entire *Tanakh* constitutes Holy
Scripture for Jews. But the Torah, as the founding constitution of Judaism
and the original source of its laws, beliefs and history, is its most
authoritative and significant element.

Beginning with the creation of the world, through the stories of Adam
and Eve, Noah and the flood, and the patriarchs Abraham, Isaac and Jacob,
the Torah tells the story of the birth of the Jewish nation and religion
through the history and pre-history of the Israelites that, regardless of
historical accuracy, forms the collective memory of the Jewish people to
this day. For Judaism is not simply a religion. With the exception of
converts, Jews are born and not made. One is born into the Jewish nation,
a nation formed in the crucible of Egyptian slavery and subsequently
redeemed miraculously as commemorated in the annual spring festival of
Passover, or *Pesach*. But the Torah is not only the source of Jewish
peoplehood. It is also the source of the Jewish religion that begins with
the revelation at Sinai where this nation is chosen by God to be bound to
a covenant based around the concept of *mitzvah* (pl. *mitzvot*) or divine
commandment. According to Rabbi Simlai in the *Babylonian Talmud*
(*bMakkot* 23b), and subsequently rabbinic tradition more generally, the
Torah contains 613 of these *mitzvot*. Believed to be the divine and eternal
commands of God that enable the Jew to live a life of holiness, many of
them remain at the very foundation of Jewish practice to this day, such as
the basis of the laws of the Sabbath and the dietary laws. The Torah then
proceeds from the Sinaitic revelation to weave together legal and narrative
elements until it ends with the death of Moses, as the people stand poised
to conquer the land of Canaan that God promised to Abraham.

Obviously the traditional view of the Torah as a work dictated to
Moses at Mount Sinai is at odds with modern academic views of the
authorship and genesis of the Bible. While the academic view is shared by
most of the progressive branches of contemporary Judaism, it is important
to understand that the internal perspective of medieval Judaism was based

on the traditional assumption of the absolute divinity of the text, a view that is upheld in Orthodox Judaism to this day. For the Jews of medieval times, the Torah was the literal and unmediated word of God that records the history and beliefs of the Jewish people and sets out the eternal *mitzvot* that form their obligations.

Yet relatively speaking, the historical information and legislation provided by the Torah are sparse. Thus, for example, Abraham is first introduced to us as a fully-grown married man. The complexity of the Sabbath laws and the central rituals of particular festivals, such as the structured night-time meal at *Pesach* known as the *seder*, cannot be gleaned simply by reading the Torah. In addition there is little if anything that would pass for systematic philosophy or theology. The Judaism of today, therefore, or even that of medieval times, looks very different from the religion of the Torah. This is because according to rabbinic tradition, alongside the 'Written Torah' of Moses there existed an 'Oral Torah', also believed to have been dictated to Moses and subsequently passed down orally through the generations in an unbroken chain of transmission. This Oral Torah, expressly *not* to be committed to writing, was the means by which the biblical system could be developed and applied to the changing historical circumstances in which the Jewish nation would find itself.

Again, while within the rabbinic tradition there are many statements that emphasise the divine origin of this Oral Torah, and a minority of literalist believers accept the idea expressed in the *Palestinian Talmud* that everything was dictated to Moses at Sinai, including what the rabbis would say in the future (Tractate *Peah*, 2: 4), it is evident from the rabbinic texts themselves that the system developed through human interpretation via accepted methods of development. Those responsible for this became the recognised transmitters and interpreters of Torah (widely defined) – the rabbis. This class of scholars emerged as a self-conscious and organised scholarly body only after the destruction of the Temple (70 CE), though they traced their origins back to the Pharisees of the Second Temple Period, who were the first to follow non-written oral traditions in their biblical interpretation.

Through interpretation and elaboration of the Torah and its *mitzvot*, the Oral Torah develops a rich and complex legal system, known as the *halakhah*, of which the biblical commandments were simply the first and most authoritative layer. Apart from the halakhic developments, the rabbis also engaged in more general theological reflection. Such multifaceted and often non-legal rabbinic exegesis was recorded in material collectively known as *aggadah* which includes biblical interpretation – *midrash* – and stories, legends and theological speculations. Eventually, committing this growing Oral Torah to writing became a necessity if the law was to be preserved from being forgotten through persecution, or split into myriad factions by opposing parties. And thus the rabbinic period, which spans the first six centuries CE, produced the second fundamental text of Judaism, the Talmud.

As the term is currently used, the Talmud is made up of two works. The first, the *Mishnah* (compiled in Palestine by R. Judah ha-Nasi circa 200) was a compilation of the Oral Torah up to that point. Though generally a halakhic work that presents statements of law and leaves aside detailed argumentation, the *Mishnah* was not a straightforward code of law and included competing opinions, leading to debates as to whether it was intended as a practical code or a legal study book. Either way, the *Mishnah* subsequently formed the basis of further detailed discussion in the rabbinic academies of Israel and Babylonia, the latter being one of the centres of diaspora Judaism since the destruction of the first Temple and subsequent Babylonian exile of 586 BCE. These discussions formed the basis of the Talmud, a title originally reserved solely for these later elaborations of the *Mishnah*. There were two versions of the Talmud, Palestinian and Babylonian, which recorded and reconstructed these further rabbinic debates. In contrast to the concise formulations of the *Mishnah*, the Talmud is a lengthy and complex work of argumentation and analysis that covers both halakhic and aggadic material.

With its long established rabbinic academies at Sura and Pumbeditha, Babylonia became the focal point of Jewish life and literature by the middle of the first millennium CE. As a result it was the *Babylonian Talmud*, redacted in the sixth century, which became *the* Talmud and the primary influence on Jewish life. With much of the biblical legislation regarding such matters as ritual purity and the sacrificial cult rendered obsolete by the destruction of the Temple, the Talmud's detailed elaboration of a now much developed rabbinic system of *halakhah* reflected a new reality, with, for example, its system of fixed daily prayer. And thus the original 613 *mitzvot* are expanded into a complex and all-encompassing behavioural system. Similarly, theological ideas almost entirely lacking in the *Tanakh* now enter into the aggadic discussions of the Talmud, with the appearance, for example, of so-called eschatological ('end of days') speculations on otherworldly and messianic redemption. So by the end of the sixth century the two most important books in Judaism, the *Tanakh* and the Talmud, are complete, with the latter in particular setting the template for the classical rabbinic form of Judaism that held sway until the nineteenth century. This rabbinic Judaism would be finally sealed and consolidated in the Geonic period (seventh–eleventh century approx.), so-called on account of the heads of the Babylonian academies of Sura and Pumbeditha – the *Geonim* (sing. *Gaon*) – during which the Talmud is seen as a closed canonical work.

The *Babylonian Talmud* attained an ascendancy and authority by the Geonic period that lasts to this day. From the legal perspective, it was seen as the ultimate basis for halakhic practice, and was at the root of an expanding post-Talmudic literature. Commentaries on the classic sources, codes of Jewish law, and responsa in which halakhic authorities appeal to Talmudic traditions and ancient cases in order to derive answers to new halakhic questions, all originated in the Geonic period and continue to be further developed by contemporary rabbinic figures. Today, however, different groupings vary widely in their understanding of what constitutes the correct form of continuity with rabbinic *halakhah* and the extent of its authority, with contemporary Orthodoxy most bound by the precedents set by the tradition.

All of the Geonic developments mentioned so far concern the halakhic system, reflecting the fact that Judaism is primarily a way of life rather than a theological or philosophical system. As we have noted, while the *Tanakh* could be said to provide much food for philosophical thought with its portrayal of God and humanity and more notably in its extended reflection on the problem of evil in the book of Job, one could hardly classify it as a philosophical work. The turn of the first century did produce Philo of Alexandria, the first Jewish thinker to confront Greek philosophy, but Philo's work led to a dead end as far as Jewish philosophy was concerned, forgotten by Judaism only to be preserved by the early Church fathers and much later reclaimed for Jewish philosophy. Thus, when the Talmud later presents arguments and certain standard argument forms, they are generally employed in the service of halakhic debate, not philosophical speculation. Again, there is certainly no lack of material that would elicit philosophical interest, but Talmudic *halakhah* is recognisably legal in a way that its *aggadah* is not recognisably philosophical, in the style, say, of an Aristotle or Augustine.

So with the closing of the Talmud, we have a highly developed and systematic halakhic system that governs Jewish life, with a far less systematic system of philosophical thought underpinning it. During the Geonic period, however, we find – Philo excepted – the first development of Jewish writing that we could classify as explicitly philosophical, and it is that development that interests us from here on.

2. MEDIEVAL JEWISH PHILOSOPHY: THE PROJECT

We have thus far been classifying historical periods from a narrowly Jewish perspective as biblical, rabbinic and Geonic. But through European eyes, even with the arguments between historians as to when exactly it begins, we are by now well into the medieval period. What interests us specifically, as the 'Golden Age' of medieval Jewish philosophy, begins in the ninth century, by which time Babylonia was part of the Islamic empire. Most Jews at this time were living under Islamic rule, and large numbers had abandoned their rural existence for city life, leading Jewish merchants to form commercial ties with their Islamic neighbours.

With Arabic becoming the dominant language of life and literature, Jews now had broader access to an Arabic civilisation that was showing a significant interest in Hellenistic philosophy and science. Most importantly for us, and indeed for Western civilisation, under the reign of the Abbasid caliph al-Ma'mun (813–33), we find the first phase of a major translation project. Based around Baghdad's *Bayt al-Hikma* (House of Wisdom) library, an enormous variety of Greek philosophical and scientific texts were translated into Arabic. This was followed in the tenth century by a second burst of translation activity, mainly from Syriac versions of the Greek originals, combined this time with the writing of original commentaries on Aristotle.

It was from the Jewish scholars working in this Arabic cultural context that medieval Jewish philosophy would emerge, as Jewish thinkers confronted similar questions to their Muslim counterparts. Indeed, the story of medieval Jewish philosophy, until the thirteenth-century shift to Christian Europe, runs so closely parallel to that of medieval Islamic philosophy that they are really two strands of a single story. Nonetheless, it is with the Jewish strand that we are concerned, and regardless of the problems we have noted with defining Jewish philosophy in general, there *is* a way of describing the shared project of these medieval Jewish philosophers.

Whether true or not of Jewish philosophy *per se*, a useful way of introducing us to medieval Jewish philosophy is found in Julius Guttmann's statement at the beginning of his classic work on Jewish philosophy:

> The Jewish people did not begin to philosophise because of an irresistible urge to do so. They received philosophy from outside, and the history of Jewish philosophy is the history of the successive absorptions of foreign ideas which were then transformed and analysed according to specific Jewish points of view.[3]

The basic idea is that medieval Jewish philosophy was generated by the clash between two opposing worldviews: the Jewish worldview and those of the external philosophical systems that emerged out of its engagement with Arabic culture. So we begin with two sets of truth claims about reality, and Jewish philosophy is somehow generated out of the conflicts that arise between them.

How might this work? Let us look at the assumptions required to generate Jewish philosophy out of this clash:

> i) Divine revelation as expressed in Jewish Scripture is a legitimate source of truth claims about God and the universe.

For our characterisation of medieval Jewish philosophy to get started, one has to accept that the texts of Judaism are presenting serious truth claims regarding philosophical questions, an assumption that is not universally accepted. In the nineteenth century Rabbi Samson Raphael Hirsch wrote that it was senseless 'to apply the term theology to the Torah... [O]f the inner essence of the Godhead and the supernatural we find in the Torah nothing at all.'[4] On such a view there could not be any conflict between the worldviews of the Torah and philosophy since the Torah does not for the most part offer us truth claims about God or a systematic worldview. The idea expressed in (i) though, is that Judaism's texts have plenty to say about topics such as the nature of God or the problem of creation from which we can generate propositions that together would make up a 'Jewish worldview'. So, for example, we could say that the Torah presents us with a God who creates the world and is then actively involved with his creation, a God who communicates with mankind, performs miracles, and rewards and punishes his creatures. Subsequent rabbinic discussions introduce further ideas, such as that of an afterlife in *Olam ha-ba* – 'The World to Come'. So we can find in the *Tanakh* and Talmud ideas that form the basis of truth claims that provide us with a 'traditional Jewish view'. And most importantly, given that these claims derive from God, we presume that they must be true.

> ii) Human reason, as expressed in philosophical systems, is a legitimate source of truth claims about God and the universe.

Revelation was not the only source of truth. The fruits of philosophical endeavour yield a rational path to truth independent of revelation, and the worldview so formed yields truth claims of its own. The most influential alternative worldview for the medieval Jewish philosophers was a version of Aristotle's philosophy as mediated by his medieval Arabic interpreters. That view is well expressed in the following passage taken from one of the classics of medieval Jewish philosophy that we will be introducing shortly – Judah Halevi's *Kuzari*.

Halevi presents the following picture as the view of 'the philosopher':

> There is no favour or dislike in [the nature of] God, because He is above desire and intention. A desire intimates a want in the person who feels it, and not till it is satisfied does he become (so to speak) complete. If it remains unfulfilled, he lacks completion. In a similar way He is, in the opinion of philosophers, above the knowledge of individuals, because the latter change with the times, whilst there is no change in God's knowledge. He therefore does not know thee, much less thy thoughts and actions, nor does he listen to thy prayers, or see thy movements. If philosophers say that He created you, they only use a metaphor, because He is the Cause of causes in the creation of all creatures, but not because this was His intention from the beginning. He never created man. For the world is without beginning, and there never arose a man otherwise than through one who came into existence before him, in whom were united forms, gifts, and characteristics inherited from father, mother, and other relations, besides the influences of climate, countries, foods and water, spheres, stars and constellations...
>
> In the perfect person a light of divine nature called Active Intellect is with him... This degree is the last and most longed for goal for the perfect man whose soul, after having been purified, has grasped the inward truths of all branches of science... Thus the soul of the perfect man and that Intellect become one... If thou hast reached such disposition of belief, be not concerned about the forms of thy humility or religion or worship, or the word or language or actions thou employest. Thou mayest even choose a religion in the way of humility, worship, and benediction, for the management of thy temperament, thy house, and [the people of thy] country, if they agree to it. Or fashion thy religion according to the laws of reason set up by

the philosophers, and strive after purity of soul. In fine, seek purity of heart in which way thou art able, provided thou hast acquired the sum total of knowledge in its real essence. (*Kuzari*, I: 1, 36–9)

Though presented here by Halevi as *the* philosophical worldview, different Jewish thinkers would grapple with different worldviews. Indeed, even this one is actually an amalgam of two schools of thought, as we will discover. But the problems should be immediately clear. For now that we have before us the Jewish worldview and the philosophical worldview, we find that:

iii) The two sources of truth apparently conflict.

The clashes between (i) and (ii) are clear and manifold. The God of Judaism is a God who creates the world and mankind. The God of the philosophers is the 'Cause of all causes' and 'never created man'. The God of Judaism speaks to man and is well aware of his every move, of which he either approves or disapproves with predictable consequences. The God of the philosophers neither communicates with us nor reacts to our actions, being unchanging and thus unaware of our behaviour and prayers. And the God of Judaism makes very specific demands of his people through the *mitzvot* that are at the very core of Judaism and the key to the 'World to Come'. The God of the philosophers, however, is not concerned with one's actions, but rather with how much philosophy one knows, and only through such knowledge will one gain the ultimate reward.

How is one to react to this clash of worldviews? What happens to the unquestioned religious certainties gained from one's religion when confronted with this alternative picture? One could of course simply dismiss Judaism as irrational superstition on account of its failure to meet the demands of reason. Alternatively, one might dismiss human rationality out of hand because it conflicts with the apparent word of God. But Maimonides shows how for one immersed in both cultures, neither of these was an option:

[H]e would remain in a state of perplexity and confusion as to whether he should follow his intellect, renounce what he knew concerning the terms in question, and consequently consider that he has renounced the foundations of the Law. Or he should hold fast to his understanding of these terms and not let himself be drawn on together with his intellect, rather turning his back on it and moving away from it, while at the same time perceiving that he had brought loss to himself and harm to his religion. He would be left with those

11

imaginary beliefs to which he owes his fear and difficulty and would not cease to suffer from heartache and great perplexity. (*Guide*, Introduction to the first part, 5–6)

If one is committed to both Judaism and reason, the conflict between the two must be resolved in a manner that will retain the integrity of both. One can neither dismiss religion, nor seek refuge in an 'Ostrich Judaism' by burying one's head in the sand when one's truth claims about God and the universe prove problematic. It is the attempt to negotiate some resolution to this conflict that is the crucial final step in producing Jewish philosophy:

iv) Since there can only be one truth, the conflict between the two sources is only apparent.

According to this assumption, medieval Jewish philosophy was born of the universalist premise that we discussed at the beginning of this introduction – that there can only be one truth. Surely there can only be one correct answer to the question regarding, for example, whether the world is created or eternal. And given that there can only be one answer, the appearance of conflict between the two worldviews must be just that – an appearance. So while it may appear as if the two worldviews cannot be reconciled, many Jewish philosophers attempted to argue that up to a point (and what precise point was a matter of great debate) there must be a way of resolving apparent conflicts.

The Jewish philosopher is therefore faced with a choice when confronted by a conflict:

(1) Resolve the conflict by upholding the Jewish view and showing the philosophical view to be somehow inadequate. In this way Judaism does not present a doctrine that is contrary to reason even when it is chosen at the expense of the philosophical worldview, for one rejects the philosophical view on philosophical grounds.

(2) Uphold the philosophical view and argue that the Jewish view is actually saying something rather different from what it appears to be saying. If one accepts the power and veracity of genuine philosophical argumentation and there are Jewish texts that, read literally, contradict its claims, the Jewish philosopher must reinterpret the texts in a non-literal fashion so that they can be seen to be making the same truth claims as the philosophical worldview. Thus, Jewish philosophers were often engaged in the philosophical interpretation of classical Jewish texts.

Even those who in many cases follow (2) will agree that reason has its limits and when these limits are reached we can rely on Judaism to fill in the gaps. In those areas where reason cannot prove the point either way, revelation can be accepted on authority in order to provide answers to supra-rational questions. But ultimately there can be no real conflict between the truths of Judaism and philosophy when either one of them is presenting a genuine truth.

Despite the above analysis, Jewish philosophy was not limited to purely religious questions. The philosophical foundations required to answer religious questions would draw Jewish philosophers into the study of other philosophical disciplines such as logic and epistemology (the theory of knowledge). So while Jewish philosophers might not have produced comprehensive metaphysical systems, they produced much more than philosophy of religion narrowly defined. The basic problem of medieval Jewish philosophy, however, remained how to negotiate the confrontation between external philosophies and the views that emerged from Judaism's canonical texts. And even then, as we will see, there were many different ways of going about negotiating the conflict, and differences between the thinkers were often quite fundamental. Many, like Judah Halevi, would be surprised that any Jewish thinker could contemplate integrating the type of philosophical view he had presented with Judaism. Yet integrate some did, and as a result Jewish philosophy has often been viewed with a degree of suspicion, especially among more conservative religionists who have always viewed it as a slightly controversial and marginal enterprise.

3. MEDIEVAL JEWISH PHILOSOPHY: THE CAST

So much then for the script – what about the cast? As noted earlier, this book is not intended to provide an exhaustive historical account of medieval Jewish philosophy. Thus, we will necessarily be working with a very selective group of thinkers who have been chosen mainly for their prominence in the study of Jewish philosophy and their accessibility to English-speaking readers. As things stand, these are the thinkers who form the main spine of any study of medieval Jewish philosophy and they do represent a broad enough spectrum to give readers a fair picture of the richness and variety of the subject. We will introduce each of the thinkers together with their main philosophical works and a word about the philosophical 'school' to which they are generally thought to belong. We will not be dealing with Jewish mysticism (or going into the argument over whether we should), which is not to deny its significance, but rather we side with those who would understand it as using methods other than those of philosophy.

i) Saadia Gaon

Most accounts of medieval Jewish philosophy begin with Saadia ben Joseph Al-Fayyumi (882–942) better known as Saadia Gaon. Saadia was born in Fayyum, Egypt, and would go on to become the head (Gaon) of the great Babylonian academy of Sura. Saadia combined great erudition – writing on science, grammar, *halakhah* and philosophy, and composing liturgical poems and biblical commentaries – with political and polemical activities. Politically, his most notable battle with David ben Zakkai, the political head of diaspora Jewry, or exilarch, led to his temporary (albeit lengthy) dismissal from the Suran Gaonate. His polemics were often reserved for the battle with the Karaites, a group of Jews who rejected the Oral Torah and thus the Judaism of the Talmud. The Karaites, who exist to this day, though they are numerically insignificant and have no impact on Judaism, were a significant threat to the rabbanite majority from Saadia's time up until the twelfth century, and his first work is directed against its founder, Anan.

Though not the first medieval Jewish philosopher, Saadia is often treated as the godfather of medieval Jewish philosophy on account of his *Kitāb al-Amānāt Wa-l- I'iqādāt*, translated into Hebrew as *Sefer Emunot ve-De'ot* and usually known in English as *The Book of Beliefs and Opinions*. As the first systematic account of Jewish thought, it became one of the most influential and important works of medieval Jewish theology and philosophy. Philosophically speaking the work is usually categorised as Jewish *kalam*.

Kalam is the term for a school of theology that arose in the eighth century to give a rational account of Islam. Its practitioners – the *mutakallimun* – are the butt of much Maimonidean invective for moulding their philosophical argumentation to pre-existing religious prejudices. They were thus very much apologetic theologians, in contrast to the *falasifa*, who saw themselves as pure philosophers engaged in rational speculation about the universe for its own sake. For *falasifa* such as al-Farabi (872–950) and Averroes (Ibn Rushd, 1126–98), religion approved the study of philosophy, which could take one beyond the surface of Scripture without compromising religious faith – or at least this was how they packaged matters for a sceptical public. But the *mutakallimun* saw such freethinking *falasifa* as a threat to religion and were instead devoted to drawing from a number of philosophical sources specifically to prove the theological views of their Scriptures. Saadia – certainly a kalamic thinker stylistically, with his tendency to exhaustively list opinions and arguments – proceeds similarly by starting with the view of Jewish Scripture and then showing how it can be rationally proven.

The two main *kalam* schools were the Ash'arites and the Mut'azilites. The latter, generally seen as the more rationalistic, was the prime influence on Saadia as can be seen from the very structure of *Emunot*. Known as 'the people of justice and unity', Mut'azilite's would begin their treatises with these central pillars of their thought – the idea of God's unity and then his justice. Similarly, after an introductory treatise on faith and reason in general, *Emunot* opens with a discussion on creation to establish the existence of God, followed by a treatise on God's attribute of unity, before moving on to topics related to God's justice.

Though arguments of the *kalam* are much in evidence, Saadia certainly does not slavishly follow their system, with one of his most significant departures from them being his rejection of atomism. This scientific view has the universe made up of tiny indivisible and indistinguishable atoms that God constantly destroys and recreates at each moment. These atoms have no properties as such, but are instead created at each instant with the specific properties that God wills. Indeed the structure of nature is entirely down to God's will at each moment. This means that atoms have no natural properties and that nature has no independent structure – there are no 'natural' laws governing the world. God's intervention is the only cause of what happens in the universe, a doctrine known as occasionalism.

Emunot is generally a rather eclectic work, as we will see in some of our discussions, and to some, Saadia's stature as a philosopher is less than his stature as a pioneer in the sophisticated systematisation of Jewish philosophy and theology. His influence, however, and that of *Emunot*, is undeniable.

ii) Isaac Israeli and Jewish Neoplatonism

One of the thinkers whose writings preceded those of Saadia was an older Egyptian contemporary of his, Isaac ben Solomon Israeli (850–932/55) who is known to have corresponded with Saadia. Like a number of medieval Jewish scholars, Israeli was a physician, and moved to Tunisia to serve al-Mahdi, the founder of the Fatimid Muslim dynasty that would (unsuccessfully) challenge the Abbasids for leadership of the Islamic world. Along with his medical writings, he composed a number of philosophical works in Arabic of which *The Book of Definitions, The Book of Substances, The Book on Spirit and Soul, The Book on the Elements* and *Chapters on the Elements*, survive in varying states of completion. Though less influential than Saadia and a far lesser figure in this book, the school of thought of which he is a representative is of immense importance. Along with the great philosopher-poet Solomon Ibn Gabirol (1021/2–1054/8, author of the *Fons Vitae – Fountain of Life*), he is the major representative of Jewish Neoplatonism, a philosophical current that would also influence the important eleventh-century pietist Bahya Ibn Paquda (c. 1050–c. 1156), author of *Hidāya 'ilā Farāid al-Qulūb*, best known by the title of its Hebrew translation *Sefer Hovot ha-Levavot* (*The Book of Direction to the Duties of the Heart*).

Medieval Neoplatonism was mainly based on the writings of two interpreters of Plato, Plotinus and Proclus. Plotinus' most famous work, *The Enneads*, was inherited by Jewish thinkers through an Arabic paraphrase of books 4–6 called the *Theology of Aristotle*, which for obvious reasons would lead to much confusion as to its author. Proclus' *Elements of Theology* was also transmitted in Arabic translation before being translated as the Latin *Liber de Causis*. As with Plotinus' *Theology of Aristotle*, the medievals attributed *Liber de Causis* to Aristotle.

The defining characteristic of Neoplatonism is its monism, that is, the belief that all of reality is one. Thus, Plotinus posited the existence of the One, or the Good, as the basic reality that transcends all existence and from which all else derives its varying levels of reality. Through a process known as emanation, a hierarchy of lower existents known as hypostases proceed from the One, though none of them are comparable to the One itself which is beyond knowledge and description, or ineffable. Moreover, all reality will eventually return to the One and be identified with it. One can clearly see the resonance this might have for a religious thinker with its talk of a transcendent existent which is somehow at the root of all reality and to which all other existents desire to return. And though we will not spend much time on the thought of the Jewish Neoplatonists in this book, we will often have cause to return to these ideas given their influence on the 'Aristotelianism' of the time.

iii) Judah Halevi

In a sense Judah Halevi is the most interesting and anomalous medieval Jewish philosopher. Indeed, classifying him as a philosopher would likely make him turn in his grave, for Halevi does not really fit into any of the medieval philosophical schools, neither *kalam*, nor Neoplatonist, nor Aristotelian. Instead, Halevi's central work, the *Kuzari*, constitutes a critique of the philosophical systems of the time. What qualifies it for study as part of the canon of medieval Jewish philosophy is its status as the thinking man's critique, so to speak, that itself reflects a philosophical perspective on the relationship between Judaism and philosophy.

Born in Toledo in Muslim Spain around 1075 and well educated in the Arabic context we have discussed, Halevi would become one of the greatest Hebrew poets in Jewish history. After the Christian conquest of Toledo he would move South to Andalusia and study at the school of one of the most important Talmudic codifiers, Isaac Alfasi. With the conquest of Andalusia by the Almoravid Islamic sect he spent much of his young life wandering between cities in Christian Spain before returning to Toledo where he would practice as a physician. In an attempt to effect the practical realisation of his philosophy through the commandment to live in the holyland, towards the end of his life Halevi set out on the journey to Israel. He certainly made it to Egypt in 1140, though it is less likely that, as legend has it, he reached the outskirts of Jerusalem only to be trampled to death by an Arab horseman with his ode to Zion – *Tziyon ha-lo Tish'ali* – on his lips.

At the mercy of Muslim and Christian conquests throughout his life, Halevi was caught between two religious superpowers struggling for political supremacy, a struggle in which Judaism was simply not a player. And thus Halevi, schooled in the ways of the philosophers, wrote his *al Kitāb Radd wa-'l-Dalīl fi'l-Dīn al-Dhalīl* – or *The Book of Refutation and Proof in Defence of the Despised Faith*, now relegated to the mere subtitle of the work that we know as the *Kuzari*. Originally written in Arabic as a response to Karaism, Halevi subsequently reworked it into the full philosophical and religious critique that we know today, and it was translated into Hebrew by Judah Ibn Tibbon as early as 1167.

The *Kuzari* is a fictional reconstruction of an actual historical event that took place between 786 and 809, during the reign of King Bulan of the Khazars, a Turkish people who at the time were sovereign over a considerable area, taking in the Volga basin and the Crimea. In his quest for a monotheistic religion the king engaged in dialogue with Muslim, Christian and Jewish scholars, leading to his conversion to Judaism and its establishment as the Khazar state religion. Halevi's work is a fictional reconstruction of these discussions, written in dialogue form. It opens with an account of a recurring dream that troubled the Khazar king, a priest of the pagan Khazar religion and well-versed in its rites and rituals. In this dream, an angel appears to him and states that while his religious intentions are worthy, his actions are not. As a result, the king decides to look into the various religious alternatives available to him, and speaks first, as we have seen above, with a philosopher, and then with a Muslim, a Christian and finally a Jewish sage.

The book is not intended as an even-handed critique of each religious alternative. After dismissing the three non-Jewish options within a matter of pages, the king continues to dialogue with the sage for four and half further books, converting at the beginning of book II. But the philosophy of Judaism and the critique of philosophy that he presents through this dialogue make for a fascinating piece of philosophical writing, taking in everything from the 'A' of Aristotelian physics that influenced Halevi in his youth, to the 'Z' of Zion that he strove to see before his death. Out of step with virtually all of the thinkers that we will be studying, Halevi is the perfect counterpoint to those who might uncritically accept the philosophical approaches of the age.

iv) Moses Maimonides

Probably the most important and most controversial of all the medieval Jewish philosophers, the towering shadow of Rabbi Moses ben Maimon (1138–1204) looms large over the entire field. From Maimonides onwards, all medieval Jewish philosophy would be by way of response to his work, whether positive or negative. He sets the syllabus for medieval Jewish philosophy that all others would follow.

Born in Cordoba in Andalusia, Maimonides was the son of a rabbinic judge. As with many of his contemporaries, his family was forced out of the land of their birth by the religious persecutions of the invading Islamic

Almohade sect and after a period wandering through Spain they settled in Fez, Morocco. The Almohades soon followed and thus Maimonides moved on, possibly passing through Israel briefly before settling in Fostat, Egypt. Originally a merchant in the family business, following the death of his brother David, Maimonides took up medicine and like Isaac Israeli served as a royal physician at the Palace of Saladin in Cairo.

Already a renowned rabbi on account of his immensely influential code of Jewish law the *Mishneh Torah* (1180) – to this day the most comprehensive such code in Jewish history – Maimonides' philosophical magnum opus, *Dalālat al-Hā'irīn*, the *Guide of the Perplexed* was completed in 1190. Written in Judeo-Arabic (Arabic in Hebrew letters) and translated during his lifetime by Samuel Ibn Tibbon as *Moreh ha-Nevukhim*, it would establish him as the foremost Jewish philosopher of his and any other age. He had already written a primer in philosophical logic, *Millot ha-Higgayon* (*Treatise on the Art of Logic*) and the *Commentary on the Mishnah*, which contained a number of philosophical introductions, most notably the introduction to Tractate *Avot* usually known as *Shemonah Perakim* (Eight Chapters) and the introduction to the tenth chapter of tractate *Sanhedrin* – the 'Introduction to *Perek Helek*'. The *Mishneh Torah* also contained much philosophical content, most notably in *Sefer ha-Madda* (*The Book of Knowledge*).

Maimonides is usually characterised as an Aristotelian and while this is certainly fair inasmuch as it correctly sets him apart from the thinkers we have so far discussed, his Arabic Aristotelianism unwittingly drew on sources other than Aristotle, most notably the aforementioned misattributed Neoplatonic works. Moreover, Maimonides was influenced by his great Islamic predecessors, most notably Al-Fārābi, Ibn Bājja (d. 1139), Averroes (Ibn Rushd) and Avicenna (Ibn Sina, 980–1037) with the former pair in particular incorporating significant Platonic elements into their thought that some scholars detect in Maimonides. When we use the term Aristotelian in this book we should bear in mind these qualifications. Nonetheless, for Maimonides, this hybrid Aristotelian structure was the towering achievement of human thought and one that Jewish thinkers had to take extremely seriously. Just *how* seriously is matter of great debate.

The *Guide*, though written in more prosaic style, is no less a literary construct than the *Kuzari* and is notoriously structured so as to throw the uninitiated off the scent. Maimonides was aware of the controversial nature of philosophy, and especially of some of the claims that he was going to make as a Jewish Aristotelian. He was also bound by the rabbinic prohibition (*Mishnah Hagigah* 2:1) on the public dissemination of *Ma'aseh Bereshit* (the *Account of the Beginning*) – the opening chapters of Genesis – and *Ma'aseh Merkavah* (*Account of the Chariot*) – the opening chapter of Ezekiel – which he identified with natural science and divine science (or metaphysics) respectively. Despite this religious requirement for discretion in revealing difficult philosophical truths, the necessity of passing on philosophical knowledge for Maimonides, lest it be forgotten, outweighed these requirements. He does, however, warn that the *Guide* is only suitable for those well versed in both Judaism and philosophy – 'It is not the purpose of this treatise to make its totality understandable to the vulgar or to beginners in philosophical speculation, nor to teach those who have engaged in…the legalistic study of the law' (*Guide*, Introduction, 5). Maimonides the philosopher appears at times to be an intellectual elitist.

Human nature being what it is though, and evidently no different eight hundred years ago, a simple warning to the masses not to read the work was never going to suffice, so Maimonides constructs the work so as to confuse those without the requisite philosophical background. As he tells us:

> If you wish to grasp the totality of what this Treatise contains…then you must connect its chapters one with another; and when reading a given chapter, your intention must be not only to understand the totality of the subject of that chapter, but also to grasp each word that occurs in it in the course of the speech, even if that word does not belong to the intention of that chapter. (*Guide*, Instruction with Respect to this Treatise, 15)

Taken literally, this would mean that one needs to read the whole book in order to understand any part of it, since one needs to connect every chapter in order to get to grips with its meaning. Moreover, Maimonides tells us that some words will appear out of place in certain chapters and this too needs to be understood. And if that were not difficult enough, the assault course that is Maimonides' *Guide* has one final surprise for the prying eyes and minds of the masses. Thus, Maimonides writes of the contradictions that find their way into the work. Of the seven reasons for literary contradiction that he lists, Maimonides says that two appear in the *Guide*. The first is a simple necessity of pedagogy. Much as someone doing a GCSE in Chemistry will learn certain things that are simplifications to the point of falsification in order to learn some of its more basic ideas, in setting out the basics Maimonides will sometimes say something that is not entirely correct about a certain matter, before 'contradicting' this later when he is writing at a more sophisticated level. But it is the seventh reason for contradiction that is the most famous, or infamous:

> In speaking about very obscure matters it is necessary to conceal some parts and to disclose others. Sometimes in the case of certain dicta this necessity requires that the discussion proceed on the basis of a certain premise, whereas in another place necessity requires that the discussion proceed on the basis of another premise contradicting the first one. In such cases the vulgar must in no way be aware of the contradiction; the author accordingly uses some device to conceal it by all means. (*Guide*, Introduction, 17)

Maimonides is here telling us that the book will contain contradictions that are expressly there to conceal certain matters from 'the vulgar'. While all of this should more than take care of the masses, the problem is that by now even the so-called experts are struggling. For before one even starts to think about its philosophical cogency, this battery of literary devices have led to an entire industry centred on what it is that Maimonides was actually saying. On the one hand there is the straightforward reading of what he writes – the exoteric reading of the book. But given what he says above, there is also an esoteric layer that is only revealed to those with the literary and philosophical subtlety to understand it. And since that view is hidden as unfit for public consumption, we need to look for the hints, clues and contradictions that will lead us this esoteric view and thus to the real Maimonides.

The problem here is that scholars differ over the degree and nature of Maimonides' esotericism as it relates to the extent to which he was or was not a thoroughgoing Aristotelian who held views that would be deemed religiously unacceptable and possibly incompatible with Judaism and indeed his own *Mishneh Torah*. And this means that when one proffers an interpretation of the *Guide*, there will be those who argue that that is just what Maimonides *wants* you to think, and suggesting that he truly believed the opposite of the view for which he has explicitly (and exoterically) argued.

It is impossible in a work of this nature not to engage with this problem to a degree. But while mention is often made of these esoteric possibilities, I have reserved detailed discussion of Maimonides' esotericism for the Appendix, where we will discuss his view of creation in the context of this exoteric/esoteric debate. I intend in the main body of the book, however, chiefly to concentrate on what Maimonides writes at the exoteric level since there is plenty there to awaken our philosophical interest; and doing so allows us to probe the arguments that he presents on either side of the debate anyway. Thus, should Maimonides actually side with the opposite view to that which he explicitly states, we might, philosophically speaking at least, know some of the reasons why. If we find that the arguments for his stated view are weak, those who wish to take it as evidence of some hidden esoteric agenda will have ample opportunity to investigate further through the additional readings.

v) Levi Gersonides

With Levi ben Gershon (1288–1344), our focus shifts from Muslim Spain and Egypt to Christian Europe, and initially to Southern France in particular. There, as a result of the Hebrew translations of Arabic philosophical texts by the Ibn Tibbon family, Jewish philosophy had become accessible to the Jewish middle class and far more widespread, a fact that would eventually lead to controversy. Though little is known of Gersonides' life, we know that he spent it in the Jewish scholarly hotbed that was medieval Provence and like so many of the thinkers we are studying, he was a master of many different subjects. Gersonides was expert in many branches of secular learning, most notably mathematics and astronomy – sponsorship for some of his astronomical work came from the Christian clergy, and he has the distinction of being the only rabbi with a crater on the moon named after him. The commentaries that he wrote on the vast majority of the books of the *Tanakh* are studied to this day and his commentary to the Torah in particular reflects the philosophical ideas that he presented in his best known philosophical work *Milhamot Adonai – Wars of the Lord*, which is the first of the works we have encountered to have been written in Hebrew.

Though also generally classed as an Aristotelian, Gersonides' Aristotelianism is mediated by the Islamic thinker Averroes, on whom Gersonides also wrote commentaries that are still in manuscript form. And it is out of his critical engagement with Averroes on the one hand, and Maimonides on the other, that Gersonides finds his own philosophical voice. Often seen as the more radical 'Aristotelian' of the two – and therefore also not immune to accusations of heresy – in *Wars* Gersonides often explicitly responds to Maimonides. In fact, *Wars* began as a work on the question of the creation of the universe, but was expanded into six treatises when Gersonides realised that other significant philosophical topics needed to be dealt with before one could tackle the creation question satisfactorily. He therefore devotes a treatise to each of the following: the immortality of the soul; dreams, divination and prophecy; divine knowledge; divine providence; the structure of the universe; and creation. Though he cannot be compared to Maimonides in terms of subsequent influence, from a purely philosophical perspective there are those who would place him above his more illustrious predecessor.

vi) Hasdai Crescas

Though his student Joseph Albo was better known, Hasdai Crescas (1340–1410/11), born in Barcelona, is usually seen as the last great thinker of the medieval period. He studied under one of the great names in Talmudic scholarship, Rabbenu Nissim Gerondi, and forged his reputation at Saragossa in Aragon through the rebuilding of a community ravaged by the anti-Jewish riots of 1391. His major Hebrew philosophical treatise *Or Adonai* (*Light of the Lord*) is the philosophical section of what was intended to be a two-part work including a halakhic critique of Maimonides called *Ner Mitzvah*. His polemical *Refutation of the Christian Principles* and his *Sermon on the Passover* also survive.

Crescas' work is particularly significant for its philosophical critique of the Aristotelian scheme that had held sway for so long. A philosophical critic of Maimonides who presents much of his work in explicit opposition to the *Guide* – the first book of *Light* is a chapter by chapter treatment of the twenty-five Aristotelian propositions that Maimonides lists in the introduction to Part II of the *Guide* – Crescas took issue with the philosophical and religious conclusions of the Aristotelians. His influences differed markedly from those of his Islamic inclined predecessors in Jewish philosophy, and his position in Saragossa brought him into close contact with Christian scholars. His lack of influence among his Jewish contemporaries is matched by his prescience for modern philosophy and science, with his anti-Aristotelianism a notable precursor of the fall of Aristotelian science that was to come. As Aviezer Ravitzky has written he was a man out of time, 'too early' for the critique of Aristotle to be seen as anything other than unconvincing, yet 'too late' in the medieval flowering of Jewish philosophy to establish a lasting Jewish philosophical 'school' in opposition to the now established Maimonidean 'orthodoxy'.[5] An influence on Spinoza,

Crescas is thus an appropriate person with whom to complete our survey of the thinkers and books that will be most prominent in what follows.

4. A FINAL NOTE

With an idea of the most important philosophical streams adapted by our medieval Jewish thinkers, though we should reiterate that terms such as 'Aristotelian' or 'Neoplatonic' hide a multitude of other influences, in what follows, each chapter will deal with a particular subject or cluster of subjects and weave a philosophical discussion around them from a selection of the thinkers and books we have discussed. There will be times when the issues raised might be of contemporary philosophical concern, and times when that is not the case. On the whole, that question is incidental to the purpose of this book. In taking a conceptual approach, we are attempting to highlight issues of philosophical interest to the medieval thinkers of the time, and by looking at the structure and content of the arguments in their own terms we hope to awaken interest in the field of medieval Jewish philosophy.

NOTES

1 Leo Strauss, 'How to Begin to Study *The Guide of the Perplexed*', in *Guide*, xi–lvi. Quotation from xiv.
2 BCE stands for 'Before the Common Era', as opposed to CE which means 'The Common Era'. These abbreviations are often used in Jewish scholarship as more neutral substitutes for BC and AD respectively.
3 Julius Guttmann, *Philosophies of Judaism*, trans. David W. Silverman (New York: Holt, Rinehart and Winston, 1964), 3.
4 Quoted in I. Grunfeld's introduction to Samson Raphael Hirsch, *Horeb*, trans. I. Grunfeld (London: Soncino Press, 1962), xlix.
5 Aviezer Ravitzky, *Crescas' Sermon on the Passover and Studies in his Philosophy* [Hebrew] (Jerusalem: Israel Academy of Sciences and Humanities, 1988), v.

FURTHER READING

There are a number of works on Jewish philosophy in general and medieval Jewish philosophy in particular that contain comprehensive accounts of the thinkers discussed in this chapter and far more besides. Though some are starting to show their age, they are all useful. The main works are:

Isaac Husik, *A History of Medieval Jewish Philosophy* (Philadelphia: Jewish Publication Society, 1958)

Julius Guttmann, *Philosophies of Judaism*, trans. David W. Silverman (New York: Holt, Rinehart and Winston, 1964)

Colette Sirat, *A History of Jewish Philosophy in the Middle Ages* (Cambridge: Cambridge University Press, 1985)

Daniel H. Frank and Oliver Leaman (eds), (1) *Routledge History of Jewish Philosophy* (London: Routledge, 1997) and (2) *The Cambridge Companion to Medieval Jewish Philosophy* (Cambridge: Cambridge University Press, 2003) Of these, Sirat is the most comprehensive and the Cambridge Companion contains some more sophisticated material that is probably best appreciated after having looked at one of the other books.

The section on Judaism provides a basic minimum to facilitate understanding of this book and there are many more comprehensive introductions to Judaism. One of the shortest and best of those specifically aimed at students is Jeremy Rosen, *Understanding Judaism* (Edinburgh: Dunedin Academic Press, 2003).

Less of a student textbook to be studied and more of a sophisticated conceptual introduction that is also a very good read is Jonathan Sacks, *Radical Then, Radical Now* (London: Harper Collins, 2000).

For an exhaustive list of suggested definitions of Jewish philosophy, see Ze'ev Levy, *Between Yafeth and Shem: On the Relationship Between Jewish and General Philosophy* (New York: Peter Lang, 1987), chapter 19.

For a good introduction to the problems in defining Jewish philosophy see Menachem Kellner, 'Is Contemporary Jewish Philosophy Possible? – No', in Norbert Samuelson, ed., *Studies in Jewish Philosophy: Collected Essays of the Academy for Jewish Philosophy, 1980–1985* (Lanham, Md.: University Press of America, 1987), 17–28.

The introduction to David Hartman, *Maimonides: Torah and Philosophic Quest* (Philadelphia: Jewish Publication Society, 1976) is also a highly accessible discussion of the nature of Jewish philosophy.

For discussion of the nature of medieval Jewish philosophy specifically, see Aviezer Ravitzky, 'On the Study of Medieval Jewish Philosophy', *History and Faith: Studies in Jewish Philosophy* (Amsterdam: J. C. Gieben, 1996).

1

The Existence of God

One would probably expect medieval Jewish thinkers to have spent an inordinate amount of time formulating and refining their arguments for the existence of God. After all, the existence of God is surely the most fundamental idea of all for monotheistic faiths. Yet arguments for the existence of God take up rather less space in the medieval Jewish philosophical corpus than most of the other topics we will be addressing. In a sense this is precisely *because* it is so fundamental. Anyone claiming to work within the Jewish tradition, and for that matter anyone working in any medieval religious setting, could not embark on a free and open enquiry into the question of whether God exists since the answer had to be a resounding 'yes'.

One might think that medieval Jewish thinkers would be similarly constrained on all issues. Surely, for example, they could not deny the creation of the world or God's foreknowledge any more than they could God's existence. As we will discover, that is not quite the case. Our thinkers arrived at quite different conclusions regarding these issues, admittedly not all equally acceptable to their coreligionists either then or now, but all capable of being integrated into a recognisably Jewish framework. On the existence of God though, there could be but one answer with little room for manoeuvre.

This might explain why arguments for the existence of God are not central in the syllabus of medieval Jewish thought, or indeed in the history of Jewish philosophy. Quite why this should be the case in the Jewish tradition, given the formidable Christian tradition of developing such arguments, and despite the foregoing considerations applying as much to Christian thinkers, is an interesting question that is beyond our scope. But regardless of the relative weight of reflection on this problem in different traditions, the real issue for all of those working in a religious milieu was whether or not one could rationally *prove* that God exists. Our purpose in looking at the arguments propounded by our thinkers then, is not to discover whether or not they believed that God exists, but to discover the manner in which they argued for the foregone conclusion, since the way they arrived at the answer reflected fundamentally different approaches to philosophy and indeed religion. It is with this in mind that we will focus in this chapter on the very different arguments found in Moses Maimonides' *Guide* and Judah Halevi's *Kuzari*.

1. MAIMONIDES' METHOD AND A WORD ABOUT ARGUMENTS

Before presenting his detailed arguments for the existence of God in the opening chapter of Part II of the *Guide*, at *Guide*, I: 71, Maimonides sets out his 'method', establishing a number of important parameters for approaching the question of God's existence, attention to which will allow us to introduce some key terms:

> The world cannot but be either eternal or created in time. If it is created in time, it undoubtedly has a creator who created it in time. For it is a first intelligible that what has appeared at a certain moment in time has not created itself in time and that its creator is other than itself. Accordingly the creator who created the world in time is the deity. If, however, the world is eternal, it follows necessarily because of this and that proof that there is an existent other than all the bodies to be found in the world; an existent who is not a body and not a force in a body and who is one, permanent and sempiternal; who has no cause and whose becoming subject to change is impossible. Accordingly he is a deity. Thus it has become manifest to you that the proofs for the existence and the oneness of the deity and of His not being a body ought to be procured from the starting point afforded by the supposition of the eternity of the world, for in this way the demonstration will be perfect, both if the world is eternal and if it is created in time. For this reason you will always find that whenever, in what I have written in the books of jurisprudence, I ... start upon establishing the existence of the deity, I establish it by discourses that adopt the way of the doctrine of the eternity

of the world. The reason is not that I believe in the eternity of the world, but that I wish to establish in our belief the existence of God, may He be exalted, through a demonstrative method as to which there is no disagreement in any respect. (*Guide*, I: 71, 181–2)

Let us begin at the end, with the notion of a demonstrative method. As mentioned in the dedicatory letter that introduces the *Guide*, the art of logic was one of many disciplines that any prospective student of the book would have to master. This art of logic was effectively discovered by Aristotle and though it has moved on considerably since then, it remains to this day the study of reasoning or arguments (in the technical rather than everyday sense of the word), with a view to establishing what constitutes a good or bad form of reasoning and why.

In his earliest work, the *Treatise on the Art of Logic*,[1] Maimonides follows in the steps of Aristotle in categorising the different forms of logical argument: demonstrative, dialectical, sophistical and, in a post-Aristotelian addition, poetic (or rhetorical). The first category – demonstrative argument – is the only form of argument that yields conclusions that are certain and unquestionable, yielding what Aristotle termed *episteme* or scientific knowledge. Though the term 'scientific' as used here does not carry with it all the modern baggage we associate with the term, it is, nonetheless, an honorific title bestowed by Aristotle on knowledge that has been proven to a degree of absolute certainty, and it is such demonstrative assurance that Maimonides requires of arguments for God's existence.

But what exactly *is* a demonstrative argument? A demonstration is a type of deductively valid argument. The time-honoured example of a deductively valid argument that graces many an introductory work is:

Socrates is a man
All men are mortal
Therefore Socrates is mortal

The discovery of this structure of argument – two premises followed by a conclusion – was termed the syllogism and was Aristotle's great founding contribution to the discipline of formal logic. And the point about *this* syllogism is that the truth of its premises *guarantees* the truth of its conclusion. Logically speaking, it cannot be that Socrates is a man and that all men are mortal yet Socrates is not mortal. A person who accepts the two premises must accept the conclusion, unless he is being somehow irrational.

Not all arguments are of this type. More often than not, the everyday 'arguments' that people advance might be more or less persuasive, or give better or worse reasons for the desired conclusions. Within logic itself the distinction is drawn between deductive arguments and inductive arguments, the equally popular example of the latter being:

The sun has risen every day so far, therefore the sun will rise tomorrow.

The premise here gives us good reason to think that the conclusion is true and the vast majority of people certainly believe in the truth of its conclusion. But accepting the premise and denying the conclusion would not be logically inconsistent (even if it might be a little pessimistic). Inductive arguments, though extremely important, are not valid in the same way that deductive arguments are. The truth of the premises of an inductive argument does not guarantee the truth of its conclusion. In contrast, if deductive arguments begin with true premises then they necessarily and mechanically churn out true conclusions.

However, our example of a deduction would not actually constitute a demonstrative syllogism for Aristotle. A demonstration begins from premises that must conform to a number of conditions. We need not discuss them in detail here, but we can say that these premises must be more than simply true – they must be absolutely certain. So, for example, we would have a demonstration when the initial premises of a deductive syllogism are what Aristotle or Maimonides would term first intelligibles, i.e. premises that are self-evidently true. According to Aristotle, these self-evident first principles are acquired by a method that, confusingly for us, he also termed induction. This induction, however, is the repeated perception of particulars through the intellectual faculty of *nous*, often translated as intuition. Among Maimonides' examples of such premises is that the whole is greater than the part (*Treatise*, VIII, 47). Such premises simply strike us as being true without requiring a demonstration.

But a demonstration needn't always start from first intelligibles. One can take the conclusion of a prior demonstration from first intelligibles, and use that as the premise of a further argument. If one argues deductively from *that* premise to a further conclusion, we have another demonstration that yields a conclusion that is also true and certain – the truth and certainty is preserved by the deductive procedure – and from that conclusion we can in turn deduce further conclusions. This builds up a 'stack' of demonstrations that can form an entire demonstrative system. The classic example of a demonstrative system that is always cited is Euclidean geometry, where one begins from a few true and certain simple axioms as primary truths (our first intelligibles) and derives all the other theorems of the system by deductive proofs. The point about such structures is that at each stage one will arrive at true and certain conclusions. They are logically impregnable edifices that yield conclusions regarding which, as Maimonides notes 'there is no tug of war and no refusal to accept a thing proven' (*Guide*, I: 31, 66).

Though this is the ultimate form of argument and the ultimate form of knowledge, medieval philosophers also dealt with areas in which demonstration was not possible. Thus, the second tier in the logical hierarchy is that of dialectical argument. These arguments proceed from premises that only have the status of generally accepted opinions. Maimonides' examples of such premises, taken from the moral sphere, are that 'uncovering the privy parts is ugly, that compensating a benefactor generously is beautiful' (*Treatise*, VIII, 47). There are further weaker forms of argument that we need not dwell upon here, but what is important is that as far as Maimonides is concerned, his proofs for the existence of God fall into the exalted category of demonstrative arguments.

The example of the existence of God is actually rather complicated in relation to the notion of demonstration given the starting points he utilises in the quote cited previously. Maimonides begins from the possible opinions regarding the origins of the universe: either it was created or it is eternal. The problem is that Maimonides does not believe that we can demonstrate either creation or eternity and thus we are not beginning from true and certain premises, and could not *demonstrate* the existence of God on the basis of such premises. However, he manages to manoeuvre around this problem as follows. As Maimonides sees it, if the world was created then one has effectively proven the existence of God by default – on the assumption that the world was created, it is but one obvious step to the existence of God, its creator. In Maimonides' opinion, this step constitutes a first intelligible. If, however, the universe was not created, there is a little more work to be done. While 'the world was created so it must have a creator' is self-evident, 'the world is eternal so there must be a God' is rather less so. There is a bigger argumentative gap to be bridged if we start from the eternity of the universe, so it is necessary to formulate an *argument* for the existence of God that begins from this premise.

Maimonides here protests that he does not himself believe in the eternity of the world, though as we shall see in the Appendix there are those who argue that he doth protest too much. But with regards to our current topic, the point is that Maimonides does not believe that one can demonstrate either creation or eternity. The arguments to these conclusions are dialectical in Maimonides' opinion. So to establish God's existence on the basis of just one of the two options would leave the proof on shaky foundations. What he must do in order to put God's existence on a firm footing is show how it follows from either of the alternatives. In order to establish the existence of God beyond all rational doubt, we must demonstrate that he exists whatever your starting point. And if we can say that we have proved the existence of God regardless of whether the world was created or eternal we will have an absolute proof of his existence. And since we know that God exists if the world was created, what Maimonides needs to do is construct an argument based on the eternity of the world.

2. MAIMONIDES' ARGUMENTS

Maimonides presents four arguments for the existence of God in *Guide*, II: 1, though Hasdai Crescas actually finds six proofs in the opening two chapters of Part II of the *Guide* and includes the 'method' encountered in the previous section among them as a 'disjunctive' proof of the existence of God. Nevertheless, as we have seen, that disjunctive proof itself depends on successfully proving the existence of God on the basis of the eternity of the world, and that is what Maimonides sets out to do in *Guide*, II: 1. Maimonides begins, however, by listing the twenty-five propositions of Aristotelian physics and metaphysics necessary for understanding the arguments he is to present, some of which we will encounter in our study and all of which he believes to have been demonstrated by Aristotle, though he is not about to repeat those demonstrations in the *Guide*. He also adds a twenty-sixth premise – the eternity of the world – which, as we know, he does not believe to have been demonstrated though he is willing to accept it here for the sake of the argument.

Maimonides' insistence on beginning from purely philosophical premises in his pursuit of the argument marks him out in his own mind from the *mutakallimun*. The *kalam*, in his opinion, began from theologically loaded premises, 'that would be useful to them with regard to their belief' (*Guide*, I: 71, 177), and, more to the point, premises that do not conform either to the empirical evidence or to the prevailing, and to Maimonides' mind, demonstrated truth of Aristotelian science. In proving the existence of God, even though one already knows the theologically loaded answer, what matters is that one can reach it through purely rational means.

The arguments themselves are all versions of the cosmological argument for the existence of God, a family of arguments in which one appeals to a general feature of the world, or even its very existence, and argues that in accounting for that feature (or the world's existence), in the final analysis we arrive at a God who must ultimately be responsible for it. We will focus on the third of Maimonides' arguments, an argument that he acknowledges as tracing back to Aristotle, though in his more immediate historical and cultural vicinity Avicenna had given it its most developed formulation.

Maimonides begins from the obvious empirical observation that we perceive that things exist. But there are three possibilities regarding the nature of their existence with respect to what is termed 'generation and corruption' – one of the fundamental explanatory concepts in the framework of underlying concepts and beliefs (or worldview) through which the classical and medieval thinkers understood the world:

> 1) None of them are subject to generation and corruption i.e. none of them have come into existence and none of them will cease to exist. All of these things are eternal.
>
> 2) All of them are subject to generation and corruption i.e. all of these things have come into existence at some point and all of them will at some point cease to exist.
>
> 3) Some of them are subject to generation and corruption (which, on the strength of (1) and (2) should be self-explanatory, though as we will see that might be an unfortunate turn of phrase).

The first alternative is dismissed as 'absurd' – we all know that there are existents that come into existence and cease to exist through the evidence of our senses. More interesting (and complicated) is his dismissal of the second alternative, which runs as follows:

> If every existent falls under generation and corruption, then all the existents and every one of them have a possibility of undergoing corruption. Now it is indubitable, as you know, that what is possible with regard to a species must necessarily come about. Thus it follows necessarily that they, I mean all existents, will necessarily undergo corruption. Now if all of them have undergone corruption, it would be impossible that anything exists, for there would remain no one who would bring anything into existence. Hence it

follows necessarily that there would be no existent thing at all. Now we perceive things that are existent. In fact we ourselves are existent. Hence it follows necessarily, according to this speculation that if there are, as we perceive, existents subject to generation and corruption, there must be a certain existent that is not subject to generation and corruption. Now in this existent that is not subject to generation and corruption, there is no possibility of corruption at all; rather, its existence is necessary, not possible. (*Guide*, II: 1, 247)

Let's take this argument step by step:

(1) If every existent falls under generation and corruption, then all the existents and every one of them have a possibility of undergoing corruption.

Maimonides begins by exploring the logical implications of accepting option two, taking the hypothetical assumption that every existent is subject to generation and corruption to obviously imply the possibility of every one of them becoming corrupted.

(2) Now it is indubitable, as you know, that what is possible with regard to a species must necessarily come about. Thus it follows necessarily that they, I mean all existents, will necessarily undergo corruption.

Having accepted that all things are possibly subject to generation and corruption, the next step is to accept the rather more controversial idea that what is possible for a species must actually happen, meaning in this case that because each individual existent can cease to exist, at some point all these existents must cease to exist at *one and the same time*.

Why the insistence that this must happen? This depends on an important assumption and an important Aristotelian principle, though Maimonides does not state them explicitly here. The assumption, which we have been expecting, is premise twenty-six – the eternity of the world, or more specifically, in medieval philosophic terms, that the world is eternal *a parte ante* (its past is eternal). The principle that arises out of this, known as the principle of plenitude in Aristotelian thought, is that the possible must at some point be realised.

The basic idea is that given infinite time, all possible permutations and combinations of existence will at some point be realised, including the one where every existent ceases to exist and, more importantly, does so at one and the same time so that there is, quite literally, nothing. This principle has subsequently been popularly expressed in variations on the arresting image of a monkey typing the complete works of Shakespeare. The serious point, a subject of mathematical proofs by probability theorists, is that over infinite time, as more and more permutations of letters are produced, the likelihood of the monkey reproducing Shakespeare's work increases. Given infinite time (and of course an immortal monkey) it becomes inevitable. Along these lines, Maimonides argues that if all existents are subject to generation and corruption, there will be a time where nothing exists. More importantly, once we have this 'state of nothingness', it would be impossible for anything to exist since there is nothing in existence out of which things can be generated, all of which he expresses as follows:

> (3) Now if all of them have undergone corruption, it would be impossible that anything exists, for there would remain no one who would bring anything into existence. Hence it follows necessarily that there would be no existent thing at all.

Thus according to Maimonides nothing would exist. But having argued for this hypothetical scenario, Maimonides goes on to argue that it is in fact impossible:

> (4) Now we perceive things that are existent. In fact we ourselves are existent. Hence it follows necessarily, according to this speculation that if there are, as we perceive, existents subject to generation and corruption, there must be a certain existent that is not subject to generation and corruption.

We know that things currently exist, not least (indeed according to one of the founders of modern philosophy Rene Descartes, most of all) ourselves. Yet – and this is the intuitive question that drives the cosmological argument – why should that be? How, to put it in classic terms, do we account for the fact that there is something rather than nothing?

Maimonides argues that if there were a time when literally nothing existed, we wouldn't be here. Since things cannot just spontaneously create themselves – 'For it is a first intelligible that what has appeared at a certain moment in time has not created itself in time' (*Guide*, I: 71, 181) – then had all existents been corrupted, that would have been the end of existents (and existence). There would have been nothing 'then' and nothing 'now'. But since we are here, that simply cannot have happened. And if it did not happen, something must have stopped it happening, meaning that there must have been something that could not go out of existence, something not subject to generation and corruption, and which kept existence ticking over (if only through its own survival). Simply put, something had to survive the corruption of all things in order to get things going again. And thus having

begun with the hypothetical acceptance of option two – that everything is
subject to generation and corruption – we end up forced to reject it in favour
of option three: that while generally things are subject to generation and
corruption, there must be something that is not. The question is – what?

> (5) Now in this existent that is not subject to generation and corruption,
> there is no possibility of corruption at all; rather, its existence is necessary,
> not possible.

This existent that is not subject to generation or corruption is said to
be a 'necessary existent' – which at this stage simply seems to mean an
eternal existent, i.e. one that neither comes into existence nor goes out of
existence. But Maimonides further probes the nature of this necessity:

> (6) With reference to this existent's being necessary of existence, there are
> two possibilities: this may be either in respect to its own essence or in respect
> to the cause of this existent. In the latter case, its existence and non-existence
> are possible in respect to its own essence, but necessary in respect to its cause.

Maimonides here makes the move into the metaphysical language of
essences and necessary and possible (or contingent) existence, derived from
Arabic philosophers such as al-Farabi and most notably Avicenna. The
precise meanings of these terms is a topic of some dispute, both in
their original Avicennan usage and their subsequent appropriation by
Maimonides, though in an introductory work such as this we can gloss over
these questions while still getting a sense for what Maimonides is saying.

How then are we to understand the idea of something that is 'possible
with respect to its own essence, but necessary in respect to its cause'? We
can begin by noting that it is perfectly natural to ask of any existent why it
exists or what accounts for its existence. Take, for example, this book. It
does exist, but that surely calls for some explanation. Something must have
caused it to exist rather than not. Whether it does or does not exist is a
contingent matter as philosophers say, and this is what is meant by saying
that its existence is possible with respect to its own essence. Its existence is
something we have to account for causally as it is not something that exists
by its nature. It is dependent on something else – in the case of this book,
my writing it.

That very dependence is captured in the other idea of something
being 'necessary in respect to its cause'. The fact that I am writing this
book accounts for its existence and thus we can say my writing it has
necessitated its existence. So this book's existence or non-existence is

possible in respect to its own essence, since we need to look beyond it to account for its existence. Yet once we look beyond it, we find there is something that determined that it did indeed come into existence, and thus we can say that it is necessary with respect to that – its cause.

Returning now to (6) above, Maimonides is dealing with eternal objects, which do not come into or go out of existence. Nonetheless, the basic idea remains the same – what accounts for the existence of these eternal objects? Let us take an eternal object and call it E. E might be eternal, but that does not mean that it accounts for its own existence. We could analyse the nature of E, and even include eternal existence as part of its nature, yet E might not have actually existed in the world. In that case we would say that had E existed, it would have been an eternal object. Given that it does exist, however, the point is that its existence is still a contingent matter that calls for explanation. The existence of E depends on something else, which we can call F. Since E is eternal, it cannot be that F existed and then caused E to come into existence at some later point in time. But E nonetheless *depends* on F for its existence. We can have a chain of eternal objects that co-exist in time but have relationships of dependence such that each one is the cause of another. Maimonides therefore says that an object such as E is 'possible in respect to its own essence, but necessary in respect to its cause', meaning that E's existence depends on something else – a cause – and thus its existence is still necessitated by something else – F.

At this point Maimonides adds the following significant premise:

(7) Now it has been demonstrated that, of necessity, there can be no doubt that there is an existent that is necessary of existence in respect to its own essence. For without it, there would be no existent at all...

Maimonides' argument here is not explicit, but he seems to be relying implicitly on the third premise in his Aristotelian introduction – that there cannot be an infinite regress of causes. Maimonides is saying that in our realm of eternal objects, we need to account for the existence of each eternal object by appealing to something else. Thus we began with E and noted that its existence needed accounting for and so we invoked F. But what of F? Surely F must also have its existence accounted for and hence we have to appeal to that on which it depends for its existence, and so on for each link in the chain. The question that then arises is where this chain stops. Can this chain go on infinitely? Most versions of the cosmological argument rely on some version of the intuitively appealing idea captured in the Aristotelian third premise that the answer to this question is 'no' – there must be a First Cause (though not necessarily first in the sense of preceding all others *in time*) that accounts for the existence of the whole, or else we have not actually answered the question of why the world exists rather than not.

What this means is that we have to trace the chain back to something that accounts for the whole and is not itself dependent on any further cause. This First Cause, which we'll call G, is therefore 'necessary of existence in respect to its own essence', which means that its existence is not dependent on anything other than itself. According to Maimonides that is what is ultimately required to account for the existence of the world at all. All the other links in the chain might exist eternally, but they are all dependent on a further cause for their existence. G exists, however, because existing is in its very nature. It is a necessary existent pure and simple in the sense that it accounts for its own existence.

At this point the basic argument is complete. Reduced to its barest bones, the essence of the argument is that everything we observe is 'possible with respect to its own essence but necessary in respect to its cause' meaning that it is dependent for its existence on something else. Once we analyse this idea, we understand that it is in fact impossible for *everything* to be dependent in this manner, so there must be a being 'necessary of existence in respect to its own essence', that ultimately accounts for its own existence and that of all other objects (and thus the world). Continuing the argument though, we see that Maimonides wants to say something more about the nature of this uncaused necessary existent G:

> (8) In anything that is necessary of existence there cannot be a multiplicity of notions, as has been mentioned in the twenty-first premise. Hence it follows necessarily that, as has been set forth in the twenty-second premise, it is not a body or a force in a body.

Being a necessary existent in the sense we have discussed brings two further important and interrelated notions along with it – unity and incorporeality. Indeed, starting with any one of the three characteristics will lead directly to the other two.

Firstly, for Maimonides, our necessary existent that we have called G can have no multiplicity. This, on the one hand, is something that flows from the definition of a necessary existent. According to the twenty-first premise, if something is made up of two (or more) parts, it exists in virtue of those two parts. They are the cause of its existence. And in that case it would not be a necessary existent since its existence would be dependent on the existence of its parts. But secondly, just as importantly, to be composed of parts is inevitably bound up with generation and corruption. If something is composed of parts, it must be a material thing, or corporeal. And to be a corporeal being with a certain composition means the inevitable possibility of decomposition. Yet we know that this necessary existent is not subject to generation and corruption – it cannot decompose by definition. So as soon as we have our definition of necessity, it follows that G cannot possibly be composed of parts (a multiplicity) and cannot possibly be corporeal (a material body).

The central philosophical view that Maimonides is putting forward here is that of unity. G is a unity, or a 'simple' being in the sense of not being composed of parts. And that in turn means that G cannot be in any way material, since all material things *can* be divided into parts. To be a material thing is therefore inevitably bound up with the idea of composition and decomposition, i.e. generation and corruption. So G, it turns out, is incorporeal, a unity and a necessary existent. As Maimonides puts it:

> (9) It thus has been demonstrated in this speculation that there is an existent that is necessary of existence and is so necessarily with respect to its own essence, and that this existent has no cause for its existence and has no composition in itself, and for this reason is neither a body nor a force in a body. It is He who is the deity, may His name be sublime.

So our G (conveniently) turns out to stand for God, and Maimonides believes he has demonstrated (given the assumption of eternity) God's existence. And for Maimonides the idea that this God is one is not a simple numerical statement. It tells us something important about God's nature – that He is a unity and is incorporeal (or at least we will put it like this for the moment, pending discussion of God's attributes in chapter 4).

The argument can certainly be questioned at a number of stages, as it has been in its various incarnations throughout the history of philosophy. The pivotal issue is the requirement that we give an account of existence that goes 'all the way down'. We seem to require some ultimate explanation, whether causal or not, for the existence of the universe. Maimonides, and many like him then and now, argued that this must lead us to a First Cause that accounts for its own existence, since if we have an infinite regress of causes we lack an overall account for the existence of the universe – having an account that goes 'all the way down' means reaching the bottom at some point. But is that necessarily the case? The alternative would be that we need not account for the universe by appeal to a First Cause since there *could* be an infinite series of causes. Here, we would have an explanation of each causal link and no requirement for a First Cause to get things started since there is no starting point by definition – the chain is infinite. Yet this still gives us an account that goes 'all the way down' since we never have a link that is unaccounted for. It is just that in this case going 'all the way down' is a never-ending task. We never reach the bottom, but we can still account for every link in the chain. Ultimately then, the suppressed premise in Maimonides' presentation – the impossibility of an infinite regress of causes – becomes the pivotal one. Whether it is true or not is a more controversial matter. Indeed, even medieval Jewish philosophers such as Hasdai Crescas believed that an infinite series of causes is possible and thus rejected Maimonides' proof for this reason (among others), though Crescas did argue for the existence of a First Cause on other grounds.

But the most significant question to ask for our immediate purpose is – what sort of God has Maimonides arrived at? Effectively, one has argued that given Maimonides' Aristotelian physics and metaphysics there must be something that lies at the source of the world's existence. As a necessary existent, this being is incorporeal and beyond our world in the manner we would expect of the God of a classical monotheistic faith such as Judaism. But is this the God that we encounter in the classical Jewish sources? Is this the God that speaks to Abraham and Moses and intervenes to split the Red Sea or plague the Egyptians? All Maimonides has shown is that there must be a necessary existent that is an incorporeal unity. This might act as a scientific or metaphysical explanation of the universe, but as is clear from Maimonides' acknowledgement of the argument's provenance, Aristotle could happily sign up to such a belief and that hardly makes Aristotle a proponent of the biblical picture of God. For Aristotle, God is pure intellect and even without knowing precisely what he means by this, it is clearly some way from the personal God of the *Tanakh*. Simply put then, there is no reason why the philosophical posit at the conclusion of Maimonides' argument should be a personal being that interacts with its 'creation'. There is nothing to identify this Necessary Existent with the God of the *Tanakh*, and that is Judah Halevi's central problem with this approach.

3. HALEVI'S 'REPLY'

Judah Halevi's *Kuzari* preceded Maimonides' *Guide*, so Halevi is not reacting directly to the specific argument that we have just discussed. As we will see, however, he can be read as responding to the sort of approach to God and religion that Maimonides exemplifies. Indeed, the very first words uttered by the Jewish sage – 'I believe in the God of Abraham, Isaac and Israel, who led the children of Israel out of Egypt with signs and miracles' (*Kuzari*, I: 11, 44) – would have been far more familiar to most Jews of the time than the God who is the logical conclusion of abstract argumentation.

As the *Kuzari*'s opening dialogue between the king and the sage continues, it becomes clear that it can be read in a number of ways and contains various overlapping themes. One way of looking at it though, which we will pursue here, is as a contrasting way of arguing for the existence of God. Indeed the king's immediate reaction to the sage's opening gambit is one of derision, apparently based on the expectation of a rather more Maimonidean approach, to which the sage responds by casting doubt on the efficacy of philosophical arguments in the realm of religion, be they cosmological or of any other type. Such 'religion based on speculation and system' is for Halevi 'open to many doubts' (*Kuzari*, I: 13, 45). But Halevi would not figure in the history of Jewish philosophy as prominently as he does if he were simply rejecting philosophical reasoning *tout court* and he goes on to justify his scepticism. In so doing, he introduces us to an altogether different approach.

Halevi begins by presenting two parables:

> Sage: If thou wert told that the king of India was an excellent man, commanding admiration, and deserving his high reputation, one whose actions were reflected in the justice which rules his country and the virtuous ways of his subjects, would this bind thee to revere him?

> Al Khazari: How could this bind me, whilst I am not sure if the justice of the Indian people is natural, and not dependent on their king, or due to the king or both? (*Kuzari*, I: 20, 45)

Evidently the king of India stands for God who rules over his dominion (presumably the world) and is responsible for the 'good order' therein, whether that be the natural or moral order of the world. Either way, the king admits he would not revere the king of India in this case. Though people may differ over the precise interpretation of the parable, the basic point being made is that philosophical argumentation would not secure his reverence for the king. Indeed, from Al-Khazari's reply it is clear that he thinks one needn't posit a king in order to account for the order that reigns in India at all.

Though Halevi's point is made about all philosophical arguments, the relevance to our foregoing discussion of Maimonides is particularly clear. As we pointed out, the cosmological argument appeals to a feature of the world and concludes that there must be a God who accounts for that feature. Halevi's point here is that there is in fact no necessity for such an inference. Philosophical arguments need not necessarily lead one from a feature of the world to the existence of God, for one might provide equally convincing naturalistic explanations of the feature in question – just ask any scientist.

So Halevi continues with a second parable:

> Sage: But if his messenger came to thee bringing presents which thou knowest to be only procurable in India, and in the royal palace, accompanied by a letter in which it is distinctly stated from whom it comes, and to which are added drugs to cure thy diseases, to preserve thy health, poisons for thy enemies, and other means to fight and kill them without battle, would this make thee beholden to him?

> Al-Khazari: Certainly. For this would remove my former doubt that the Indians have a king. I should also acknowledge that a proof of his power and dominion has reached me. (*Kuzari*, I: 21, 46)

The parable here admits of a particularly Jewish interpretation. The king (still God) this time sends a messenger (Moses) with an authentic letter (the Torah) that contains all sorts of prescriptions (*mitzvot*) for one's well being and victory over one's enemies. Most importantly, says Al-Khazari, this would certainly convince him of the king's existence, from which Halevi goes on to show that Al-Khazari had been too quick to dismiss the sage's opening Bible stories, for they exemplify the approach to God that the Khazar king has just accepted. As Halevi puts it:

> Now in the same style I answered thee, a Prince of the Khazars, when thou didst ask me about my creed. I answered thee as was fitting, and is fitting for the whole of Israel who knew these things, first from personal experience, and afterwards through uninterrupted tradition, which is equal to the former. (*Kuzari*, I: 25, 46–7)

The central point that Halevi has been setting up carefully throughout the earlier encounters and goes on to reinforce at length throughout the *Kuzari*, is that religious experience is a far better guarantor of the veracity of revelation, and in this case the existence of God, than any form of philosophic speculation. Our knowledge of God's existence depends on people having had these miraculous experiences that were evident to their senses, not simply their intellects. More importantly, the argument that God exists because you have experienced his miraculous revelation refutes any philosophical speculation that would have one believe that such experience is impossible. Experience trumps all such rational speculation. That is not to say that these experiences reveal any information about God's nature or essence – a very problematic topic as we will see in due course – but they do guarantee that God exists and communicates with certain human beings.

Of course, not simply any religious experience can play this fundamental role. Throughout the opening exchanges between the king and his various interlocutors Halevi is keen to emphasise the controls necessary to guarantee the veracity of such experiences. Thus, for example, he has already dismissed his Muslim interlocutor on account of the lack of the first control - sufficient evidence for his claims regarding God having communicated with humanity through the Koran. In the case of Sinai, however, the whole of the nation of Israel saw with their own eyes the public and miraculous revelation of God, an event the occurrence of which the Christian and Muslim also accept. The public nature of the event and its acceptance across religious divides, is highly significant for Halevi. The power of testimony is increased markedly as the number of witnesses rises, and in this case Halevi follows the traditional reading according to which there were 600,000 witnesses to God's miracles in the wilderness (*Kuzari*, I: 86, 60).

The second control that Halevi mentions is that of tradition. Much as good arguments are vehicles for transmitting knowledge from a set of premises to a conclusion, reliable tradition is the vehicle for transmitting the knowledge supplied by sense experience to a further generation. And in Halevi's eyes, the Sinai revelation is an experience that has been reliably transmitted without interruption since it took place more than 2000 years earlier, leaving us with the position that publicly verified sense experiences that are reliably transmitted are the soundest grounds for establishing religious truths such as the existence of God. The demonstrative arguments of Maimonides are far less reliable for establishing such conclusions.

There are basically two elements then to Halevi's argument. Firstly, we can only be guaranteed that God exists as a personal being who communicates with humanity through the actual experience of revelation. Secondly, those who did not experience such an event must rely on authentic tradition – the reliable transmission of the knowledge gained through that experience of the original revelation.

The former idea that sense experience is as much a source of knowledge as demonstrative argument is not at all unusual in medieval Jewish philosophy. In his epistemological discussion in the introduction to *Emunot ve-De'ot*, Saadia Gaon lists the three main sources of knowledge as 1) sense perception; 2) intellectual intuitions (parallel to Maimonides' first intelligibles); and 3) knowledge inferred by logical necessity (where Maimonidean demonstration would be the – literally – perfect example, though for Saadia this category is wider than just demonstrative argument).

Notably for the latter element of Halevi's approach, Saadia then adds:

> The community of monotheists … add a fourth source … which has thus become for us a further principle. That is [to say, we believe in] the validity of authentic tradition, by reason of the fact that it is based upon the knowledge of the senses as well as that of reason. (*Emunot*, Intro: V, 18)

Yet at both levels of the argument serious philosophical issues are raised. Firstly, one has to consider whether or not the notion of religious experience is as powerful as Halevi thinks. It is clear that appeals to sense experience, and our reliance on its veracity, are second nature to us. We rely on it virtually every moment of every day. But God is usually taken to be beyond our sense experience rather than an object of it. So how reliable can that experience be as proof of God's existence? Arguments from silence are never that convincing, but given that none of the thinkers we will be studying would have denied the reality of the Sinai revelation, it is interesting that so many of them refrain from taking this route.

The second question relates to the idea of knowledge gained through tradition. From a modern perspective it is of course easy to question the assertion that there has been an uninterrupted tradition since the revelation at Sinai, which would anyway require accepting that the revelation at Sinai took place at all. But concerns about tradition are not just a modern problem. Maimonides himself notes in the *Treatise on the Art of Logic* that 'a tradition in one group may be lacking in another' (*Treatise*, VIII, 48), though at that time one might argue that all of the three main traditions accepted that this particular event had occurred. Even though the different religions believed that the *authentic* tradition continues in a rather different direction, each could presumably have subscribed to the proof of the existence of God that Halevi is putting forward, even if they would have to reject Halevi's further claim that it is also proof of the exclusive authenticity of Jewish revelation.

The real point at issue between Halevi and Maimonides therefore is the appropriate sphere of application for different sources of knowledge. Indeed, it is notable that in the eighth chapter of the *Treatise on the Art of Logic*, Maimonides enumerates the same four starting points for knowledge as does Saadia. Maimonides does not therefore dispute that sense experience can be a reliable starting point for gaining knowledge. What it cannot do is reach beyond the corporeal world to God. Similarly, Halevi is not disputing the power of demonstration, claiming more than once that the Torah does not contradict either sense experience or demonstration (*Kuzari*, I: 67, 54). He has been termed the anti-philosopher in the history of medieval Jewish philosophy, but this cannot be in the sense of being anti-philosophy, for his work is highly philosophical. What it does signify is his scepticism regarding how far philosophy can take you when it comes to knowing the truths of revelation. Rather than undermining all attempts at human reasoning, therefore, as Colette Sirat writes, Halevi is arguing for 'the inclusion of philosophy in another system that transcends it.'[2] The question is whether philosophical reasoning is appropriate for arriving at the fundamental truths of religion.

For Halevi, demonstrative reasoning is severely limited in its ability to provide satisfactory answers to central religious questions, not only for proving the existence of God, but also notably for answering the very question that set the king of the Khazars on his quest in the first place – how we are to act. Halevi's claim is that the contemplative detachment of the rationalist and the God with which he ends up are simply at odds with the practical nature of Judaism and the personal nature of the God at its foundation. The fact that God is always 'the God who brought you out of the Land of Egypt' in the Torah is not accidental for Halevi but expresses an important truth about how one approaches questions concerning God's existence, if one indeed wishes to establish the existence of a God who can directly intervene in human affairs. The point for Halevi is that his method is in fact the only reliable method for arriving at the God of Abraham.

What we have here therefore, is not only a fundamental philosophical divide over which is the more reliable source of religious knowledge – rational argument or sense experience – but also over the sort of God that Judaism requires. As Julius Guttmann noted:

> Judah Ha-Levi … emphatically distinguishes the God of Israel, who works miracles and freely intervenes in the course of the world he created, from the god of philosophy, the first cause of the world, acting by an inner necessity.[3]

The experiential approach solves the problems raised for the cosmological argument regarding the sort of God that one has shown to exist. Where Maimonides' proof of a necessary existent brought with it unity and incorporeality, and allowed us to understand the existence of contingent existents, Halevi's proof from experience and tradition brings with it the personal living God of the *Tanakh* and allows us to understand that God communicates with humanity and intervenes in history. Philosophical speculation from nature will only lead us to know that the world has a ruler, yielding knowledge of God as *Elohim*, a generic term for ruler or governor applied to God here in that capacity, as the Supreme Being of philosophical argument. To go beyond that level of knowledge requires that we transcend philosophical speculation altogether. Halevi claims that only the actual experiences of prophets and the people of Israel allow us to know God by his proper name YHWH, the Tetragrammaton, signifying the intimate knowledge of a God who created the world and reveals himself to humanity (*Kuzari*, IV: 1–16, 198–223).

The arguments for the existence of God that we have looked at in this chapter, then, highlight two central questions – what is the appropriate philosophical method for arguing for God's existence (and for religious truths more generally) and what notion of God does Judaism require? On the former question, Halevi stands alone in the canon of medieval Jewish philosophy. As we will see, many of the thinkers differed in the precise application of philosophical apparatus to Judaism, but none were as limiting of it from a methodological perspective as Halevi. What Halevi achieves though, more than any other medieval Jewish thinker, is a highlighting of exactly what is at stake if one goes down the more Aristotelian route. And that is at the centre of many of the disputes surrounding medieval Jewish philosophy, not least the question of creation that is the subject of the next chapter.

NOTES

1   References to the *Treatise* are to the translation by Israel Efros in *Proceedings of the American Academy for Jewish Research*, 8 (1937–38), 1–136. References are by chapter and page number of this translation.
2   Colette Sirat, *A History of Jewish Philosophy in the Middle Ages* (Cambridge: Cambridge University Press, 1990), 117.
3   Julius Guttmann, *Philosophies of Judaism*, trans. D. W. Silverman (New York: Holt, Rinehart and Winston, 1964), 132.

FURTHER READING

Most discussions of Maimonides' proofs are rather advanced so it is best to first gain some understanding of the cosmological argument in general. Brian Davies, *An Introduction to the Philosophy of Religion*, 2nd edition (Oxford: Oxford University Press, 2004), chapter 3, is an excellent place to start.

For a discussion of proofs (especially cosmological) for the existence of God in Jewish philosophy, see H. A. Wolfson, 'Notes on Proofs of the Existence of God in Jewish Philosophy', in *Studies in the History of Philosophy and Religion*, (ed.) I. Twersky and G. H. Williams, 2 vols (Cambridge: Harvard University Press, 1975), I: 561–82.

For a general contrast between Maimonides and Halevi see Wolfson, 'Maimonides and Halevi: A Study in Typical Jewish Attitudes Towards Greek Philosophy in the Middle Ages', in *Studies in the History of Philosophy and Religion*. II: 120–60. A highly readable, though more applied discussion of these two thinkers that puts them to polemical use can be found in David Hartman, *Israelis and the Jewish Tradition: An Ancient People Debating its Future* (New Haven: Yale University Press, 2000).

I have read Maimonides' third argument as implicitly based upon the eternity of the world (premise 26) and the impossibility of an infinite regress of causes (premise 3). This follows the reading of Crescas (and a number of others). Maimonides' argument along with Crescas' interpretation and critique are further discussed in Warren Zev Harvey, *Physics and Metaphysics in Hasdai Crescas* (Amsterdam: J. C. Gieben, 1998), chapter 3.

However, as signalled in this chapter, the move Maimonides makes from the physical question of 'generation and corruption' to metaphysical distinctions between necessity and possibility means that some interpret it along the lines of Avicenna's metaphysical argument based on the conceptual analysis of the concepts of necessity and possibility. For an introduction to Avicenna's understanding of these terms, see Oliver Leaman, *Averroes and his Philosophy* (Richmond: Curzon, 1998), 104–16.

Detailed analysis of Avicenna's original argument and Maimonides' interpretation of it along the lines we have followed can be found in Herbert Davidson, *Proofs for Eternity, Creation and the Existence of God in Medieval Islamic and Jewish Philosophy* (Oxford: Oxford University Press, 1987), chapters 9 and 12.

2

God and Creation

As mentioned in chapter 1, the cosmological argument for the existence
of God was motivated in part by the question of how we account for there
being something rather than nothing. Having established why there is
indeed 'something', at least to the satisfaction of some of the medievals, a
further question that troubled them is how we got quite so much. One
might expect that from a Jewish perspective, the same simple answer is
available – God. The Torah in Genesis 1–2 states that God created our
diverse world in six days and according to rabbinic tradition did so some
5768 years ago as I write. Yet matters are rather less simple as soon as one
starts down the philosophical road of the previous chapter. How, for
example, does the incorporeal necessary First Cause of the Maimonidean
argument produce a corporeal world of physical things? What possible
link can there be between a perfect unity that transcends all materiality
and such physical things as mud and hair (to use two relatively inoffensive
examples)? Even those unfamiliar with philosophical ideas such as
incorporeality might simply wonder what, if anything, existed *before*
creation. Did God have any raw materials to work with? The text of
Genesis itself is certainly not unequivocal on this as evidenced by the
variety of views in early rabbinic literature. The question of how our
physical world proceeds from a transcendent God was thus one of the
central problems in medieval philosophy and one to which there were a
whole raft of answers – Saadia Gaon gives an exhaustive, and exhausting,
refutation of *twelve* different theories of creation in *Emunot ve-De'ot* (II: 3).

The question of the origins of the universe, or cosmogony, is now more the preserve of science than philosophy, so many of these medieval arguments are primarily of historic interest. Yet there remain issues of philosophical significance in the medieval discussion. Some of them emerge when we look at what Gersonides calls 'the major difficulties pertaining to this question' (*Wars*, VI: 1, 1, 217) at the beginning of the sixth and longest treatise of *Wars of the Lord* devoted exclusively to creation. Firstly:

> It is incumbent on such an investigator to know the nature of existent things in their entirety and the various properties, so that he will be able to determine if anything in reality exhibits a property that entails the eternity of the world, or if there is some feature of reality that entails the creation of the world, or if there is no such feature that entails either creation or eternity. (*Wars*, VI: 1, 1, 217–18)

Thus, it seems that we must master science in its entirety, which Gersonides acknowledges is no easy task. It also makes the question of the limits of scientific knowledge significant, even for the strongest supporters of human philosophical endeavour, and in far more subtle fashion than that exemplified by Halevi in the previous chapter. Secondly:

> Anyone who wants to make a comprehensive treatment of this issue (as far as possible) should know the essence of God, as far as this is possible, so that he will be able to arrive at a true judgment whether God can be active at one time but not another or whether this is impossible. But this makes the whole inquiry difficult... (*Wars*, VI: 1, 1, 217–18)

Something of an understatement. Not only do we need to know science, but we also need to know God. And the particular thing that we need to know is the sort of God he can be, an issue that is particularly to the fore in Maimonides' discussion of creation, for as he makes very clear, it is more than the simple mechanics of creation that one is putting on the line here. One's perspective on creation has all manner of other implications:

> The belief in eternity the way Aristotle sees it... destroys the Law in its principle, necessarily gives the lie to every miracle, and reduces to inanity all the hopes and threats that the Law has held out... Know that with a belief in the creation of the world in time, all the miracles become possible and the Law becomes possible, and all questions that may be asked on this subject vanish. (*Guide*, II: 25, 328–9)

We ended chapter 1 with the question of what is at stake if one goes down an Aristotelian route when dealing with religious matters. The question of whether the world was eternal or created brings that issue to the fore very starkly, for whichever view one took, one was buying into a package that included a conception of God's relationship to the universe. For this reason, the question of creation was absolutely central for the medievals. But before we look at some of the arguments for creation, we need to know a little about what the medievals thought the world looked like, their more general theory of the structure of the universe – their cosmology.

1. A COSMOLOGICAL INTRODUCTION

The basic Aristotelian worldview that the medievals inherited, places the earth at the centre of a finite universe made up of concentric spheres nested within in each other that Maimonides compares in structure to the layers of an onion.[1] Without entering into the finer details, on Maimonides' Aristotelian model, the 'sublunar' realm contains the earth and its atmosphere, or at least what passes for 'atmosphere' in Aristotle's cosmology, which are the elements of water, air and fire. At the most basic level of description, this is surrounded by the heavenly or celestial realm that consists of nine transparent spheres that begin with the sphere of the moon and that are themselves divided into further spheres. All the various celestial bodies – the sun, the planets and in the outermost sphere the so-called 'fixed stars' – are attached in permanent positions to the first eight of the main spheres, which all move around the earth in an eternal circular motion carrying these celestial bodies with them. Since, as we will see, the world was eternal according to Aristotle, accounting for its creation was not an issue. Accounting for this eternal motion certainly was, but Aristotle took care of this with his God, the unmoved First Mover who is the ultimate cause of all motion.

So far, so Aristotelian. We have a universe composed of spheres that revolve around the earth with God as the First Cause of this motion. There are, however, problems with this Aristotelian picture. For we have an incorporeal God who is apparently the First Cause of the movement of the spheres, and the question that in various forms has troubled philosophers through the centuries is how an incorporeal God can get any foothold in an essentially physical concept like causation. What will become particularly significant for us is that the movement of the spheres that God causes does not require his activity. God is an object of love for the spheres – the celestial spheres are living intelligent beings – and it is their desire to emulate God that causes their circular motion. He does not actually have to *do* anything. Though this seems strange at first, we can at least gain some understanding of it by seeing that God is acting as what Aristotle would have termed a 'final cause'.

A final cause explains something by being the end or purpose at which it aims. The simplest examples come from human action. One of Aristotle's own examples is someone who is walking in order to be healthy. Here the purpose or goal of the action – health – explains the taking of the walk, so health is said to be the final cause of the action. Similarly here, the goal – to be like the Unmoved Mover, God – explains the circular motion of the celestial spheres (we needn't go into how this motion makes them in any way 'like' God). God is therefore the final cause of the motion and does not have to 'do' anything since the simple desire of the spheres to be like God 'causes' them to move, just as my desire to be healthy 'causes' me to walk. Yet returning to the example, fulfilling our desire to go for a walk also requires us to have the physical capacity to do so. So we cannot easily divorce the idea of final causation from the more everyday physical understanding of causation, such as when a ball hits another and causes it to move. Aristotle accounts for this physical idea with the idea of efficient causation, where the actual 'push' given by the first ball, initiates the movement of the second ball, rather than any 'final cause'. The first ball is said to be the efficient cause of the movement of the second. But transferring this sort of talk to an incorporeal God, who cannot come into *physical* contact with anything, is obviously problematic. How can we talk of God physically causing the movement of the spheres? This is parallel to the more general problem to which we have already alluded of how we get our corporeal world from a simple incorporeal starting point, since it is again a question of crossing the boundary between the incorporeal and the corporeal. This problem appears in different forms within philosophical debates to this day. In the philosophy of mind, for example, dualists who wish to argue that a person consists of both a physical body and a non-physical mind continue to have great difficulty accounting for the interaction between these two entirely different types of substance. How do mental events like beliefs and desires, if they are 'located' in the mind and are non-physical, cause physical actions? This, in microcosm, is the same problem of crossing boundaries.

This causal problem did trouble Maimonides, for whom God obviously could not be an efficient cause in any ordinary sense of the term.

Maimonides therefore speaks of God acting like 'an overflowing spring of water' (*Guide*, II: 12, 279), with the world being a result of that 'overflow'. Now this language is again only intended as a simile, more rarefied than the physical language of causation, but also not to be taken literally. Yet it is more than just a figure of speech for medieval thinkers since it is drawn from the Neoplatonic theory of emanation.

By medieval times Neoplatonism, especially the system of emanation that is at its core, had infiltrated Aristotelian cosmology. For Plotinus, the One, the highest perfection, is 'beyond being', which basically means that it is beyond any sort of limitation or indeed characterisation. Yet the One 'overflows' as a natural result of its perfection, since any infinite perfect being could not prevent its perfection from overflowing. Perfection just can't help itself, so to speak. As a result, the One is the cause or ground of lower levels of being, called hypostases, and the process of overflow that results in these hypostases is termed emanation. Plotinus explains this process of emanation in great detail, with the significant hypostases being firstly the intellect that emanates directly from the One, then the Soul, which in similar manner emanates from the intellect, and finally our material world that emanates from the Soul. This series of intermediaries gradually introduces more and more diversity into a system that has its ultimate source in the simple unity of the One but culminates in our material world in all its complexity.

This process of emanation was helpful in answering the question of how we get to our corporeal world from an incorporeal God. God's 'overflow' produces a hierarchy of ever more complex beings and eventually we end up with our material world. And where Aristotle had explained the *motion* of the universe, the system of emanation gave us a causal account for its *existence*. Suddenly, God is not simply the Unmoved Mover of the first intelligence, but also the cause of its existence through emanation.

In truth, combining the One of Plotinus, which is beyond being, with the causally effective God of Aristotle, yields a less than stable hybrid. Yet due to the misattribution of the *Theology of Aristotle* mentioned in our introductory chapter, the two pictures were combined in medieval Arabic and Jewish thought and the resulting hybrid gives us the following. God emanates a first intellect and the system continues with a further emanation from that intellect. What happens is that the first intellect reflects on (or thinks about) God, and as a result emanates a second intellect. But the first intellect also reflects on itself, which leads to the emanation of a sphere, and so it goes on with this second intellect similarly emanating a further intellect and sphere depending on what it is thinking about. Through this Neoplatonic system of emanation we account for the existence of the different spheres of Aristotelian cosmology and the fact that they each have a so-called Separate Intellect 'attached' to them. Maimonides even identified the angels of biblical and rabbinic tradition with these Separate Intellects.

Despite reservations about this whole system of emanation that we will deal with in due course, Maimonides therefore presents the following picture:

> The overflow coming from Him, may He be exalted, for the bringing into being of separate intellects, overflows likewise from these intellects, so that one of them brings another one into being and this continues up to the Active Intellect. With the latter, the bringing into being of separate intellects comes to an end. Moreover a certain other act of bringing into being overflows from every separate intellect until the spheres come to an end with the sphere of the moon. (*Guide*, II: 11, 275–6)

Notably, it is not only moderns that might find this bizarre. Halevi was certainly less than impressed, famously criticising the idea that an intellect/angel will emanate either a further intellect/angel or sphere depending on what it's thinking about with almost satirical relish:

> When Aristotle asserts that he was conscious of his existence, one may consistently expect that a sphere should emanate from him, and when he asserts that he recognised the Prime Cause, an angel should emanate. (*Kuzari*, IV: 25, 239)

Despite such criticism, the scheme was highly influential. In accounting for the existence of the world, the language of emanation was thought by certain Jewish thinkers to be a perfect way of giving philosophical expression to religious ideas, especially that of creation.

2. THE THREE VIEWS

Though not the only views considered, the three most prominent cosmogonies for medieval Jewish thinkers were creation *ex nihilo*, the Aristotelian view of the eternity of the world, and the Platonic view of creation from eternal matter. The latter two labels have become part of the vocabulary of the subject that we will retain, despite real questions as to whether they are correctly attributed from a historical point of view.

We will begin with what most people instinctively take to be the 'Jewish' view, and the view that Maimonides attributes to 'all who believe in the Law of Moses our Master':

> [T]he world as a whole – I mean to say every existent other than God ... – was brought into existence by God after having been purely and absolutely nonexistent, and that God ... had existed alone, and nothing else – neither an angel nor a sphere not what subsists within the sphere. Afterwards, through His will and His volition, He brought into existence out of nothing all the beings as they are, time itself being one of the created things. (*Guide*, II: 13, 281)

This view, usually termed 'creation *ex nihilo*', says that God created the world after it had been absolutely nonexistent. For Maimonides, despite his using the temporal term 'after', the act of creation *ex nihilo* includes God's creation of time, in which case existence cannot in any literal sense have come *after* nonexistence. Maimonides subscribed to the Aristotelian view that time is the measure of motion and is therefore consequent on there being things in motion. While for Aristotle this meant that the world and time were both eternal, for Maimonides it meant that both were created together. There could only be time once there was creation and thus objects in motion.

We can try to gain some understanding of this view by reflecting on our perception of time and asking whether we would notice time passing at all if the universe were changeless (since for Aristotle motion is understood more generally as change). Would we be aware of time if there were no change in the world, including no change in our own inner world? Most likely we would conclude that we could not be conscious of time in such a situation. Aristotle is taking this idea further. He is not just saying that we do not *notice* time if nothing changes – he is saying that there is *no such thing* as time if nothing changes. On Maimonides' Aristotelian picture therefore, there can be no time if there is nothing that is in motion (or changing), and hence no time without creation.

So God creates time and the world *ex nihilo*. Yet not only does God create the world *ex nihilo*, but he also freely chose to create the world in this manner. In philosophic terms, the creation of the world is not only *ex nihilo*, but also *de novo* – it was a free act of God's will. This emphasis on will, or volition, is particularly important for the conceptions of God that have already featured in our discussions. For it implies that God decided to bring the world into existence as an act of free choice, the very free choice that defines the God of the *Tanakh*, who can choose to intervene in the world he created. That is why creation *ex nihilo* and *de novo* brings with it the package that Maimonides notes in *Guide*, II: 25; the possibility of the existence of the type of God that Judah Halevi was so keen to prove in the previous chapter. Establishing the truth of this view of creation thus becomes all the more significant.

Maimonides' account of Aristotle on the other hand yields a very different picture.

> This being as a whole, such as it is, has never ceased to be and will never do so; that the permanent thing not subject to generation and passing-away, namely, the heaven, likewise does not cease to be; that time and motion are perpetual and everlasting and not subject to generation and passing-away; and also that the thing subject to generation and passing-away, namely, that which is beneath the sphere of the moon, does not cease to be. I mean to say that its first matter is not subject in its essence to generation and passing-away, but that various forms succeed each other in it in such a way that it divests itself of one form and assumes another… Accordingly it follows necessarily that this being as a whole has never ceased to be as it is at present and will be as it is in the future eternity. (*Guide*, II: 13, 284)

The starting point here is that it is impossible for something to be created out of nothing, a principle that Aristotle notes was 'common to nearly all the natural philosophers.' (*Metaphysics*, XI. 6, 1062b25). That is not to limit God's power, but simply to state that God cannot do the impossible, such as create a square whose diagonal is equal in length to one of its sides (see *Guide*, III: 15, 460), to use Maimonides' example. So, for Aristotle, God cannot have created the world *ex nihilo*. Rather, God is the First Cause of a world that is neither created *ex nihilo* nor *de novo* but is instead eternal and unchanging. This obviously does not mean that nothing can change in any way. There is no question of the table that I am sitting at being eternal. What is eternal is the structure of our world: its matter and the natural laws that govern it.

In his presentation of the Aristotelian view, however, Maimonides writes that

> all that exists has been brought into existence, in the state in which it is at present, by God through his volition, but that it was not produced after having been in a state of nonexistence. (*Guide*, II: 13, 284)

Strictly speaking, if the world exists eternally by God's side as an effect of his causal activity, it is not clear that God can be described as actually *bringing* anything into existence at all. God is the First Cause of this eternal universe, but as First Cause he does not decide to cause the universe anymore than a ball 'decides' to hit another and cause it to move. On this view the world was not *created* at all and the idea of God bringing anything into existence through his volition seems out of place. As Philo wrote well before the medievals, Aristotle posits 'God existing in a state of complete inactivity' (*De Opificio Mundi*, II: 7).[2]

This, however, is where the Neoplatonic elements of the medieval picture become influential. Given their Neoplatonised version of Aristotelianism, thinkers like al-Farabi and Avicenna understood Aristotelian eternity as eternal emanation, the idea being that the world is eternal, but only because God is eternally emanating it. This is the view that Maimonides reflects when he writes of God bringing the world into existence. The Aristotelian view is understood here as one where God is and always has been creating the world through his continuous creative act.

The most famous Jewish Neoplatonists to fully adapt this system to Jewish ends were Isaac Israeli and Solomon Ibn Gabirol. In Israeli, for example, we find a typical Plotinian scheme whereby God through his 'power', or his 'power and will' creates the First Matter and First Form, which are combined to form the intellect (unlike in Plotinus where Intellect emanates directly from the One). From this point on, we have a series of emanations that follow necessarily from each other until we reach the world itself. Nonetheless, God is described by Israeli as the Creator, and the first stage in the process – the creation of First Matter and First Form – is creation *ex nihilo* rather than the necessary emanation that he ascribes to the rest of the process. Thus, Israeli attempts to combine the Neoplatonic scheme of emanation with the biblical view of creation *ex nihilo*.

However one dresses it up though, Maimonides is aware that this picture does not sit easily with the view of God as a free agent who intentionally brings the world into existence. Maimonides, whose reference to Israeli as 'only a physician'[3] tells you all you need to know about his opinion of Israeli's philosophy, exploits precisely this tension between the free activity implied by creation *ex nihilo* and the necessary procession of emanatory beings, in a proof that he formulates for creation *ex nihilo*. In condensed form the argument runs as follows:

> It is impossible that anything but a single simple thing should proceed from a simple thing... In accordance with this proposition, Aristotle says that what first proceeded from God was constituted by a single simple intellect... With regard to Aristotle's statement that the first intellect is the cause of the second, the second of the third, and so on – even if there were thousands of degrees, the last intellect would indubitably still be simple. How then can the composition have come to exist, the composition existing – as Aristotle believes – in the beings in virtue of necessity? (*Guide*, II: 22, 317)

Appealing to the principle that 'It is impossible that anything but a single simple thing should proceed from a simple thing' (*ibid.*), Maimonides hoists the Neoplatonists by their own petard, showing that their system cannot answer one of the very questions it was designed to overcome – how do we get to a complex material world from simple incorporeal beginnings? One cannot account for the transition from simple intellects to the complex objects of the sublunar sphere on the 'natural' schemes of Neoplatonic emanation that proceed necessarily. Maimonides' argument is that if we start with an incorporeal God and can only appeal to the necessary process of emanation where only 'simple' or non-composite things can proceed from other simple things, we cannot account for the introduction of matter into existence. We can only make sense of the introduction of matter if we have recourse to a free and omnipotent God who can decide to introduce something new into the process.

Thus, while the language of emanation may have soothed the consciences of certain religious thinkers, it really leads us to a God who is 'acting' by virtue of necessity. His emanation of the first intellect is a necessary emanation of his perfection; 'creating' the world is not therefore something he has decided to do. As Maimonides writes:

> For to me a combination between existing in virtue of necessity and being produced in time in virtue of a purpose and a will... comes near to a combination of two contraries. For the meaning of necessity, as Aristotle believes it, is that everything among the beings, which is not an artifact, cannot but have a cause necessitating that particular thing – a cause that has brought it into being as it is – and that this cause has a second cause and this second cause similarly a third one, until finally a first cause is reached from which everything is necessarily derived... For this First Cause... cannot will anything contrary to this. Now this is not called purpose, and the notion of purpose is not included in it. (*Guide*, II: 21, 313–14)

Regardless of whether God is the final cause of the motion of the world or the being who necessarily and involuntarily emanates further hypostases, he is not a free agent who can voluntarily perform miracles or reveal his will to a people at the bottom of a mountain. Belief in eternity 'is the belief according to which the world exists in virtue of necessity, that no nature changes at all, and that the customary course of events cannot be modified with regard to anything' (*Guide*, II: 25, 328). On this picture therefore, God cannot intervene in nature since God is simply not that sort of being. Indeed, 'if He wished to lengthen a fly's wing or shorten a worm's foot, he would not be able to do it' (*Guide*, II: 22, 319). The God of Aristotelian eternity is the necessary physical or metaphysical posit that makes existence possible. But that is far from the idea of a personal God who has decided to create a world of his own free volition, such that he can subsequently intervene at will.

The final view for us to consider is the Platonic view, which like that of Aristotle dismisses creation *ex nihilo* as 'absurd'. Rather, there is eternal matter that is the 'clay' to God's 'potter':

> Hence they believe that there exists a certain matter that is eternal as the deity is eternal; and that He does not exist without it, nor does it exist without Him. They do not believe that it has the same rank in what exists as He, may He be exalted, but that He is the cause of its existence; and that it has the same relation toward Him as, for instance, clay has toward a potter...and that He creates in it whatever He wishes. (*Guide*, II: 13, 283)

On this view everything 'is subject to generation and corruption', but it is not generated out of nothing, nor does it pass away into nothing. There is an eternal matter that coexists with God, though it depends on God for its existence and not *vice versa*, and God can do with it as he wills. Most importantly, he forms it into our world in an act of creation.

While there is some controversy as to the implications of this view (see Appendix), Maimonides does state that such a view would not have the same dire consequences for traditional religionists as Aristotle's. Since on this Platonic view God does 'intervene' to form eternal matter into heaven and earth, we still have an interventionist picture of God that would allow for miracles and revelation. In the philosophic terms used above, this allows for the creation of the world *de novo* that is so important in opposing the necessity-based view that comes with an Aristotelian cosmogony. The Platonic view 'would not destroy the foundations of the Law and would be followed not by the lie being given to miracles, but by their becoming admissible' (*Guide*, II: 25, 328). We know, however, that Maimonides is scathing towards the *kalam* for basing their scientific views on religious presuppositions. So if he is going to end up with the theology he apparently wants, it will need to be based on good philosophical and scientific grounds rather than any special religious pleading. The main question we need to consider therefore is whether these philosophical grounds existed or not.

3. CREATION AND THE LIMITS OF SCIENCE

While most of our thinkers attempt to argue for their views on rational grounds, they differ in their evaluation of what they have succeeded in doing. While Gersonides is happy that he can provide a demonstration of creation, Maimonides does not believe that one can demonstrate any of the views on offer. Instead he formulates lesser dialectical arguments for some pretty modest claims regarding the philosophical superiority of creation *ex nihilo*. His discussion of creation has probably been subject to more conflicting interpretations than any other, as scholars try to ascertain whether to take him at his admittedly low-key word when he writes of creation that he 'shall begin to make it prevail...by means of speculative proof over any other affirmations' (*Guide*, II: 16, 294). We will take him at his word in our discussion here, leaving considerations of esotericism for the Appendix.

Maimonides begins his discussion by setting out Aristotle's arguments for the eternity of the world and showing how they fail as demonstrations, as we will see shortly. In doing this Maimonides believes he has cleared a logical space for the possibility that creation *ex nihilo* is the true view, and he goes on to fill this space with what he claims are 'arguments that come close to being a demonstration' (*Guide*, II: 19, 303). The first of those arguments is an argument from particularisation, a form of argument that had been popular among the *kalam*, but that Maimonides bases on Aristotelian science rather than on the specious kalamic alternative. The argument appeals to certain 'anomalies' in the heavenly spheres. Since the celestial spheres are all composed of the same matter – the so-called quintessence or fifth element, *aether* – they ought to revolve around the earth in the same direction and at the same speed. The fact that they do not requires explanation, and ultimately no explanation is forthcoming on the principles of Aristotelian science. Similarly the apparently anomalous existence and distribution of the stars within the spheres cannot be accounted for.

Gersonides' argument to show that the universe was generated gives a more explicit illustration of what is going on here. He takes the best candidates for eternal existence – the heavenly bodies – and shows that they have three features that provide conclusive proof that the heavens must have been generated. It is the second of these features – that generated things 'manifest properties that do not necessarily follow from their natures or essences' (*Wars*, VI: 1, 6, 241) – that Maimonides has used in his argument.

These properties are not essential properties of the heavenly bodies, but rather properties that they just happen to have, termed accidental properties. For example, a triangle can be any colour – colour is an accidental property of the triangle. But its internal angles must add up to 180 degrees or it is simply not a triangle. This is therefore an essential property of the triangle. The important point for the argument is that these essential properties follow naturally and necessarily from the essence of something. That the angles of a triangle add up to 180 degrees follows from the very nature of a triangle and is true of all triangles – we require no explanation as to why the triangle should have this property. But if the triangle happens to be red, we need to explain why it is red rather than, say, green. Its colour does not 'follow' necessarily from its nature.

Applying this distinction to our concern, the heavenly bodies are all made of the same matter and therefore share the same nature, yet they have different properties. But why should they, for example, be different sizes and emit different colours? If these were essential properties of the bodies then they would be shared by all of them and we would to be able to explain them as natural and necessary properties of the heavens – but we can't. So we cannot explain these properties on the assumption of the eternity of the universe, for this would require that they follow naturally as part of the necessary scientific picture that the eternity thesis brings with it. They are accidental properties, and for Gersonides the existence of such accidental properties is evidence of generation. We can only account for them if they have been created by an agent 'by choice and voluntarily' (*Wars*, VI: 1, 8, 257).

Maimonides is using the very same idea in arguing that since we cannot appeal to the laws of nature to explain anomalous features of the heavens, we must instead appeal to a God who can freely create the world as he sees fit, and thus 'particularise' things in this way:

> On the basis of our opinion, that is, the opinion of the community of those who affirm the production of the world in time, all this becomes easy and is consistent with our principles. For we say that there is a being that has particularised, just as it willed, every sphere in regard to its motion and rapidity; but we do not know in what respect there is wisdom in making these things exist in this fashion. (*Guide*, II: 19, 308)

Maimonides admits that God's choices here are beyond our own understanding, but the very fact that a personal being is making choices can at least explain what is beyond explanation for Aristotle.

Looking at the merits of the argument itself, there are reasons why it is of limited philosophical interest, based as it is on an outdated Aristotelian cosmology. It might also be criticised for the assumption that in the absence of a scientific explanation for certain phenomena, God as creator is the only possible fallback position. Given the religious context in which Maimonides is working and the fact that he has already proved the existence of God, resorting to God as the explanation of these anomalies becomes more understandable. But Maimonides is not just blithely bringing God into the picture in the absence of a scientific account. Science is too crucial for Maimonides' understanding of the world for that to be the case. As he states, with a swipe at the kalamic 'science' developed to suit preconceived opinions, the *only* legitimate basis for a particularisation argument is Aristotelian science since:

> Everything that Aristotle has said about all that exists from beneath the sphere of the moon to the center of the earth is indubitably correct, and no one will deviate from it unless he does not understand it or unless he has preconceived opinions that he wishes to defend or that lead him to a denial of a thing that is manifest. (*Guide*, II: 22, 319)

The truth of Aristotle's account of the world, a world which runs according to a stable rational structure, is essential to Maimonides' worldview and reflects God's perfection. Moreover, *we* rely on our scientific understanding of the natural world for everything from taking a walk in the park to developing cures for cancer. Without it, we would be at the mercy of arbitrary events and not know anything. You could not rely on the book you are reading, or indeed the place you are sitting, not suddenly and inexplicably rising up to heaven or disappearing. And yet, for Maimonides, even if we use legitimate Aristotelian science, we end up going beyond our limits if we try to extend it to the heavenly realm:

> On the other hand, everything that Aristotle expounds with regard to the sphere of the moon and that which is above it is, except for certain things, something analogous to guessing and conjecturing. (*Guide*, II: 22, 319)

On reaching the heavens, we reach the limits of science for Maimonides, and we can but appeal to God if we wish to indicate how one might in principle make sense of them. Maimonides seems to suggest a principle of humility regarding knowledge – what we will term the principle of epistemological humility – where we cannot simply assume that we can apply our current knowledge of science from one sphere to another.

This all stems from what Maimonides refers to in the *Guide* as the 'true perplexity', which is the clash between Aristotelian science and Ptolemaic astronomy. Maimonides accepts that Ptolemaic astronomy had come up with mathematical models that accounted almost perfectly for astronomical observations regarding the motions and positions of the planets. The problem was that this Ptolemaic model was inconsistent with Aristotelian physics. So a correct description of astronomy entails dismissing Aristotle's physics – a major problem if one accepts that Aristotle's physics is correct. Maimonides therefore writes

> The Heavens are the heavens of the Lord, but the earth hath He given to the sons of man [*Psalms*, 115: 16]. I mean thereby that the deity alone fully knows the true reality, the nature, the substance, the form, the motions, the causes of the heavens. But He has enabled man to have knowledge of what is beneath the heavens, for that is his world and his dwelling place in which he has been placed and of which he himself is a part. This is the truth. (*Guide*, II: 24, 326–7)

Aristotelian physics cannot be rejected, but it also cannot be extended to the celestial realm. Thus, it appears from the above as if Maimonides thought we could not gain scientific knowledge of the celestial realm, though there are inevitably some who dispute this reading and argue that Maimonides countenances the possibility that in the future a scientist might find a 'demonstration by means of which the true reality of what is obscure for me will become clear to him' (*Guide*, II: 24, 327).

For all the problems with the argument from particularisation, Maimonides is making an interesting philosophical point about the limits of our scientific schemas when applied to the celestial realm. There is a real question concerning how we are to apply a scientific scheme derived from our empirical observations regarding the universe, to a heavenly realm that is altogether different. As Maimonides warns:

> And to fatigue the minds with notions that cannot be grasped by them and for the grasp of which they have no instrument, is a defect in one's inborn disposition or some sort of temptation. Let us then stop at a point that is within our capacity... (*Guide*, II: 24, 327)

Notably, Gersonides is rather more optimistic about the extent of our scientific knowledge. As mentioned, his particularisation argument appeals to more than just the accidental properties of the heavens. For Gersonides the first and 'most distinctive feature of a generated substance is that it is made for some end' (*Wars*, VI: 1, 6, 239). Gersonides here takes the Aristotelian notion of a final cause that we have already encountered (**2.1**), and argues that nature as a whole is structured for certain purposes, or teleologically. All natural phenomena can be seen to serve some end, and Gersonides argues that if something has a certain end, it must have been directed towards that goal by some agent – an intelligent being must have directed it in that fashion. Since, in the Gersonidean scheme of things, this applies as much to the heavenly bodies as to anything else, their teleological structure is a further argument for the conclusion that they must have been generated.

What is particularly interesting on Gersonides' scheme is his view that all the features of the heavenly realm are directed towards the perfection of the sublunar realm:

> For example, the distance between the heavenly domain and the earth is absolutely perfect in order that the activity necessary for the perfection of earthly phenomena emanate [from the heavenly bodies]. (*Wars*, VI: 1, 7, 243)

Thus, it seems as if Gersonides pushes man into a more prominent position in the universe than does Maimonides. For Gersonides, the universe is structured for the benefit of our world and neither God nor the celestial realms are entirely beyond our cognitive capacities. This is not to suggest that our 'knowledge' of this structure is on a par with that of God. But it is to say that we can know about the structure of the heavenly realm and the manner in which God has created it. For Maimonides, neither of these claims is true.

Gersonides' argument might not ultimately be any more convincing than that of Maimonides. In a post-Darwinian world, we are used to the idea that natural objects can give the impression of purposeful design without appealing to an intelligent being to account for them. Ignoring these problems though, we can see that the difference between the way that Maimonides and Gersonides present their arguments is more than a mere detail. Where Maimonides simply posits God as an explanation of the unexplainable without giving any positive explanation of God's actions, Gersonides believes that he can actually explain why the heavenly bodies are thus and so – it is because that is how they must be if they are to perfect our sublunar realm. His integrated scientific account of the universe allows him to give details of the 'particularisation' of the heavens that God decided upon. Thus, their arguments have broader implications regarding the limits of our knowledge and man's importance in the cosmos. But these differences lead to a more fundamental disagreement on the question of creation itself.

Even if we were to accept the argument from particularisation, it only proves the creation of the world, not its creation *ex nihilo*. There is nothing to rule out the Platonic view that there was an eternal matter from which God created the world, since this would still allow for the particularisation that is fundamental to the argument. It is no coincidence therefore that while Maimonides, exoterically at least, argues for creation *ex nihilo*, Gersonides ends up arguing for a version of the Platonic view. For at the root of this divergence are their differing views on the limits of human knowledge. We can best appreciate this by turning first to their arguments against Aristotelian eternity.

4. ETERNITY AND THE LIMITS OF SCIENCE

Given that Maimonides is convinced by Aristotelian science, what are his problems with its account of the origins of the universe? Maimonides divides the Aristotelian arguments for eternity into two categories: arguments from the nature of the world and arguments from the nature of God, though we should note that according to Maimonides, Aristotle himself realised that these were not demonstrations and only his followers misrepresented them as such. We will for the moment confine ourselves to the arguments from nature, which appeal to our scientific knowledge of the world in order to show that it cannot have been brought into existence (and must therefore be eternal). So, for example, the second argument

Maimonides presents, an argument that Gersonides also reproduces at *Wars*, VI: 1, 3, 227, is from the nature of matter:

> The first matter ... is not subject to generation and passing away. For if the first matter were subject to generation, it would have to have a matter out of which it would be generated. And it necessarily would follow that the generated matter would have to be endowed with form, for the latter is the true reality of generation. But we have assumed that the matter in question was matter not endowed with form. Now such matter necessarily must not be generated from some thing. It is consequently eternal and not liable to be destroyed. (*Guide*, II: 14, 286)

First an explanatory note. The matter/form distinction is one of the most important in ancient Greek philosophy. If we begin with our understanding of everyday objects, we can talk about their matter and form in an equally everyday manner. To take one of Aristotle's favourite examples, a bronze statue is made of bronze (its matter) and is formed into a certain shape (its form). What though if the bronze were not shaped into a statue and was simply scrap? According to Aristotle it would still have the form of being a pile of scrap. The idea is that matter and form are not two separable parts of an object. You cannot encounter 'bare' matter without form. The two are each (real) features of substances, which we can separate conceptually but not in reality. What is true, however, is that when objects change, it is their form that changes rather than their matter. The same matter, the bronze for example, might be a statue at one point, then a bowl, and then a pile of scrap. In each case the matter is taking on successive different forms. Aristotle has far more to say about this distinction, but for our current purposes these basics suffice.

Maimonides now presents Aristotle's argument as follows. Breaking it down to its most basic elements, the argument is that matter is either generated, in which case it must be generated from some other matter, or since here it is presumed to be the first unformed matter and not generated, it must be eternal. To flesh this out a little, if the First Matter, the most basic stuff of the universe, had been generated, it must have been generated from some other matter, since as we have seen, it was accepted that matter cannot simply be brought into existence out of nothing. To account for any matter always requires that we appeal to some underlying matter out of which it was generated. What, though, if we claim that this First Matter has no form and is indeed pure matter, the underlying bedrock of creation? The problem is that this too cannot have been generated. As we've seen, though the matter/form distinction is a useful conceptual tool and refers to a real distinction, one cannot actually encounter sheer unformed matter. So once we are in the realm of actual generated things, we must be talking of matter with form – true generation *means* having matter with form. But in that case, since generation means bringing form to matter, the first unformed matter cannot have been generated. It must therefore be eternal.

Ultimately, this argument relies on the idea that the coming into existence of matter out of nothing is impossible. This is taken either to be self-evident, or something that we know from our repeated perception of the world around us – we have never seen something come from nothing. The most notable thing is that both Maimonides and Gersonides agree with all of this. For Maimonides, however, it is only true of the empirical world. Given what we know of matter, Aristotle is absolutely correct about its nature. However, that does not rule out creation *ex nihilo* for Maimonides, who goes on to present a famous analogy.

Imagine, he says, a man on an island who originally had a wife who bore him a child. The mother dies and the child grows up to ask the question that all parents dread – 'Daddy, how did I get here?' Skimming over the embarrassing part as most parents do, Maimonides has the father tell him that he, and all beings like him, began as a small body inside a female of the species and grew there and was fed there until he reached such a size that 'an opening was opened up for him in the lower part of the body, from which he issued and came forth' (*Guide*, II: 17, 295). The child asks if the small body ate, drank or drew breath during this time to which the father answers in the negative. The child, perfectly logically, wonders how he, who cannot go without food, drink and most certainly air, for anything but a short period of time, could have existed in a sack of liquid for nine months. The child therefore dismisses the whole idea as impossible (much to the relief of the father, no doubt, who can wait a little longer for the awkward conversation). And yet, of course, the father was telling the truth. Maimonides' point is that the child understandably dismisses the truth as impossible on account of his empirical knowledge. But that is because his empirical knowledge is irrelevant to the case at hand. Aristotle similarly, on account of his empirical knowledge of matter, dismisses the possibility of the creation of matter *ex nihilo*. But this is because his empirical knowledge is similarly irrelevant to the case at hand. Maimonides sets this out in the following principle:

> No inference can be drawn in any respect from the nature of a thing after it has been generated, has attained its final state, and has achieved stability in

its most perfect state, to the state of the thing while it moved toward being generated. Nor can an inference be drawn from the state of the thing when it moves toward being generated to its state before it begins to move thus. (*Guide*, II: 17, 295)

The child of the parable, in rejecting the truth, has done so for very good reason. But while he is correct that no human being could survive in the conditions of the foetus, we cannot make inferences about our foetal development from what we know of our development as fully formed human beings. Similarly, we cannot make inferences from our knowledge of how matter is generated in this world in order to understand the generation of matter in the initial act of creation. Aristotle's argument regarding matter is correct for Maimonides, as long as it remains limited to the generation of matter within the world. But he cannot make claims from this empirical knowledge to the very origins of matter under circumstances inconceivably different to those from which we gained that knowledge.

One might argue that there is a sense in which the argument is circular. It is saying that we cannot infer anything from the nature of matter as we know it now, to its nature when it came into being. But that is to assume that there *was* a point at which it did come into being, which is precisely the question at issue. Thus Maimonides is assuming there was an 'origin' in formulating his very principle. At the same time, it could be argued that the eternity theorist is making the assumption that matter simply cannot be generated from nothing in order to argue that it must be eternal. But that again could be construed as simply rejecting the other side of the argument before you begin. So both sides are assuming what they want to prove. Maimonides would remind us, however, of the principle of epistemological humility. We have already seen that we cannot apply the principles of sublunar physics to the celestial sphere, so in the same way maybe, we should not assume that they are absolute truths about the nature of reality as such, especially when very different from our current reality. Once again, the principle of epistemological humility is at the very heart of what Maimonides is saying here.

Gersonides again provides us with a rather different take on all of this. We have already seen that he is less radical than Maimonides in his epistemological views, believing that we can know more about the heavens than Maimonides thought possible. Similarly, while Gersonides rejects many of the Aristotelian arguments for eternity on similar grounds to Maimonides, accepting that we cannot assume that an existent thing in its completed state will have the same properties as an existent thing in the process of generation, on his own version of the principle 'this is not true in every respect; for it is possible that there are features that are common to the generation of a whole and the generation of a part' (*Wars*, VI: 1, 4, 235).

Gersonides reads Maimonides' principle in a limited manner as saying that one cannot draw inferences from the generation of the parts of something to conclusions about the generation of the whole. But there are elements of existent things that Gersonides does accept as necessary features of existence *per se* and that do not depend either on what stage of generation an existent has reached or on the part/whole distinction. For Gersonides 'whatever is necessary of something [simply] because it exists, [no matter] which attributes it may have, must be present in it at the moment of its generation' (*Wars*, VI: 1, 17, 328). Certain features of existence are so fundamental for Gersonides that anything we can conceive of as existing must answer to them. Most significantly, 'it is assumed as a self-evident axiom in physics that nothing is generated from nothing' (*Wars*, VI: 1, 17, 325). This, and various other scientific considerations, such as the impossibility of a vacuum, led him to argue against creation *ex nihilo*.

> It is therefore evident that the view of the Torah is that the world is created; but it doesn't follow from this that it is created absolutely from nothing. Indeed, it would seem that the Torah throughout describes creation as something from something, except in the case of the Intelligences... The world is created from something in so far as it is generated from [some kind of] body; it is created from nothing in so far as this body is devoid of form. (*Wars*, VI: 1, 17, 329–30)

The argument that we cannot apply *any* of our scientific theories to the moment of creation is one that Gersonides does not accept. Instead, Gersonides concludes in favour of creation from pre-existent matter, though he distinguishes his view from that of Plato since Gersonidean pre-existent matter is formless, unlike Plato's. When we speak of generation therefore, according to Gersonides we are speaking of the bestowal of form, not the creation of matter out of nothing. So where Maimonides goes for the 'traditional view' of creation *ex nihilo*, Gersonides accepts a version of the Platonic view. And at the basis of this divergence is a dispute over the limits of our scientific knowledge. While Maimonides does not believe that we can use our scientific knowledge to rule out the possibility of creation *ex nihilo*, Gersonides thinks we can know enough about the nature of reality *per se* to do just that.

5. CREATION, ETERNITY AND INFINITY

Having demonstrated that the heavens were generated, Gersonides argues separately that time and motion must have been generated. On this occasion though he appeals to the final strand of cosmogonic argumentation that we will consider: the question of infinity. Prior to Gersonides, Saadia Gaon, who seems less constrained by concerns about the limits of knowledge, dealt with this issue in two of the four arguments he presents in *Emunot*.

Saadia's first argument for creation runs as follows:

> It is certain that heaven and earth are both finite, because the earth is in the center of the universe and the heaven revolves around it. It therefore follows, of necessity, that the force inhering in them be finite, since it is impossible for an infinite force to reside in a finite body, for such a possibility is rejected by all that is known. Now, since the force that maintains these two is finite, it follows necessarily that they must have a beginning and an end. (*Emunot*, II: 1, 41)

In this argument Saadia begins with the Aristotelian view discussed earlier, which places the earth at the centre of a finite universe. Given that the universe is finite, it can only contain a finite force, the twelfth of the Aristotelian premises cited by Maimonides in the introduction to Part II of the *Guide*. And given that we only have a finite force, this 'battery' only has a limited shelf life, so the existence of the world it is powering must be finite, i.e. it must have a beginning and end.

All that this argument actually proves, however, is that the universe cannot sustain *itself* since it can only have finite power. It does not rule out the possibility of a finite universe that is eternal through being given infinite motion by something external to it such as God. In fact, that is precisely the picture that Aristotle would accept – the universe is finite but eternal since it has an eternal Unmoved Mover. The only way that the argument can actually prove that the universe must have been created is by smuggling in some further Aristotelian principles familiar from the previous chapter.

Firstly, we should recall that the universe considered in itself is only possible of existence, to utilise a term that we have already encountered (1.2). Its existence and non-existence are possible, so its existence must be accounted for by appeal to something external to it. Secondly, we should recall the principle of plenitude – that all possibilities are realised over infinite time. With these additions, Saadia can reach his desired conclusion. Since the universe has the possibility of non-existence, and according to the principle of plenitude that must have been realised at some time in the infinite past, the world must have been brought into existence at some point. Notably, as Herbert Davidson has shown, the arguments we are considering are based on those of a sixth-century critic of Aristotle – John Philoponus – who specialised in turning Aristotelian philosophy back on itself, and filled these gaps in argumentation in his own writings.

Regardless of the validity of the argument itself, we can see that by bringing in the principle of plenitude, it assumes that time is infinite. The problem for Saadia is that his fourth argument for creation proves the *impossibility* of infinite time. Beginning from the present point in time, he proceeds:

> Let it be supposed that a person should desire mentally to advance in time above this point. He would be unable to do it for the reason that time is infinite, and what is infinite cannot be completely traversed mentally in a fashion ascending [backward to the beginning].
>
> Now this same reason makes it impossible for existence to have traversed infinity in descending fashion so as to reach us. But if existence had not reached us, we would not have come into being. The necessary conclusion from this premise would, then, have been that we, the company of those that are, are not, and that those that exist do not exist. Since, however, I find that I do exist, I know that existence has traversed the whole length of time until it reached me and that, if it were not for the fact that time is finite, existence could not have traversed it. (*Emunot*, II: 1, 45)

If we begin with the fact that we exist, we can ask how we ever arrived at this point. Creation gives us an easy answer – God created the world a finite amount of time ago, and that amount of time has now passed, or as Saadia puts it 'existence has traversed the whole length of time', so that we now find ourselves at this point. What though if time were infinite? Saadia's point is that existence cannot traverse an infinite amount of time. The intuitive point he is trying to get across is that if time has no beginning, then how did we ever reach this point? We would basically be claiming that we had reached the end of an infinite amount of time. But how does one understand the traversing of an infinite past? It would be like coming across a fatigued jogger who, when asked why he is so exhausted claims to have just completed an infinite running race. But how could one possibly perform such a feat? How are we to understand the completion of something that stretches back to *infinity*? And it is on account of the purported impossibility of such an idea that Saadia draws the conclusion that God must have created the world a finite amount of time ago, or else we cannot account for our existing now.

So Saadia assumes that time is infinite for his first argument, and that it cannot be for the fourth. One could argue that Saadia did not realise that the first argument assumes that time is infinite and has not therefore seen the contradiction – a distinct possibility given that he does not mention infinite time in his presentation of the argument. This might shore up Sirat's view that Saadia 'used his sources without considering them deeply or criticizing them'.[4] A more charitable interpretation would be that he is using the sort of disjunctive method that we saw Maimonides using in the previous chapter – he is proving that the world must have been created whether you begin from the premise that time is finite or from the premise that time is infinite, though it has to be admitted that unlike Maimonides he makes no claims that this is how he is proceeding. Either way, Saadia brings to our attention the centrality of the notions of finitude and infinitude for this subject.

Gersonides has rather more to say on this question, and presents a plethora of proofs for the finitude of time and motion. Taking one example from, *Wars*, VI: 1, 11, he argues that according to the astronomical system of the period, different heavenly spheres rotated at different speeds. Clearly then, those that rotate faster would have more rotations in a specified period of time than a sphere that rotated more slowly. So common sense would tell us that one of the spheres had more rotations than the other. The problem is that on the assumption that time is infinite in the past, both spheres would have an infinite number of rotations, which would mean that each have an equal number of rotations – infinity – with Gersonides here invoking the principle that no infinite can be greater than another infinite (*Wars*, VI: 1, 11, 291). But that contradicts our common sense idea that one must have rotated more than the other.

Though this again relies on an outdated cosmology, the basic problem of the infinite that it exhibits can be made independently of the cosmology. For example, while we would say that by the end of the month, time will have advanced an extra month and by the end of next month a further month will have been added, if time is infinite in the past, what we actually have are two infinite magnitudes and one cannot be greater than the other. Whether we measure time from 31 March 2008 infinitely backwards or starting on 30 April 2008 going backwards, given that we are going backwards infinitely, we cannot put a cap on how much time we have traversed 'altogether', and it is therefore meaningless to say that one of these lengths of time is greater than the other, despite this one-month gap. On both, an infinite number of days have passed. So if time is infinite, we end up with some very strange conclusions that seem to go against commonsense assumptions. We are forced to say that despite the passing of a month, the age of the world has not changed. While now there are set theorists who would accept these counterintuitive conclusions for infinite sets, for Gersonides, these paradoxes show that time cannot be infinite and thus, given the link between time and motion that we noted previously, the world must have been created at some point together with time.

6. CONCLUSION: CREATION AND THE LIMITS OF THEOLOGY

While it remains difficult to understand how the arguments we have studied could *prove* that God created the universe, the philosophical issues raised during the discussion are significant. The idea that our scientific laws might not apply to the origins of the universe find modern expression in the idea of the 'singularity' with which our universe began, discussed by Big Bang theorists. And though we have only presented the arguments against infinite time, even in the late medieval period Hasdai Crescas argued contra Gersonides for a view of time as infinite. Disagreements remain to this day over infinite time and whether or not an infinite number of past events can exist, all as part of the debate over the possibility of what is termed an 'actual infinite' (though there are also disputes over whether time can be defined as an actual infinite!). This is one for the interested reader to investigate further.

Even for the medievals, however, we have seen how differing perspectives on these issues meant that no definitive answer was reached. A fascinating comment in the *Kuzari* suggests that maybe this stalemate should have been expected. In discussing creation, Halevi puts the following analysis of Aristotle's arguments into the mouth of the sage:

> He exerted his mind because he had no tradition from any reliable source at his disposal. He meditated on the beginning and end of the world, but found as much difficulty in the theory of a beginning as in that of eternity. Finally, these abstract speculations which made for eternity, prevailed, and he found no reason to inquire into the chronology or derivation of those who lived before him. Had he lived among a people with well-authenticated and generally acknowledged traditions, he would have applied his deductions and arguments to establish the theory of creation,

however difficult, instead of eternity, which is even more difficult to accept. (*Kuzari*, I: 65, 53–4)

We have already seen that Halevi has strong reservations about the power of rational argument in the religious sphere, and here he seems to say that an apparently 'neutral' rational proof can often in fact be prejudiced, whether consciously or (more likely) not, by the intellectual or cultural baggage that one brings to it. Thus, in a passage that would resonate with many contemporary thinkers, he notes that had Aristotle been predisposed by his tradition to creation *ex nihilo*, he doubtless would have formulated a proof for that conclusion rather than for the eternity of the world. Arguments for the existence of God are a perfect case in point. The cosmological argument often seems obvious to religious thinkers who believe that the existence of the world cannot just be a 'brute fact' and must have a First Cause. But it seems just as obvious to a secular thinker that there is absolutely no need for such an account and that the argument therefore does not work.

Though he sees no philosophical reason to prefer one view of creation to another, Halevi is not about to slip into a postmodern claim that there is no truth of the matter. There is, in his opinion, an absolute reason to believe in one of the views on account of its prophetic origins in the Torah, a point that Maimonides also makes rather more guardedly (*Guide*, II: 16, 294). Yet it is not clear that there was an official 'prophetic' view prior to the medieval period. Differences over the interpretation of the opening verses of Genesis abound in traditional rabbinic literature and all of the thinkers we have looked at in this chapter include detailed comments on Genesis in their philosophical works that indicate its ambiguities.

As a mere taster, Saadia has to reject the idea of the eternity of water and air that some had based on Genesis, 1: 2 – 'And the earth was empty and void (*tohu va-vohu*) and darkness was upon the face of the deep and the wind of God hovered over the face of the water.' Maimonides is forced to deal with the view that God creates and destroys an infinite number of successive worlds, if only to dismiss apparent midrashic affirmations of it by Rabbi Abahu in *Genesis Rabbah*: 'the Holy One, may His name be blessed, used to create worlds and to destroy them' (*Guide*, II: 30, 349). Yet this very view was perfectly acceptable to Hasdai Crescas who quotes the same *midrash* in support of it.[5] And Gersonides devotes the second part of *Wars*, VI, to showing that his Platonic view fits best with the biblical text. Even the most influential of all biblical commentators, Rashi (1040–1105), can be read as saying that God was working with all manner of pre-existent raw materials, not least the 'empty' and 'void' earth of Genesis, 1: 2. So even if we accept that reason is limited and that we should turn to 'the Jewish view', it is not at all clear what that is. The appearance of creation *ex nihilo* in Saadia and Maimonides was itself highly influential in establishing it as *the* canonical view in Judaism. What appears clearer is the nature of the God that each view brings with it, as we have seen. Or is it?

Both Maimonides and Gersonides agree that we can interpret biblical texts in accordance with Plato's view. More controversially maybe, Maimonides writes that if Aristotelian eternity were to be demonstrated, we could reinterpret the texts figuratively to accommodate that. At the same time it would necessitate a rather radical rethink: 'the Law as whole would become void and a shift to other opinions would take place' (*Guide*, II: 25, 330). At first glance the very countenancing of this possibility seems beyond anything that would remain recognisably Jewish. It is worth, however, remaining with Maimonides for the last word on this and returning to a significant element of his discussion of eternity that we have missed out – his refutation of arguments for eternity from the nature of God.

To simplify one of the arguments somewhat, if God made the world at a certain point, why had he not made it until that point? As Maimonides writes, there must either have been something stopping him, or something that suddenly motivated him to act. But we would then have something causing God to change his mind, so to speak, as if something turned out to be a good reason for God only after giving it some thought. But God, as a perfect being cannot be subject to such external influence. The very idea that God changes his mind at all is highly problematic for philosophers, since if God is perfect, a change can only move him in one direction, and that is away from perfection – or else, a change of mind implies he was not perfect in the first place. Ultimately neither of these is terribly helpful in application to God. As Maimonides himself puts it in a paraphrase of the argument 'does not the supposition that one wishes at one time and does not wish at another time imply in itself a change?' (*Guide*, II: 18, 301). If the world is eternal, all of these problems disappear since there is no change in a God who eternally causes an eternal world.

Gersonides' refutation of this argument (*Wars*, VI: 1, 18, 342–3), is based on the inherently defective nature of the matter with which God is working. Since matter is defective, the 'goodness' it exhibits when formed into our world cannot possibly be eternally present in it. So it is not that God changes his mind. God's intention that the matter should take this perfected form is eternal. But matter simply cannot be the bearer of eternal goodness since it has a defective nature. In contrast, Maimonides' refutation of these arguments follows the pattern of epistemological humility that we have traced throughout the chapter, though here it is even more severe in its application. It boils down to the point that when we speak of God, we cannot apply the same logic that we apply to our ordinary language. As Maimonides puts it

> If the will in question belongs to a material being...then the will is subject to change because of impediments and supervening accidents. But as for a being separate from matter, its will...is not subject to change. The fact that it may wish one thing now and another thing tomorrow does not constitute a change in its essence and does not call for another cause... It is only by equivocation that our will and that of a being separate from matter are both designated as 'will,' for there is no likeness between the two wills. (*Guide*, II: 18, 301)

Again we find a version of the idea that has been central to Maimonides throughout: we cannot apply what we know from our experience to what is in principle beyond our experience. But whereas we can at least proffer arguments for creation, when it comes to our knowledge of God, the limits are stretched beyond breaking point – 'there is no likeness between the two wills'. In our attempts to characterise how God is viewed in each creation package, some, including Maimonides at the exoteric level, have been arguing that certain conceptions are more acceptable than others. Yet if he is serious in placing these radical limits on our knowledge of God, it is not clear that any of our characterisations are particularly appropriate. Gersonides is again less pessimistic about the possibility of making limited claims about God. But this issue suddenly becomes highly significant. If there is no rational argument that demonstrates creation over eternity, their respective theological implications might become rather more significant. And while the view of God as a voluntary agent appeared fundamental to both Maimonides and Gersonides, we are now faced with the question of the extent to which we can characterise God in this way at all. And so we turn next to this very question.

NOTES

1   Details of Maimonides' version of this cosmology can be found in *Mishneh Torah*, 'Laws of the Foundations of the Torah', chapter III.

2   In *The Works of Philo: Complete and Unabridged*, New Updated Edition, trans. C. D. Yonge (Peabody, MA: Hendrickson, 1993), 3

3   A. Marx, 'Texts by and about Maimonides', *Jewish Quarterly Review*, vol. 25 (1934–5), 371–428. Quotation from 378.

4   Colette Sirat, *A History of Jewish Philosophy in the Middle Ages* (Cambridge: Cambridge University Press, 1990), 24.

5   Hasdai Crescas, *Light*, IIIA: 1, 5, translated in Warren Zev Harvey, *Physics and Metaphysics in Hasdai Crescas* (Amsterdam: J. C. Gieben, 1998), 41–3.

FURTHER READING

This chapter has only dipped into some of the arguments discussed by these thinkers. The following deal with these arguments and more, and contain detailed bibliographies:

For an account of Isaac Israeli's Neoplatonic approach, see A. Altmann and S. M. Stern, *Isaac Israeli* (Oxford: Oxford University Press, 1958), especially Part IIA.

Maimonides' approach and his sources are given a book-length treatment in Kenneth Seeskin, *Maimonides on the Origin of the World* (Cambridge: Cambridge University Press, 2005).

Gersonides' arguments, are treated in detail in Seymour Feldman, 'Gersonides' Proofs for the Creation of the Universe', Proceedings of the American Academy for Jewish Research 35 (1967), 113–37.

A variety of views, together with detailed consideration of their relationship with the nature of time and infinity can be found in Tamar Rudavsky, *Time Matters: Time Creation and Cosmology in Medieval Jewish Philosophy* (Albany: SUNY Press, 2000), chapters 1 and 2.

All of the arguments and their sources are discussed in detail in Herbert Davidson, *Proofs for Eternity, Creation and the Existence of God in Medieval Islamic and Jewish Philosophy* (Oxford: Oxford University Press, 1987), chapters 2–6.

If you want to look further into the possibility of an actual infinite, a good place to start is with the famous Hilbert's hotel example, discussed (and supported) by William Lane Craig in his 'The Existence of God and The Beginning of the Universe', It can be found at http://www.origins.org/articles/craig_existencegodbeginning.html

For Maimonides' esoteric views, see the Further Reading section of the Appendix.

3

Divine Attributes

In attempting to speak of the One in his *Enneads*, Plotinus famously described it as 'above being'. The One is unknowable and ineffable – beyond our knowledge and beyond description or characterisation. We know *that* the One exists, but we can know nothing of *what* its essence is. Given the Neoplatonic currents in medieval Jewish philosophy, it will come as little surprise that this view had a profound influence on the way in which our thinkers would understand language relating to God. Thus, according to Saadia, the idea of God

> must of necessity be subtler than the subtlest and more recondite than the most recondite and more abstract than the most abstract and profounder than the most profound ... so that it would be impossible to fathom its character at all. (*Emunot*, II: Exordium, 92)

And during his discussion of divine attributes, Maimonides quotes Psalms, 65: 2 – 'Silence is praise to Thee' – and expands:

> This is a most perfectly put phrase regarding this matter. For of whatever we say intending to magnify and exalt, on the one hand we find that it can have some application to Him, may He be exalted, and on the other we perceive in it some deficiency. Accordingly, silence and limiting oneself to the apprehension of the intellects are more appropriate. (*Guide*, I: 59, 139–40)

This could be a very short chapter.

Yet pronouncements on the nature of God abound in classical Jewish sources. Despite the lack of explicit philosophical discourse in the *Tanakh* and Talmud, when it comes to descriptions of God there is certainly no lack of source material. The problem is that much of it portrays God in a manner that is as far from the rarefied 'above being' of Plotinus as it is possible to get. So, for example, we are told that God wrote the Ten Commandments on the tablets of stone with his own finger (Exodus, 31: 18), which was presumably at the end of 'the mighty hand and the outstretched arm' (Deuteronomy, 7: 19) with which he delivered the Israelites from Egypt. Other indirect physical descriptions have him, for example, walking (Genesis, 3: 8) or sitting (Lamentations, 5: 19). And aside from the physical images, we are also told of his character traits by no less an authority than God himself at Exodus, 34: 6, where he states that he is, among other things, 'mighty, merciful and gracious, longsuffering, and abundant in love and truth'. And of course God – who 'by wisdom founded the earth; by understanding he established the heavens' (Proverbs, 3: 19) – has incomparable knowledge and wisdom.

Similar anthropomorphisms – the attributing of human form or characteristics to God – are found in rabbinic sources. The Talmud, for example, famously describes God as wearing *tefillin* (*bBerakhot* 6a), usually translated as phylacteries, which are the black leather boxes with attached straps that are worn by men on their head and arm when praying in the morning. Most radically, an early mystical text – the *Shiur Komah* (lit. *Measure of the Body*) – details the measurements of each of God's limbs, even if disputes abound over whether or not these measurements were intended to be taken literally. The Talmudic tractate *Baba Metzia* at 59b even has God laughing, thereby adding, in the context, an ironic sense of humour to his list of personality traits. And neither the *Tanakh* nor the Talmud are averse to anthropopathism, the ascribing of human feelings to God, as we know from numerous references to his getting angry (Exodus, 32: 10) or upset (Genesis, 6: 7), to mention just two examples.

Certainly many Jews, then and now, would stare blankly if confronted by technical philosophical language describing God as 'above being'. But all Jews, regardless of their philosophical leanings, believed in a God who was incomparably greater than any other being – for 'there is none like thee, O Lord' (Jeremiah, 10: 6). The idea of God as a perfect being wholly other than man was not, therefore, confined to philosophers, and the corporeal language used to describe God in the texts was bound to raise questions. What *was* the preserve of the philosophers, however, was the detailed analysis of the issues this use of language raised. That said, belief in God's incorporeality was not a given, even at this stage of Jewish history. In a well-known critical gloss to Maimonides' claim that those who attribute corporeality to God are heretics, Rabbi Abraham ben David of Posquierres, better known by the acronym Rabad, refers to those 'greater and better' than Maimonides who have believed in God's corporeality.[1] Nonetheless, those who do so provoke the following from Maimonides:

> [W]hen you believe in the doctrine of the corporeality of God or believe that one of the states of the body belongs to Him, you *provoke His jealousy and anger, kindle the fire of His wrath*, and are *a hater, an enemy, and an adversary* of God, much more so than an *idolater*. (*Guide*, I: 36, 84)

For Maimonides, the ascription of corporeality to God is worse than the cardinal sin of idolatry. Notably, in a late responsum he maintained that he had never believed that *Shiur Komah* had been written by the sages, and advises that it should be destroyed.[2]

Philosophically speaking, then, it had been demonstrated that God was wholly non-corporeal, and thus for our thinkers physical descriptions of God defied reason. It is also worth noting the heightened polemical aspect to this particular medieval discussion. The Karaites, who utilised Greek categories of thought, as well as the Muslims and the Christians, ridiculed rabbinic anthropomorphism. It certainly looked remarkably unsophisticated in comparison to the stress on incorporeality in the Muslim world, the absolute unity of God being a central tenet of Mut'azilite belief for example. Moreover, belief in incorporeality might even have had political implications for Jews in the Islamic world, helping to safeguard their protected *dhimmi* status in those territories.[3] With regard to Christianity, it is probably no coincidence that Saadia dedicates *Emunot ve-De'ot*, II: 5 to picking apart the Christian Trinitarian view of God as implying corporeality.

Whichever way one looks at it, there were evidently serious problems with the sort of 'God-talk' we find in classic Jewish texts and on closer inspection we find two different, albeit related problems. The first is a straightforward question of meaning – a semantic question – asking what these words mean when applied to God. If God is unique and non-physical, he obviously cannot have arms or hands and these terms will require reinterpretation. But we also get our only purchase on the meaning of terms like 'power' or 'knowledge' in a human context. Can these terms therefore be applied beyond that context to God? Surely, for example, the term 'knowledge' in all of its human contexts refers to a knowledge that is highly limited and thus to say that his knowledge is comparable to ours in any way surely belittles God. So there is a real problem in understanding what our words mean when we displace them from their usual context and apply them to a context beyond direct human experience in talking about God. Can we really preserve the uniqueness of God when all we have at our disposal is our ordinary language?

The second question arises out of the metaphysical connotations of this use of language, which begin, but do not end, with the problem of corporeality. It should be obvious that asserting that God has physical attributes implies a corporeal God, with all the associated imperfections that corporeality brings. The deeper foundation of this problem, however, was the manner in which it infected divine unity. Thus, Saadia's discussion of the language of the *Tanakh* is preceded by a discourse on God's one-ness and Maimonides states: 'there is no profession of unity unless the doctrine of God's corporeality is denied' (*Guide*, I: 35, 81). But the concept of unity for the medievals goes much further than incorporeality. The idea that God is an absolutely simple being with no multiplicity or complexity was not only used to rule out language that falsely implied physical composition in God. As we will see, certain thinkers believed that the attribution of *any* property to God introduced an unacceptable level of complexity into his essence, which could mislead us as to the nature of God.

This type of problem regarding the nature of what exists is what philosophers would call an ontological problem, and questions surrounding divine attributes also have this ontological dimension. Thus, if one believed that God really had a hand, this would obviously have problematic ontological implications. Similarly, anthropopathic descriptions of God's feelings of anger or pleasure imply corporeality for Maimonides and Saadia, with the latter noting that those who 'insist on arrogating for Him ... anger or good will or the like, they really arrogate for Him a corporeal character by way of implication' (*Emunot*, II: Exordium, 93). Where the ontological dimension of attributes is most controversial, however, is with the so-called essential attributes of God, such as the references to God's 'knowledge' or 'will'. Whether the use of such terms introduces multiplicity into God's essence and is metaphysically problematic was a matter of dispute, as we will see.

We have seen then that 'God-talk' throws out two related problems – what does it mean and how does it impact on our understanding of God's nature? Most importantly, we need to investigate the extent to which the medievals thought we could preserve meaning for the words without encroaching on God's unity. It is to these questions that we address ourselves in this chapter, focusing mainly on the dispute between Maimonides and Gersonides, though we begin with Saadia's and Maimonides' 'guides' to reading the *Tanakh*.

1. HOW TO READ THE *TANAKH*: SAADIA AND MAIMONIDES

The first obstacle to a correct philosophic understanding of God is the language of Scripture itself and Saadia and Maimonides address themselves to this early on in their philosophical works. Thus, Maimonides begins the *Guide* by stating that its first purpose 'is to explain the meanings of certain terms occurring in the books of prophecy', (*Guide*, Introduction to the First Part, 5). As one might expect, Maimonides elsewhere speaks of other purposes, but mastering the problematic terms in the *Tanakh* is certainly the 'first' required skill for any of the further purposes he cites, such as understanding the biblical texts that make up *Ma'aseh Bereshit* and *Ma'aseh Merkavah*.

The sorts of biblical terms requiring explanation is very clear both to Saadia and Maimonides, who state their criteria for reading (or rereading) Scripture. As Saadia writes:

> whenever there is encountered ... an expression pertaining to the description of our Creator or His handiwork which stands in contradiction to the requirement of sound reason, there can be no doubt about it that that expression was meant to be taken in a figurative sense, which the diligent students will find if they seek it. (*Emunot*, II: 3, 100)

For Maimonides the barrier is more strictly defined: we only appeal to a figurative reading if there is a strict *demonstration* that goes contrary to the literal reading. Exoterically at least, he refuses to read the creation account figuratively precisely because in his opinion there is no available demonstration to the contrary. Since the incorporeality of God had been demonstrated, however, there is a need for reinterpretation in all cases where God is spoken of in corporeal terms, whether directly or by implication. Indeed, all of the thinkers that interest us would be agreed upon the need for a figurative reading of descriptions ascribing corporeality to God. They differ, however, over which descriptions actually imply corporeality.

Maimonides begins the *Guide* with a lengthy discussion of the problem of God's attributes that falls into two main divisions. Chapters 1–49 are, on the whole, a guide to understanding biblical language used about God. The section is basically devoted to lexicography, and many of the chapters discuss possible meanings of a word and specify how it is to be understood when applied to God in a way that removes any suggestion of corporeality. For example, Genesis, 1: 26 – 'Let us make man in our image' – proves a very early obstacle to thinking of God as incorporeal. As Maimonides remarks, many have believed that God must have a body on account of this verse (though God would obviously be bigger). So this is his starting point in the first chapter of the *Guide* and he initially notes that the term for the *physical* form of something is the Hebrew *to'ar*, a term never used of God. At Genesis, 1: 26, therefore, the word *tzelem* is used, which is not to be understood in a physical sense. Instead, *tzelem* denotes the form of something in the Aristotelian sense we have discussed previously (**2.4**). There, however, we did not note the most important characteristic of an Aristotelian form – that it is 'the notion in virtue of which a thing is constituted as a substance and becomes what it is' (*Guide*, I: 1, 22), or the essential property of something without which it would not be that thing, such as the sum of the internal angles of the triangle, to take the example from **2.3**. In this case, the form of man is his rationality and thus the term *tzelem* here denotes man's rational faculty, his intellect.

Saadia takes a less intellectualistic route for this particular verse, and rather than translating the word *tzelem* itself, he looks at the idea expressed in the verse as a whole where the language used is 'merely a way of conferring honor' (*Emunot*, II: 9, 114). By saying that man alone is made in God's image, the Torah is conferring special honour on man among all of his creations. So the common denominator between Saadia and Maimonides is the wish to give interpretations of problematic biblical terms that eliminate any corporeal implications. Saadia deals with many of these terms in his biblical commentaries, but *Emunot* is the first work to engage with the problem of anthropomorphism within a systematic philosophical discussion of God's unity.

Saadia actually frames his philosophical discussion here in Aristotelian terms, using Aristotle's scheme of classification known as the categories. In medieval times, as a result of Aristotle's logic, sentences were understood as subject-predicate combinations – they were of the form 's is P'. So, for example we might predicate a quality of a person by saying that he is angry

– 'Daniel is angry' – or we might predicate a relation of that person by saying that he is a father – 'Daniel is a father'. The former predicate falls under the category of quality and the latter under the category of relation. So predicates are simply the words we use to describe subjects and Aristotle listed ten categories of predicate. Saadia proceeds to discuss the predicates used to describe God under each of these categories, and a couple of examples will give us an indication of some of the approaches he adopted.

Beginning with bodily parts attributed to God, discussed under the category of quantity, Saadia shows how these words are employed in the *Tanakh* in a non-material fashion even when not being used to speak of God. So, for example, the Hebrew word for 'hand' is used to speak of inanimate objects – 'the hand (lit.) of the river' (Daniel, 10: 4) – or to denote power in human contexts – 'their inhabitants were short of hand (lit.)' (II [Kings], 19: 26). Thus, as Saadia notes:

> Since, then, at certain times we find such expressions used of human beings, in a non-material sense how much more fittingly should they be construed in this non-material sense when applied to the Creator! (*Emunot*, II: 9, 119)

In this case then, Saadia's work is almost done for him. The non-corporeal interpretation of the words as they relate to God is prefigured in their non-corporeal use in other contexts.

Saadia goes on to discuss classic anthropopathisms like 'anger' or 'pleasure' under the category of quality, and anticipating Maimonides' more developed account, he writes that rather than actually attributing emotions to God, they are to be understood as referring to what is happening to human beings:

> whenever happiness and reward are decreed for some of God's creatures, that is characterised as God's pleasure … [W]hen some of them are deserving of hardship and punishment, that is characterised as God's anger. (*Emunot*, II: 11, 123)

For Saadia – and Halevi makes a similar point at *Kuzari*, II: 2, 83 – God is not actually angry; we just say that he is when we see things happening to people that we would usually understand to be produced by anger.

Maimonides' exegetical chapters give rather more detailed accounts of the meanings of specified terms and we will again just take a few illustrations. *Guide*, I: 19 discusses the word *malleh* – to fill. It can take its usual physical meaning such as when Rebecca the biblical matriarch fills her pitcher with water (Genesis, 24: 16). It can also mean the 'completion of a measurable period of time' as in 'And her days were fulfilled' (Genesis, 25: 24). But it is also used

> to signify the achievement of perfection in virtue of the latter's ultimate end... In this sense it is said: *The whole earth is full of His glory* [Isaiah, 6: 3]; the meaning of this verse being that the whole earth bears witness to His perfection... (*Guide*, I: 19, 46)

This is an example of an equivocal term, i.e. one word bearing different meanings, such as 'bank', which could refer to the bank of a river or a financial institution. Here similarly, the same word can take on different meanings, but only one of those meanings can be applied when the word is used to describe God. Other more general examples of figurative interpretation abound, as in Maimonides' explanation of how the term 'sitting' can be used in the ordinary everyday sense, or can be 'used figuratively to denote all steady, stable and changeless states' (*Guide*, I: 11, 37). Whenever the term is used of God, it is evidently to be understood in this latter sense since God cannot sit in the literal sense. So for Maimonides:

> *He that sitteth in heaven* [Psalms, 2: 4]. That is, the stable One who undergoes no manner of change, neither a change in his Essence... nor a change in His relation to what is other than Himself... (*ibid.*, 37–8)

Notably Saadia also anticipates this interpretation, understanding 'sitting' as referring to God's permanence (*Emunot*, II: 11, 127), though Maimonides does not mention this as an influence.

The obvious question that arises is why the misleading corporeal terms are used in the first place. Saadia indicates that were we to limit ourselves to 'true' descriptions and not speak of God in anthropomorphisms 'there would be nothing left for us to affirm except the fact of His existence' (*Emunot*, II: 10, 118). Given the quote regarding silence that we encountered at the beginning of this chapter, one might think that for Maimonides this would be no bad thing. Yet Maimonides himself admits that such language is necessary, explaining at *Guide*, I: 26 that 'The Torah speaks in the language of the sons of man' (*bYevamot* 71a). This Talmudic statement (which Maimonides has to reinterpret in order to use in the manner he wishes!) is taken to imply that since most people associate existence with physical existence and find it difficult to comprehend the existence of a non-corporeal being such as God, the Torah 'speaks their language', ascribing corporeal properties to God in order to make his existence evident to the masses. If the Torah had been written as a philosophical treatise on God's incorporeality, the likelihood of ordinary people understanding it, let alone subscribing to it, would be vanishingly small.

Along similarly pragmatic lines, the Torah only attributes terms to God that the masses would consider perfections and does not use words that would be thought of as imperfections from a human perspective. So, while talk of God 'seeing' or 'sitting' are allowed, the negative impact that talk of God 'sleeping' or 'eating' would have is enough to render these types of word impermissible, even though there is no substantive difference between any of these words in terms of their metaphysical implications. They all ultimately imply corporeality.

Such concessions made by the Torah, and hence by God himself, to accommodate the masses are a theme that we will encounter a number of times in Maimonides. In this specific case it is a concession to establish the existence of God firmly in the minds of the masses since 'it is not within their power to understand these matters as they truly are' (*Guide*, I: 33, 71). Maimonides' exegetical approach is helping them on the first steps to a more accurate understanding of God which might, with the requisite training, be taken further.

Treating biblical exegesis in chapters 1–49 before moving to the more philosophical stage of the discussion, it has been suggested that Maimonides is writing here for all possible readers of the *Guide*, whether philosophically trained or not. Certainly Maimonides constantly reiterates that

> the negation of the doctrine of the corporeality of God and the denial of His having a likeness to created things and of His being subject to affections are matters that ought to be made clear and explained to everyone according to his capacity and ought to be inculcated in virtue of traditional authority upon children, women, stupid ones, and those of a defective natural disposition, just as they adopt the notion that God is one, that He is eternal, and that none but He should be worshipped. (*Guide*, I: 35, 81)

Political correctness was of course not a concern in medieval times, so ignoring the attitudes that were a product of his time, Maimonides' point is that *everyone* needs to be aware of this level of biblical interpretation so as not to fall into the error of ascribing gross corporeality to God, an easy error to make given the language that the *Tanakh* uses. So Maimonides begins the *Guide* with this relatively uncontroversial lexicon that will allow all Jews to reinterpret problematic descriptions of God in a manner that emphasises his perfection. He might have been hoping that less philosophically inclined readers would fall away before they went on to the second section of his discussion, which they might have found rather more troubling.

2. MAIMONIDES ON EQUIVOCATION AND NEGATION

From chapter 50 onwards in Part I of the *Guide*, Maimonides switches mode and takes us into the realm of philosophical analysis, leading to a far more radical view than that implied in the exegetical chapters. This further step is necessitated by the limits on what Maimonides has achieved so far. For up to this point he has managed to reinterpret words that obviously imply corporeality – such as that God has a hand or that God sits – in a manner that appears to eliminate such concerns. So, as we have seen, 'sitting' refers to God's stability and we can therefore say that God is unchanging or stable. But we still have to ask what words like 'stable' and 'unchanging' mean when predicated of God, for they are, after all, also taken from our ordinary human discourse. It is this further level of analysis with which Maimonides engages in his philosophical discussion, and we will attempt to set out his views in this section before looking at some of the issues they raise in the next.

Maimonides begins with the following division of attributes:

> An attribute may be only one of two things. It is either the essence of the thing of which it is predicated, in which case it is an explanation of a term … Or the attribute is different from the thing of which it is predicated, being a notion superadded to that thing. This would lead to the conclusion that that attribute is an accident belonging to that essence. (*Guide*, I: 51, 113)

So, to use a distinction with which we should by now be familiar, an attribute might be essential or it might be accidental. The question is what we are to do with this distinction when speaking of God.

Generally, when we speak of the essence of something we speak of the attributes that make up that essence. Maimonides' own example – the definition of man as a rational animal – clearly shows how a definition introduces a level of complexity into the essence of something and thus Maimonides warns us against attempting analogous definitions in God's case. In his list of the five types of attribute that can be predicated of a subject, therefore, the first two – a predicate that is a definition or a predicate that is a partial definition – are dismissed as introducing multiplicity into God:

> For there is no oneness at all except in believing that there is one simple
> essence in which there is no complexity or multiplication of notions, but
> one notion only; so that from whatever angle you regard it and from whatever
> point of view you consider it, you will find that it is one, not divided in any
> way and by any cause into two notions; and you will not find therein any
> multiplicity either in the thing as it is outside of the mind or as it is in the
> mind... (*Guide*, I: 51, 113)

As we have seen, Maimonides is extremely strict regarding God's unity. Though we will return to this idea later, for the moment we simply note that for Maimonides any definition, whether total or partial, encroaches upon this unity. If God were, for example, a rational living being, then we have introduced multiplicity into his essence as God would now be both a living being and a rational being and our definition of God becomes dependent on these attributes. So God cannot be defined by any essential attributes if his absolute simplicity is to be preserved. Those who think God can be so defined cannot genuinely believe that God is One, whatever their protestations to the contrary. Any formulation that might fudge this, such as that God has attributes but they are 'neither His essence nor a thing external to His essence' (*Guide*, I: 51, 113), or the Christian notion that God can somehow be one and three (*Guide*, I: 50, 111), Maimonides dismisses with a set of withering putdowns, as mere sophistry that transforms individually meaningful words into meaningless combinations.

What of non-essential attributes? Maimonides deals with three further types of predicate here. The first to go are accidental qualities, including moral dispositions such as kindness, natural faculties such as strength or weakness, and what Maimonides terms 'affections' – feelings such as anger. All of the medievals agreed that such predicates introduce multiplicity in God since they imply that God has an essence to which various qualities may or may not attach themselves. We make God the subject of separable properties, which yields multiplicity. It is at this point that we begin to see quite how far Maimonides is willing to take his notion of God's utter transcendence and uniqueness and just how limited we are in what we can legitimately say about God. It is also not difficult to imagine how this might play with the religious masses.

Their concerns would multiply with the fourth group of predicates, those of relation, whether to people, times or places. As Maimonides admits, such attributes do not introduce multiplicity into their subject. I am a father, but that does not introduce multiplicity into my essence, and nor does my being in my office on a specific August afternoon. Yet, as Maimonides writes:

> How ... can a relation be represented between Him and what is other than he when there is no notion comprising any respect of the two, inasmuch as existence is, in our opinion, affirmed of Him, may he be exalted, and of what is other than He merely by way of absolute equivocation. There is, in truth, no relation in any respect between Him and any of his creatures. (*Guide*, I: 52, 117–18)

Though time is actually ruled out on different grounds, this statement regarding relations shows us just how extreme Maimonides' views were. He writes that just as there can be no relation between the intellect and colour, which we can at least say have the same level of reality or existence, there can be no relation between things that are as radically different as God and his creation.[4]

At this point then, the limits on what we can say of God have been very tightly drawn. The final group of predicates however – those of action – give us a little leeway, for Maimonides is willing to allow such predicates of God since 'this kind of attribute is remote from the essence of the thing of which it is predicated' (*Guide*, I: 52, 119). So we can say what God does, even if we cannot say anything about what God is. Nonetheless, even here when speaking of acts, we must limit ourselves to the acts themselves and not use them to imply any quality in the agent. So while in the case of a person who carried out a skilful act, we would attribute that skill to the person, we cannot do that for God, for then we are ascribing qualities to Him, which as we have seen is forbidden. We must limit ourselves to the act itself and cannot say that it is the consequence of a certain character trait in God, especially since his many different actions might lead to many different attributes, though as Maimonides points out 'there need not be a diversity in the notions subsisting in an agent because of the diversity of his various actions' (*Guide*, I: 53, 120).

This concession gives us some latitude for speaking of God, especially since we can use the same idea in reverse to understand moral qualities attributed to God. Thus, while we cannot say that God is merciful, for example, since that would imply a separable quality that he happens to have, we can use such terms if we understand them as telling us something about his actions rather than something about his nature. Whereas if someone does something gracious, we would say that they *were* gracious, if the Torah says God is gracious, we are *not* to understand it as saying that God has that characteristic. So when we say that God is merciful, this is not to be read as telling us anything about God's character. Instead this should be 'translated' into a statement about God's actions, which incidentally, for Maimonides, are to be equated with the natural causal course of nature. So when we say 'God is gracious', we are actually saying that the 'acts' of nature that we are witnessing are the sort of thing that we would usually associate with the attribute of graciousness. Basically, the use of these attributes is shorthand for speaking about God's actions, but instead of writing that a certain natural event is the sort of thing we usually associate with the attribute of graciousness, the *Tanakh* simply writes that God is gracious. Similarly, saying that God is angry is simply to report on the calamities that have befallen those who have suffered, as we have seen previously with Saadia. At this point then, we can speak of God's actions and can say things like 'God is gracious' as long as we reinterpret such statements as indicating God's actions. But we cannot literally ascribe any quality to God. We can only talk about what he does.

What though of the essential attributes that, despite Maimonides' statements about definitions, are nonetheless ascribed to God – 'that He is existent, living, possessing power, knowing, and willing' (*Guide*, I: 56, 130)? We know that they cannot represent any genuinely differing notions in God's essence which is 'one and simple' (*Guide*, I: 53, 122). Indeed, Maimonides is very strict about the formulations that we can use in explaining these attributes, ruling out saying 'that He possesses power because of his essence, possesses knowledge because of his essence' (*Guide*, I: 53, 121). Maimonides' formulation is that 'He exists, but not through an existence other than his essence ... He is powerful, but not through power' (*Guide*, I: 57, 132), and so it goes on. For Maimonides, this is to indicate that these words, when used in application to ourselves and God, are absolutely equivocal. They 'have nothing in common in any respect or in any mode; these attributions have in common only the name and nothing else' (*Guide*, I: 56, 131). We are not to give these terms any sort of analogous meaning to the extent that you overstep the bounds 'if you say that, with one knowledge and with this changeless knowledge that has no multiplicity in it, He knows the multiple and changeable things that are constantly being renewed,' for then 'you have clearly stated that he knows with a knowledge that is not like our knowledge' (*Guide*, I: 60, 144).

What then are we to make of these words as applied to God in the *Tanakh* itself? Maimonides' discussion is leading us to the linguistic 'final frontier' of negating all such positive attributes. The formulations above in which we say that 'He is powerful, but not through power' have only been pointing us in the right direction. In using these phrases, all that we do is 'give the gist of the notion and give the mind the correct direction toward the true reality of the matter' (*Guide*, I: 57, 133). Using these positive attributes, even in an absolutely equivocal way, is not ultimately the correct approach for Maimonides, who instead concludes 'that the description of God, may He be cherished and exalted, by means of negation is the correct description' (*Guide*, I: 58, 134).

Maimonides has already shown that we are to 'negate' any affections or privations – a privation being a lack of something – with reference to God, but the idea of negation is now given a more technical sense in relation to the essential attributes. When we say that God is eternal, for example, what we mean is that 'no cause has brought Him into existence' and when we say that God is One, that is simply 'the denial of multiplicity' (*Guide*, I: 59, 136). This is the formula we should follow for any purported positive description of God's essence. All should be understood as negative attributes. In this way, Maimonides believes we are not saying anything to characterise God's essence, for all we are saying is what God is not. We are negating a lack or, in Maimonidean terms, a privation, in God. We are saying that God does not have this privation, whether it is the privation of finitude, ignorance, etc.

All of this makes it clear that we should move on from designations such as 'stable' and 'permanent' that Maimonides had previously used in his exegetical discussion, for the use of such terms still implies that God has certain positive attributes, even if we are unable to describe them further. We should rather understand such descriptions as negations. So in summary

> every attribute that we predicate of Him is an attribute of action or, if the attribute is intended for the apprehension of his essence and not of His action, it signifies the negation of the privation of the attribute in question. (*Guide*, I: 58, 136)

At this point one might naturally wonder whether this is simply a semantic fudge. Surely if I say that God is not a multiplicity, then I am effectively just saying that God is One; by negating an attribute such as ignorance, I surely just affirm God's knowledge. But Maimonides does not take the negations in this manner. In denying *any* comparison between God and his creatures, our negation of ignorance is, for Maimonides, a negation of something 'that cannot fittingly exist in it. Thus we say of a wall that it is not endowed with sight' (*Guide*, I: 58, 136). To explain: walls do not have sight, but they are not the sorts of things that *could* have. It is not as if a wall might naturally have sight but has been deprived of it, as would be the case for a blind person. In the same way we negate attributes of God. In saying that God is not ignorant, we are saying that God is not the type of thing to which the term ignorance could possibly apply. Indeed, God is not a 'type' at all. So we are not saying that since God is not ignorant he therefore has knowledge. Instead our negation removes God from the very class of things that could be ignorant *or* knowledgeable.

Maimonides goes on to make a number of claims regarding the 'knowledge' of God to which this approach can lead. Thus he ascribes Moses' superior knowledge of God to his demonstration of more negations, and he illustrates this using the analogy of a person who knows that a ship exists but knows nothing of what a ship is. Different individuals each discover that a ship 'is not an accident…not a mineral…not a living being…not a plant…does not possess a simple shape', and many more such negations until 'the last individual has nearly achieved, by means of these negative attributes, the representation of the ship as it is' (*Guide*, I: 60, 143). Similarly, Maimonides claims, one comes closer to knowledge of God the more one multiplies negative attributes. It seems, however, that Maimonides is being a little disingenuous here. With the ship, one works through a process of elimination, which narrows down the possibilities, until all that is left is a positive picture of the ship. With God, though, we go on negating *ad infinitum* and thus the narrowing down of possibilities never leaves us with any positive content. Thus, as Hasdai Crescas argued, additional negations do not actually increase one's knowledge of God. Having said that, Maimonides does note that even in the case of the ship analogy above, we have at best 'nearly achieved' a representation of the ship. With God, the gap between achievement and true representation must remain infinite.

In the final analysis, it seems that Maimonides' position is that while negations do not yield knowledge of the true reality of God, they do lead towards an ever increasing realisation of the fact that this reality cannot be known. Presumably, the more one negates, the greater that realisation. But Maimonides reminds us nonetheless that 'negation does not give knowledge in any respect of the true reality of the thing with regard to which the particular matter in question has been negated' (*Guide*, I: 59, 139). Indeed, that is the very attraction of negation for Maimonides. It is far less likely to mislead us into thinking that we *could* gain positive knowledge, since negations do not indicate unknown positive attributes within God's essence that are waiting to be discovered.

Maimonides ends up then with the statement regarding silence being the best option, for language will inevitably mislead when speaking of God:

> These subtle notions that very clearly elude the minds cannot be considered through the instrumentality of the customary words, which are the greatest among the causes leading unto error. For the bounds of expression in all languages are very narrow indeed, so that we cannot represent this notion to ourselves except through a certain looseness of expression. (*Guide*, I: 57, 132–3)

Yet of course, as a rabbi who is obligated to pray three times a day in the basically anthropomorphic and anthropopathic language of rabbinic Judaism, Maimonides has to make certain concessions to this 'looseness of expression'. As human beings, language is the tool with which we think and express ourselves and Maimonides has to take a more pragmatic line with actual living worship. The very texts that are the foundation of his faith are replete with problematic affirmative assertions, as are the prayers that Maimonides would have recited on a daily basis.

Maimonides simply acknowledges the terms used in prayer to be sanctioned by tradition in order to deal with the 'necessity to address men in such terms as would make them achieve some representation', though we must 'draw a line at using these expressions and not to apply them to Him except only in reading the Torah [or] ... to pronounce only these attributes when saying our prayers' (*Guide*, I: 59, 140). Only those terms used in the Torah itself and subsequently affirmed by the men of the Great Assembly in Temple times are to be used. Not even the additional terms used in the books of the Prophets can be appropriated for liturgical use. Maimonides is scathing towards those 'poets and preachers' whose words variously constitute 'an absolute denial of faith' or 'rubbish and perverse imaginings' (*Guide*, I: 59, 141). Thus, he is full of praise for the 'perfect one' Rabbi Haninah who pointedly objected when someone added his own epithets of praise to God in his prayers (*bBerakhot* 33b).

Though it appears as if, ideally, Maimonides would prefer us to confine language to the realm where it can get some purchase, it cannot help but end up overreaching itself in the religious sphere. For Maimonides, though, everything that is said must be purified by philosophical interpretation. One can but wonder what would be going through his mind when saying thrice daily in his private *Amidah* prayer 'the great, mighty and revered God, God most high, generous and kind, owner of all things'. Suffice to say that it was unlikely to be the same as the person he was sitting next to.

3. GERSONIDES ON DIVINE ATTRIBUTES

In *Wars of the Lord*, III: 3, Gersonides offers a critique of the Maimonidean position just discussed, as well as giving his own positive account of divine attributes (which he continues in Book V, Part III, chapter 12). His discussion takes place in the context of an examination of divine knowledge specifically, more of which in chapter 6, but the critique is more general and applies beyond that particular attribute.

Gersonides first argues that, as Maimonides concedes, we begin with our own perfections and on account of their being perfections in human beings, apply them to God. So if the word 'knowledge' denotes a perfection in man, we apply it to God. But, Gersonides asks, why make this extension if the meanings of the term share nothing in common whatsoever? If there is *absolutely no meaning* in common between the word 'knows' in the propositions 'man knows' and 'God knows' then how can one take the term from the first proposition and extend its use to the second? The second statement might as well be 'God smells' for all that the word 'knows' has in common in these two instances. Gersonides writes that it would be just as valid to infer 'that man is intelligent from the fact that body is a continuous magnitude' (*Wars*, III: 3, 109) – i.e. not very. So the fact that we do apply the term in the two cases must mean that there is at least some limited relationship between its meanings in the two propositions.

To this criticism, if indeed it is a criticism as opposed to a simple presentation of Gersonides' opposing view, it seems Maimonides would have a perfectly good rejoinder – that we should not ascribe knowledge to God. Ideally we are not to ascribe positive attributes to God at all, but should stick with negative attributes. When classical Jewish texts do use positive attributes, we are to understand them negatively. So Maimonides could agree that the inference from human knowledge to divine knowledge is wrongheaded and thus he could reject Gersonides' starting point – that 'we say that God knows because of the knowledge found in us' (*Wars*, III: 3, 108). The problem is that Maimonides himself does talk of God's knowledge at some length at *Guide*, III: 20–1. Notably though, even here he spends most of these chapters telling us what God's knowledge is *not*. Thus, 'it is not true that new knowledge should come to Him ... that he should have many and numerous insights' (*Guide*, III: 20, 480). Nonetheless, this is a recurrent problem for Maimonides, who does speak about God throughout the *Guide*. Either we have to say that he intended us to use his theory of negation to interpret his own references to God, which is entirely possible given the esoteric manner in which he wrote the *Guide*, or we have to concede that it is simply not possible to remain within these strictures, though we should always be aware of the absolutely equivocal nature of the terms.

Yet Gersonides' further development of his theme questions Maimonides' right to draw the distinction between positive and negative attributes as he does. Gersonides writes that we would say, for example, (a) God is immovable. But why is that? It is because, Gersonides suggests, (b) bodies are movable. Since God is not a body, we obviously want to deny that he is movable. But that means that we are only stating 'God is immovable' because the word 'movable', as used in (b), has some relation to its ordinary meaning. Otherwise, why bother to deny that God is movable? But that means that the terms we deny of God are *not* absolutely equivocal. They must have some relation to the ordinary word or else we would not bother to deny them. Similarly, when we deny the proposition 'God is corporeal' we presumably do so on an understanding of the word 'corporeal' that is related to our ordinary understanding of it, or else why bother to deny it? So Gersonides is arguing that if the meaning of the attributes we apply or deny to God bear no relationship whatsoever to the ordinary meaning of the terms, why prefer affirmation to negation, or one predicate over another? If terms used of God are absolutely equivocal, it makes no difference what we actually say. As Gersonides writes:

> In general, if the terms used in affirming predicates of Him were absolutely equivocal, there would be no term applicable to things in our world that would be more appropriate to deny than to affirm of God or [more appropriate] to affirm than to deny of Him ... [O]ne could say 'God does not have knowledge' since the term 'knowledge' would not [on this view] have the same meaning for him in this statement as it does for us. (*Wars*, III: 3, 111)

So, for Gersonides it only makes sense to deny certain propositions about God if we allow that there is some continuity of meaning between the words we are using. And once that has been conceded, we might as well use positive attributes with some continuity of meaning, suitably understood, which is precisely what Gersonides proposes, as we will see.

But first, what are we to make of this critique? On the one hand, Gersonides seems to make a mistake in assuming that Maimonides would deny 'God is corporeal' on account of taking the word 'corporeal' in a sense that is related to its ordinary meaning. Firstly, as discussed earlier, Maimonides does not want us to understand negations such as 'God is not corporeal' as a simple denial of the property of corporeality to God. Rather, he takes it to exclude God from the entire category of existents that can or cannot have such a property. Secondly, when Maimonides wishes to stop using positive attributes to speak of God, he does not wish to stop using just the 'bad' ones, like corporeality. He wants us to stop using positive attributes altogether. So he could deny 'God has knowledge' as much as he would deny 'God is corporeal'. And the reason for this is that all such formulations are problematic, for 'attributes of affirmation...indicate a part of the thing the knowledge of which is sought, that part being either a part of its substance or one of its accidents' (*Guide*, I: 58, 135). Thus, as mentioned earlier, saying something positive about God is far more likely to tempt one into thinking that God *has* certain properties; negating attributes is less liable to lead to such misrepresentation. If this is so, then Maimonides is not rejecting 'God is corporeal' because he takes the term 'corporeal' in its ordinary sense. Rather, he rejects it for the same reason that he would reject any positive attribute – it implies that God has a certain property.

Despite all of the above, there might still be something to Gersonides' criticism, for one could argue that if words are being used in an absolutely equivocal sense, it makes no difference which words we *deny*. Why could 'God is not powerful' not perform the same task as 'God is not powerless'? Both of these propositions could be read as excluding God from the class of things that could be powerful or powerless. There is actually a sense in which, from a purely logical perspective, I think Maimonides would agree with this. But it is at this point that the streak of pragmatism and the multiple layers that run through his presentation come into play.

Maimonides recognises that words or propositions can have psychological effects on those that use them, whether in speaking, hearing, or reading them. They can be used in what Charles Stevenson once called a 'dynamic' as well as 'descriptive' manner. So, for example, Stevenson famously wrote of the emotive meaning of words, referring to the emotional colouring that words can impart over and above what they communicate at a purely descriptive level.[5] One could, for example, describe someone as 'shy'. The same descriptive information could, however, be packaged in words with a more negative or more positive emotional colouring – by, for example, describing the person as 'timid' or 'modest'. Though this is not the place for a critical discussion of the distinction between descriptive and emotive meaning, it is difficult to deny that language can affect us in a variety of ways, and while one should not for one moment anachronistically attribute a theory of emotive meaning to Maimonides, it is a useful way of illustrating the concerns he has with certain propositions.

Effectively, I think that it is his concern with the effects of certain propositions that is at the root of the distinctions he makes. So, logically speaking, Maimonides would agree that any negations applied to God are as meaningful – or should that be meaningless? – as any other. But humans are not pure intellect (shame though that is in Maimonides' opinion) and they are affected therefore in other ways by language. If one were to allow saying, for example, 'God is not knowledgeable', though logically speaking as meaningful as saying 'God is not corporeal', the effect the former would have on its hearers would be extremely damaging. And this, it seems, is the point that Maimonides wishes to make by excluding the attribution of any deficiency to God, whether by affirmation or negation. Since we cannot escape the effects that language has upon us, we cannot actually talk as if the only issue were pure logic devoid of any further associations that propositions might bring with them, especially for those non-philosophers whose emotional reactions might not be kept in check by their intellects to the same extent as Maimonides and his philosophically sophisticated readers. If we cannot be silent, then we have to allow for the limitations that come with the use of language.

So it appears as if Maimonides can answer Gersonides' critique. He can distinguish between positive attributes and negations and can invoke pragmatic considerations to explain why propositions that might, strictly speaking, be logically equivalent have been variously ruled 'in' and ruled 'out'. At the same time, a Gersonidean might argue that a Maimonidean is on shaky ground if he wants to start appealing to the damaging effects that certain words have on our understanding of God. A Gersonidean could easily turn this pragmatic perspective back on Maimonides, arguing that surely an inability to characterise God in positive terms would be far more destructive to religious worshippers than allowing certain limited positive attributes. Ultimately, whether Maimonides ever fully resolves the tensions between his negative theology and the demands of the religious life remains much debated.

Gersonides' own view therefore is that we *can* speak of God's attributes positively 'in the sense of prior and posterior predication', a view that he shared with many of the thinkers of the period, most notably his prime influence Averroes. What this means he explains as follows:

> For in God knowledge is identical with His essence, whereas in anyone else knowledge is the effect of God's knowledge. In such a case the term is applied to God in a prior sense and to other things in a posterior sense. The same is true with regard to such terms as 'exists,' 'one,' 'essence,' and the like... Hence it seems that the difference between divine and human cognition is a difference in terms of greater perfection, for this is what is implied by prior and posterior predication. (*Wars*, III: 3, 108)

According to Gersonides, there is some limited meaning that we can give to the terms we use to speak about God, which obviously means that we cannot predicate imperfections of God for the simple reason that God does not have these properties. What Gersonides proposes is that predicates used to describe God's essential attributes should be understood according to the model of what was termed *pros hens* equivocation rather than absolute equivocation. When we predicate essential attributes of God, we are saying that he is somehow the cause, or better the ground, of the existence of these attributes in us, though of course God exemplifies this attribute in a unique and infinitely more perfect way. Thus, Gersonides writes with respect to 'existent', for example, that 'God is the most truly described as "existent"' (*Wars*, V: III: 12, 174), and Gersonides is therefore happy for us to affirm certain things of God and not retreat into negations. Moreover there is some very limited link between our use of these terms with reference to ourselves and to God, at least to the extent of affirming that God is the ground of our possessing certain attributes, though this should not be taken to imply any similarity between ourselves and God.

4. UNITY, SIMPLICITY AND DIVINE ATTRIBUTES

As mentioned in the introduction to this chapter, one of the central issues driving much of this discussion of attributes was that of God's unity, and this was as much a concern for Gersonides as for Maimonides. Certainly all of the medievals accepted that there was a problem with accidental attributes. If we say, for example, that DR is angry, then we are saying that we have a subject – DR – and he has an attribute – anger. But this attribute, since it is not essential to DR, becomes a separable component of DR, who would still be DR even if he was not angry. And so it is with God. If we say that God has any accidental attributes, then they are by definition separable and we have a God who is composed of 'parts', a God who is a substratum for various different and separable elements and is therefore not a perfect unity.

What though of his essential attributes? This time, by definition, we are dealing with non-separable attributes that are part of the nature of their subject. Without those attributes, the subject would not *be* that subject. Do they, however, violate God's unity? Not according to Gersonides who argues that

> not every proposition about the essence of something implies a plurality in that thing. It does imply a plurality in the thing if one part of [the proposition] serves as a real subject [i.e., genus] for the other part [of the proposition]. But if [the former part] is not a real subject, although it is a linguistic subject, the proposition does not imply a plurality. For example, when we say 'this redness is a red color,' it does not follow from this assertion that the redness is composed of color and red, for the color is not a thing existing [by itself and serving as] a [real] subject for red. It is only a linguistic subject... Accordingly, it is evident that when God (may He be blessed) is described by any attribute or by many attributes, these attributes do not imply in Him any plurality, for He has no subject [i.e., genus]. Hence, all of these attributes denote only one simple thing. (*Wars*, III: 3, 112–14)

Gersonides here is arguing that just because we have a linguistic plurality of subject and predicate, we need not think that this implies an actual plurality in the nature of what exists, what philosophers would call ontological plurality. So for Gersonides these words explain something about the meaning of the subject without saying anything about how it exists. When we say God is powerful, we should not take that to imply anything about the manner in which God exists, i.e. that he exists as a subject with an attribute that is separate from his essence. For Gersonides, it is simply a way of saying something about God's perfection as the ground of all existence.

Ultimately then, the dispute between Maimonides and Gersonides comes down to whether or not the use of essential attributes violates God's unity. But we might wonder why anyone thought that a definition implies that we can somehow 'split' God into parts? We cannot be worried about multiplicity in a literal physical sense since everybody is agreed that God is incorporeal and cannot literally be split into parts. What then *is* the problem?

Let us approach this by recalling that God is a necessary being, which, in good Maimonidean fashion we can construe negatively – he is not dependent on anything for his existence. It is this 'negative attribute' of non-dependence that distinguishes God from all other existents. But if this is the case, then according to Maimonides God cannot have any parts or any attributes. If God is a complex being with parts or attributes, then he is composed of, or defined by, those parts or attributes. And if that is the case, then he is *dependent* on these parts or attributes. Even if this does not violate his unity in the sense of making him into a corporeal being, it does violate his absolute simplicity, since we can now give some analysis, however limited, of the concept of God. The claim is that predicating any attribute of God introduces this unacceptable level of complexity into God, giving us attributes that he is *composed* of or *depends* on for his definition.

Gersonides would argue that there is no such implication, but for Maimonides, as soon as we engage in this type of analysis, it immediately gives us ground for comparison with other beings. This appears to be Maimonides' underlying concern, a concern that in a limited sense could lead us back down the road to corporeality. To give the simplest illustration, if we start to define God through predicating essential attributes to him, he is then subject to some form of definition and we are saying what God *is* in some sense. As soon as we do this, we might be tempted to classify him as a 'kind' – a 'genus' – even if he is the only representative of that genus with no subordinate species. So while the genus of 'animal' has various species, including 'man', the God 'genus' uniquely classifies God. The problem that nonetheless remains is that this makes God one of many different types of genus that exist in the world, and he therefore now falls under a common classification – that of 'genus'. It is important to note that both Maimonides and Gersonides would deny that there is any such genus to which God belongs. But while Gersonides denies that our use of words implies that God is a 'kind', and he seems confident that linguistic predication will not detract from God's absolute transcendence, Maimonides appears to believe that any linguistic representation of God is inevitably a misrepresentation that leads us to associate him with his creatures, however limited that association might be, and that is unacceptable to Maimonides who wishes to emphasise his utter transcendence without qualification. Even the seemingly innocent use of essential attributes is enough to violate the idea of God's uniqueness and incomparability to all other existents. Any use of ordinary language to describe God that might lead us to think that we can understand him is the beginning of the temptation to anthropomorphism, which is but a step away from the ultimate sin of idolatry.

In conclusion, it is evident that using ordinary language in relation to God troubled many of the medievals greatly, and while precisely how far one had to veer from its everyday meaning was a matter of dispute, it is clear from our discussion that none were willing to take the language used at face value. Yet whatever their reservations, as adherents of the religion, our thinkers could not avoid talking about God. For some, such as Maimonides, such talk is at best a necessary evil. For others, it is plain necessary. Thus, in his discussion of God as living, omniscient and omnipotent, Saadia writes that while these are not distinct attributes in God, 'our tongues are unable to convey them with one word… It was only our *need* to transmit it that impelled us to formulate this concept in three expressions' (*Emunot*, II: 4, 101–2, emphasis added).

Ultimately, even for Maimonides, while silence might be the best option, articulation is nonetheless inevitable. To take but one example, even for Maimonides, God's free will is the cause of all existence:

> It is very clear that everything that is produced in time must necessarily have a proximate cause, which has produced it. In its turn that cause has a cause and so forth till finally one comes to the First Cause of all things, I mean God's will and free choice. (*Guide*, II: 48, 409)

As we have seen in the previous chapter, the idea that God is a free agent is central to Maimonides' discussion of creation. Given what we now know, however, even ascribing such freewill to God suddenly becomes rather more difficult to understand. It would appear as if the description of God as free might have to be interpreted as a rejection of the idea that God's relationship to the world is governed by the necessity that governs the relationships between all other existents. The 'relationship' of creation is therefore again to be read negatively as implying God's difference as 'creator' from all else, which is 'creation'. Interestingly, Plotinus believed that to say that the One is the ultimate cause of all of the beings that emanate from it, is actually to say something about those beings rather than to say something about the One – that they are all dependent and do not account for their own existence or reality. Ultimately, all 'God-talk' should only be understood as pointing to God's utter transcendence and difference from all other existents.

Misrepresenting God through language violates Maimonides' combined religious/philosophical commitment to truth. For him, the only explicit concessions to the human need for language are those already established in the *Tanakh* and subsequently prescribed for prayer. Gersonides, on the other hand, seems less concerned that such attributions are liable to mislead in quite such a damaging way. While he agrees that whatever we say of God must in no way detract from his utter transcendence, Gersonides seems less convinced that the use of positive predicates that bear some relation to ordinary language places us at the summit of a slippery slope. If it does, it is a summit that even Maimonides struggles to avoid. But whether we ultimately need silence or interpretation, we can see that medieval Jewish philosophers did not shy away from dealing with difficult questions that would profoundly affect their understanding of their classical texts.

NOTES

1   See his hasagah (gloss) on Maimonides' *Mishneh Torah*, 'Laws of Repentance', III: 7. R. Joseph Caro, in his *Kesef Mishneh* commentary there, cites approvingly a source containing a more polite version of the gloss.

2   Maimonides' *Responsa* [Hebrew] (ed.) and trans. Joshua Blau, 4 vols (Jerusalem: Meqitsei Nirdamim, 1989) vol. 1, no. 117, 200–1.

3   See Daniel J. Silver, *Maimonidean Criticism and the Maimonidean Controversy* (Leiden: E.J. Brill, 1965), 162.

4   We will briefly pick up the question of God's creation of the world, which surely is just such a relation, towards the end of the chapter.

5   Charles L. Stevenson, 'The Emotive Meaning of Ethical Terms', *Mind*, vol. 46, no. 181 (1937), 14–31.

FURTHER READING

A fuller discussion of Saadia's approach to anthropomorphism can be found in Simon Rawidowicz, 'Saadya's Purification of the Idea of God', in Erwin I. J. Rosenthal (ed.), *Saadya Studies* (Manchester: Manchester University Press, 1943).

For accounts of Maimonides' approach, start with Arthur Hyman, 'Maimonides on Religious Language', in Joel L. Kraemer (ed.), *Perspectives on Maimonides* (Oxford: The Littman Library of Jewish Civilization, 1991), 175–91. One could then move onto the series of papers by Harry Austryn Wolfson that appear in his collected papers: I. Twersky and G. H. Williams (eds), *Studies in the History of Philosophy and Religion* vol. 2 (Cambridge, Mass: Harvard University Press, 1977). The relevant chapters are 'Maimonides on Negative Attributes', 195–230; 'Maimonides and Gersonides on Divine Attributes as Ambiguous Terms', 231–46. Also included in this collection is 'Crescas on the Problem of Divine Attributes', 247–337, which deals with Crescas' interesting critique of Maimonides, which we have not discussed in this chapter, partly because the relevant parts of *Or Adonai* are not available in English translation.

For interesting discussion of some of the tensions arising out of Maimonides' negative theology see Hannah Kasher, 'Self-Cognizing Intellect and Negative Attributes in Maimonides' Theology', *Harvard Theological Review*, vol. 87, no. 4 (1994), 461–72; and Ehud Benor, 'Meaning and Reference in Maimonides' Negative Theology', *Harvard Theological Review*, vol. 88, no. 3 (1995), 339–60.

There is also plenty of interesting material on many of the philosophical issues raised by the topic in Moshe Halbertal and Avishai Margalit, *Idolatry*, trans. Naomi Goldblum (Cambridge Mass: Harvard University Press, 1992), especially in chapters 2, 4 and 5.

4

Prophecy

Prophecy is commonly thought to be about being able to predict the future. Hence the adage – if you keep saying that bad things will happen for long enough, you will eventually become a prophet. But prophecy, in the context of medieval Jewish philosophy, was also about the human reception of God's revelation more generally, the direct communication of the word of God to a human being on any topic. Basically, if God had something to communicate, it was the prophets who somehow received this communication and transmitted it to the masses. The question, of course, was how.

This question is particularly pressing considering that we have just spent a chapter discussing both the difficulties involved in knowing God and the limits on what we can say about him, to the extent that for some thinkers we cannot put our knowledge of God into words at all. It is worth noting, however, that there is an important difference between the claim that we cannot properly *articulate* our knowledge of God and the claim that we cannot *have* any knowledge of God. Reality might outstrip our powers of expression, but we might be able to know God, even if we are unable to set this knowledge out in propositional form. As Moshe Halbertal and Avishai Margalit have pointed out, there are other ways of knowing something, such as through acquaintance. Thus we might be able to *know* God's essence through our direct acquaintance with God – through 'meeting' him in some sense – rather than through philosophical speculation expressed in propositions.[1] They offer this view as a possible reading of Maimonides, but it seems closer to that of Halevi who writes

> The meaning of *Elohim* can be grasped by way of speculation, because a Guide and Manager of the world is a postulate of Reason... The meaning of *Adonai* [YHWH] however, cannot be grasped by speculation, but only by that intuition and prophetic vision which separates man, so to speak, from his kind, and brings him in contact with angelic beings... (*Kuzari*, IV: 15, 222)

If any group is a candidate for making God's acquaintance, it would be the prophets, and this quote indeed tells us that one knows God by his proper name, so to speak, or makes God's acquaintance as a result of *prophetic* vision. Now of course the prophets were not necessarily communicating information *about* God. The most important prophet of all – Moses – was concerned with communicating God's message – the Torah – which was more about the story of the Jewish people and how they were commanded to behave. The point that we can take from Halbertal and Margalit, however, is that even if Moses was unable to *articulate* his knowledge of God in propositional form, he might nonetheless have *known* God through acquaintance, which would allow him to receive and communicate God's message in his role as a prophet.

While the *Tanakh* seems to present this as a simple process for those granted 'prophetic vision', the little philosophy that we have covered so far might make us suspect that things are unlikely to be quite so clear-cut for our thinkers. Following some of the philosophical strands of the last chapter, the whole question of people, even those designated as prophets, communicating this intimately with God, not to mention then transmitting the knowledge thus gained in ordinary language to the masses, becomes far less straightforward. And as we are coming to expect, when grappling with the nature of prophecy, our medieval thinkers arrived at markedly different conclusions. These views are the topic under discussion in this chapter.

1. JUDAH HALEVI: PROPHECY AND THE SUPERNATURAL

We should begin with a brief account of the theory of prophecy that one might glean from a surface reading of the *Tanakh*. Indeed, theory might be too grand a word, for after reading the *Tanakh* one would probably end up with the following straightforward view: God miraculously chooses certain people with whom to communicate, usually as a result of their moral or 'religious' standing, and does so in ordinary language that can then be reported back to the people verbatim. At times these prophetic communications come in the form of visions that require interpretation, at other times they are simple and direct communications that these privileged individuals are enabled to have with God.

Ultimately, this is the type of view that one can find at the heart of Saadia Gaon's *Emunot ve-De'ot* and Judah Halevi's *Kuzari*, though neither present their accounts of prophecy systematically and one has to piece them together from remarks scattered throughout their works. In doing this, however, one finds a fairly detailed account of the nature of prophecy. In what follows, we will focus on Judah Halevi's *Kuzari*.

The foundation of Halevi's view follows on directly from the opening discussion between the king and the sage that we reviewed in chapter 1. For having spoken of the revelation of God to the Israelites at Sinai, the king points out perceptively that if God reveals himself in this manner to the Israelites, surely this means that only they are the beneficiaries of God's revelation, to which the sage replies

> Yes; but any Gentile who joins us unconditionally shares our good fortune, without, however, being quite equal to us. (*Kuzari*, I: 27, 47)

It will come as no surprise that the king is rather taken aback, if not offended – and says so – prompting the sage to explain his views on human nature, which form the essential foundation for his view of prophecy.

Halevi begins by taking us through the hierarchy of creation following a basically Aristotelian view of the 'powers' of the soul (*psuche*), as presented in *De Anima*. One of Aristotle's characterisations of the soul casts it as that which makes something a living thing – 'what has soul in it differs from what has not in that the former displays life' (*De Anima*, II. 2, 413a21). The soul is the life force that gives living things the characteristics that *make* them living things. For Aristotle, the 'powers' it supplies included nutrition, which brought with it growth and reproduction, locomotion, sense perception, desire and thought (or reason). So for Aristotle, a soul could have some or all of these aspects. Indeed, on this view a plant has a soul, for a plant is a living thing, though we might find it a bit strange to speak of plants having souls. Ultimately, that just shows that 'soul' might not be the ideal translation of *psuche*, but it also gives us a good indication of the sort of hierarchy of 'souls' that one would encounter on this system, and it is this hierarchy that serves Halevi's purpose so well.

Thus, the sage begins by explaining that plants and animals share the natural capacities for nutrition, growth and reproduction (*Kuzari*, I: 31, 47), while only animals have 'movement, will power, external as well as internal senses and such like' (*ibid.*, 33). Humans are unique inasmuch as they have all of this but also have intellect, at which point the sage asks whether there is any higher form of being. The king answers that at the top of the pyramid we find those individuals of great wisdom, but the sage rejects this as a mere quantitative difference among humans – some people have enough knowledge to qualify them for the title, others do not. What the sage was asking for was a qualitative difference, like that between plants and animals, or animals and humans, to which the king replies that there is no higher being than the human. The sage, as we might expect, takes us beyond these Aristotelian structures, however, moving us into a further realm beyond the natural:

> Sage: If we find a man who walks into the fire without hurt, or abstains from food for some time without starving, on whose face a light shines which the eye cannot bear, who is never ill, nor ages, until having reached his life's natural end, who dies spontaneously just as a man retires to his couch to sleep on an appointed day and hour, equipped with the knowledge of what is hidden as to past and future: is such a degree not visibly distinguished from the ordinary human degree?

> Al-Khazari: This is, indeed, the divine and seraphic degree, if it exists at all. It belongs to the province of the divine influence ['*amr ilahi*], but not to that of the intellectual, human, or natural world.

> Sage: These are some of the characteristics of the undoubted prophets through whom God made Himself manifest, and who also made known that there is a God who guides them as He wishes, according to their obedience or disobedience. He revealed to those prophets that which was hidden, and taught them how the world was created... (*Kuzari*, I: 41–43, 48)

This exchange yields some very important information about the nature of prophecy for Halevi. In building on the original Aristotelian scheme in a manner that has been identified as having a distinct Shi'ite, or more specifically Isma'ili influence,[2] Halevi begins, as ever, with empirical evidence, this time of human beings that are in some way superhuman. There are people who seem to do things that are beyond what we would expect from our understanding of nature, that the king speaks of as belonging 'to the province of the *'amr ilahi*', a term that has caused translators no end of trouble and that is rendered here as 'divine influence'. This term, which we will explain but continue to use untranslated, is pivotal to Halevi's philosophy.

While the term is used in a number of different senses, we are here interested in its use in describing a real differentiating factor among humans. Those who have it are separated from ordinary humans, just as humans are from lower animals, and animals are from plants. Those with the *'amr ilahi* are, effectively, a different species altogether. Thus, Halevi goes on to describe how this *'amr ilahi* was transmitted down a particular genealogical line, from Adam to Noah via Seth and Enosh, and then on to Shem, Ever, and through the patriarchs to Jacob and then, for the first time, to a whole group – the twelve tribes – and thus Israel as a nation. It is an inherited characteristic that we might compare in contemporary terms to an inherited gene. And just as with genetic heredity, it can show up differently in different individuals – 'an ungodly man received consideration in proportion to the minuteness of the essence with which he was endowed' (*Kuzari*, I: 95, 66).

The most important thing about the *'amr ilahi* for our purposes is that it is the feature with which certain human beings have been endowed in virtue of which they are able to receive prophecy. This *'amr ilahi* is necessary if people are to communicate with God and receive the truths that they would be unable to reach unaided, such as the truth about creation and more importantly the entire divine revelation that contains that truth – the Torah. In this context the *'amr ilahi* is a real property, a holy property, that relates to the divine and differentiates prophets from ordinary people and indeed Jews from non-Jews.

A useful and picturesque way of illustrating this, which we will keep in our armoury for what follows, is Menachem Kellner's 'holiness counter'. Just as a Geiger counter measures radioactivity, which really exists in the physical world though we cannot see it, a holiness counter would similarly measure the really existent yet invisible property of holiness such that 'it would click every time its wand came near something holy, just as a Geiger counter clicks in the presence of radioactivity'.[3] Put simply then, the holiness counter measures real objective 'holiness' that exists out in the world, and it would click every time it was near a Jew, since it would pick up the presence of the *'amr ilahi*. A non-Jew, in contrast, would simply not register.

Ironically perhaps, given the intimacy with God that the *'amr ilahi* allows, all of this actually fits rather well with the strand of thought discussed in the previous chapter that applies severe limits to our knowledge of God. For Halevi is saying that human beings can only come into direct contact with God, and thus know what he wishes to communicate, if they have a certain supra-rational faculty, a quasi-mystical prophetic faculty that is only vouchsafed to a particular genealogical line and even then only actualised in certain individuals under certain conditions, as we will see. So clearly, the capacity to receive revelation is quite literally God-given – it is something that he endows, and not something that an ordinary man can strive to achieve through his own natural endeavours. It should not therefore surprise us that 'ordinary' human beings, who only have reason and philosophical speculation at their disposal, cannot know or have contact with God. Indeed, for Halevi one who 'strives by speculation and deduction to prepare the conditions for the reception of this inspiration...is an unbeliever' (*Kuzari*, I: 79, 56). If humans do not have the *'amr ilahi*, then they would be bound by all the restrictions on knowing God, let alone being able to communicate with him, that we encountered in the previous chapter. Prophetic knowledge cannot be grasped by pure human effort.

The further conditions that have to be fulfilled for actualising this prophetic faculty take us further into realms that we would probably classify as mystical. For example, prophecy can only take place 'either in the [Holy] Land, or concerning it' (*Kuzari*, II: 14, 89). Israel, which thankfully for Moses included Sinai and Paran, has a literal holiness for Halevi: it is 'especially distinguished by the Lord of Israel, and no function can be perfect except there' (*Kuzari*, V: 23, 293). Thus, if I have a handful of soil from London and a handful of soil from Jerusalem, these two piles of soil really differ. The latter would have our holiness counter clicking furiously; the former would not give rise to any activity. So the land of Israel is *really* holy, as indeed is the Hebrew language, which means that Israel is the only place in which one is able to pick up God's transmissions perfectly. A Jew is rather like a radio receiver without a signal until he reaches the land of Israel and the signal becomes crystal clear. Certainly exilic prophets like Ezekiel and Daniel could also prophesy, but this was because they 'had seen the *Shekhinah*' (*Kuzari*, II: 14, 89), the divine presence that dwelt on earth when the first Temple stood in Israel and whose influence lasted for 'about forty years during the second Temple' (*Kuzari*, III: 39, 172 and 65, 186). And it is clear that Halevi, following a similarly realist line to that taken above, understands the *Shekhinah* as a real manifestation of God's immanence, one that was at times 'visible' (*Kuzari*, V: 23, 293). With the *Shekhinah* gone, a lower form of communication was made possible between God and the rabbis through the heavenly voice or '*Bat Kol*' (lit. daughter of a voice), spoken of in rabbinic texts.

Not only is location important, but also only those who perform God's commandments can receive direct prophetic communications from God. The commandments, in Halevi's opinion, have real ontological effects on the people who have been commanded to perform them, i.e. the Jewish nation, and they produce genuine changes in the nature of the ontologically real connection between the people and God that could again be picked up by the holiness counter. Notably, this connection and these changes would only transpire in the performance of the commandments by Jews. The commandments and the '*amr ilahi* are, quite literally, made for each other, such that a non-Jew who performs the commandments would not forge any such connection.

There are clearly implications of Halevi's view that would be uncomfortable from a modern perspective. As the king points out, and the sage admits, born Jews remain qualitatively distinguished from all other people, converts included:

> Those, however, who become Jews do not take equal rank with born Israelites, who are specially privileged to attain to prophecy, whilst the former can only achieve something by learning from them, and can only become pious and learned, but never prophets. (*Kuzari*, I: 114, 79)

Thus, on Halevi's view, all Jews have an added quality that was initially bestowed upon them by God and is lacking in all other people – the '*amr ilahi*. It distinguishes Jew from non-Jew and is a necessary condition for prophecy which momentarily at Sinai was the gift of an entire nation, though quite how this mass revelation took place is 'too deep for me to fathom' (*Kuzari*, I: 91, 63), the sage admits.

We end up then with a picture whereby those with the '*amr ilahi* who are totally obedient to God's law and correctly located in the Holy Land of Israel, or have at least had contact with the *Shekhinah* there, might be called as prophets by God. But even when all these conditions are met, prophecy is not something that these individuals can simply summon. As Halevi states the 'conditions which render man fit to receive this divine influence do not lie within him' (*Kuzari*, I: 79, 56). Thus prophecy remains a gift of God, which is presumably the 'get-out clause' that Halevi can invoke to deal with counterexamples. Thus, pre-Sinaitic prophets, Moses included, who received prophecy before they could have performed the commandments which were only revealed at Sinai, and the non-Jewish (and thus *'amr ilahi*-less) biblical prophet Balaam, could be accounted for by God's special intervention. Indeed, though he is not mentioned by name, we are told that Balaam 'was specially privileged to become a prophet' (*Kuzari*, I: 115, 80). It seems, therefore, as if it remains in God's hands whether and when he contacts those who have the necessary 'qualifications'. In Saadia's words, God

> permitted them…to obtain that knowledge at certain times, so that it might thereby become clear that all this was conferred upon them by the Creator and…it was not brought about by themselves. (*Emunot*, III: 4, 150)

A born Jew will inherit the *'amr ilahi,* and can choose to fulfil the commandments in Israel, but ultimately there are no self-made prophets. It is always God who acts directly, and without intermediaries, to freely choose to bestow the divine gift of prophecy, generally, but not exclusively, on those who fulfil the necessary conditions for receiving such a bequest.

2. MAIMONIDES' NATURALISTIC VIEW OF PROPHECY

Halevi's account of prophecy could be seen as a direct reaction to the philosophic opinion that he put into the mouth of the philosopher at the beginning of the *Kuzari*. There, though it was not termed prophecy, communication with the divine was accounted for entirely naturalistically. For the philosopher, the perfect individual is the one whose intellect has united with the Active Intellect, the final intellect in the chain of intellects that emanate from the First Cause in the manner discussed at **2.1**, and the one that is related to our sublunar world. This intellectual effort, and not the performance of practical commandments, is the route to communication with the Divine. As the king notes in typical Halevi fashion however, the accumulated empirical evidence of history goes against this view. Historically it has not been philosophers that have been granted the gift of prophecy, the king points out, for how many philosophers have been prophets? Yet Maimonides and Gersonides would gladly provide him with a list – and it would include all of the prophets of the *Tanakh*.

For Maimonides and Gersonides, a far more naturalistic picture of the prophet and his experience emerges. We will here focus on the Maimonidean discussion.[4]

Maimonides points out that, as with creation (and the Appendix will make rather more of the comparison than we will here), there were three views of prophecy:

> The first opinion – that of the multitude of those among the Pagans who considered prophecy as true and also believed by some of the common people professing our Law – is that God … chooses whom He wishes from among men, turns him into a prophet, and sends him with a mission …
>
> The second opinion is that of the philosophers. It affirms that prophecy is a certain perfection in the nature of man. This perfection is not achieved in any individual from among men except after training that makes that which exists in the potentiality of the species pass into actuality, provided an obstacle due to temperament or to some external cause does not hinder this … According to this opinion it is not possible that an ignoramus should turn into a prophet; nor can a man not be a prophet on a certain evening and be a prophet on the following morning, as though he had made some find. Things are rather as follows: When, in the case of a superior individual, who is perfect with respect to his rational and moral qualities, his imaginative faculty is in its most perfect state and when he has been prepared in the way that you will hear, he will necessarily become a prophet, inasmuch as this is a perfection that belongs to us by nature …
>
> The third opinion is the opinion of our Law and the foundation of our doctrine. It is identical with the philosophic opinion except in one thing. For we believe that it may happen that one who is fit for prophecy and prepared for it should not become a prophet, namely on account of the divine will. (*Guide*, II: 32, 360–1)

Taking each of these in turn, it certainly seems as if the first opinion corresponds to the view that many would take as that of the Torah. God chooses those whom he deems worthy of being prophets to deliver specific messages. As Maimonides also points out, those that hold this view 'also posit as a condition his having a certain goodness and sound morality' (*ibid.*), though the question of the person's intellectual abilities, his 'knowledge or ignorance', does not make a difference. Again, this seems to correlate relatively well with the traditional rabbinic image of many biblical prophets – none of them are praised for their great philosophical acumen, but, for example, Moses was famously described as the humblest of all men (Numbers, 12:3). There are also important elements of this view that correspond with that of Halevi, for whom it is God who chooses who is to be a prophet, and for whom a person's goodness, in the sense of their performance of the commandments, is a condition of being chosen. Yet to Maimonides, somewhat surprisingly in view of what we have just said, this is a Pagan view, only professed by the 'common' among the Jews.

The second view, in direct contrast, views prophecy as a purely natural phenomenon. Here, one becomes a prophet on account of one's moral and intellectual perfection. It is not something that God has to grant through direct action but is a state that man can naturally achieve through his own efforts. Thus, God is 'responsible' for prophecy only in the indirect sense that he was responsible for creating human nature with all its potentialities. It is then up to man to actualise this potential, though besides intellectual and moral perfection, on this naturalistic view the imaginative faculty must also be in a perfect state if one is to 'qualify' for prophecy. As we will see, imagination is a bodily faculty according to Maimonides, and 'the perfection of the bodily faculties ... is consequent upon the best possible temperament, the best possible size, and the purest possible matter' (*Guide*, II: 36, 369). So presumably some individuals will simply be physically incapable of attaining the rank of prophet. Nonetheless, on this view, 'it is not possible that an individual should be fit for prophecy and prepared for it and not become a prophet' (*Guide*, II: 32, 361). Prophecy here is the natural and inevitable result of human perfection – physical, moral and intellectual.

Though very close to it, apparently this is not the true Jewish view in Maimonides' opinion. The view of the Torah, though otherwise identical, does not have the implication that one who has achieved the various perfections will automatically become a prophet, for it is possible that God will withhold prophecy from such an individual by an act of will. God can prevent one who is deemed to have achieved the requisite levels of natural human perfection from becoming a prophet. This act of God, which involves intervening in the natural course of things, is a miracle like any other according to Maimonides.

That all of this would be a startling view for his coreligionists is evident. Maimonides finds it 'indubitable' that moral and rational perfection is required of prophets, and 'proves' it by quoting the Talmudic dictum 'Prophecy only rests upon a wise, strong, and rich man' (*bShabbat* 92a; *bNedarim* 38a), which, as he indicates, he has interpreted as referring to intellectual and moral perfection in earlier writings.[5] Certainly it goes without saying that the idea that the patriarchs, Moses, and all the other prophets of the *Tanakh* were experts in Aristotelian philosophy, which would be the qualification required to achieve intellectual perfection, rather strains credibility on any straightforward or even quite detailed reading of the *Tanakh*. Moreover, Moses is the greatest of all prophets for Maimonides, yet given the traditional rabbinic view of him as a stammerer, whether Moses would be thought to have had the perfect material constitution necessary for a perfect imaginative faculty is questionable. While his privileged status is certainly *not* questionable in Maimonides' mind, the problem again is reconciling his basically naturalistic view of prophecy with the exoteric sense of the biblical and rabbinic traditions. As the biblical exegete and thinker Isaac Abrabanel (1437–1508) wrote in his commentary on the *Guide*, 'it is clear from Scripture that prophecy is not a natural occurrence, but a miracle'.[6] Maimonides does attempt to make some problematic biblical verses compatible with his view as the discussion continues, but completing that task would require an almost total rereading of the *Tanakh*. Nonetheless this simply has to be the correct esoteric reading of the *Tanakh* for Maimonides, given that God's revelation must contain the truth.

Maimonides does, of course, appear to retain a role for divine intervention in his view, since God's will can prevent one who is naturally constituted for prophecy from achieving this perfection, and we have mentioned that he speaks of the miraculous nature of this divine act. Many, however, do not believe that in reality Maimonides' view differs from that of the philosophers. While we are on the whole not giving detailed consideration to Maimonides' esotericism in the main body of this book, on this occasion a discussion of this viewpoint is necessary.

Firstly, the examples Maimonides gives to illustrate his view immediately reinforce the suspicion that all is not as it seems. His first example – Jeremiah's scribe Baruch the son of Neriah – who according to Maimonides was Jeremiah's prophetic 'apprentice', was one of those 'prevented' from receiving prophecy. Yet when Maimonides quotes God's instruction to Jeremiah to inform the weary Baruch: 'And seekest thou great things for thyself? Seek them not' (Jer., 45: 5), he indicates that 'it is possible to say that this is a clear statement that prophecy is too great a thing for Baruch' (*Guide*, II: 32, 362). But of course, if it is too great a thing for him, that implies that Baruch had not achieved the perfection that was necessary. It was not, on this reading, that he was perfectly qualified and that God prevented him from becoming a prophet, but that Baruch had not gained the necessary perfection and thus was not fully qualified. He was prevented from becoming a prophet by the entirely natural obstacles that would have prevented him from becoming a prophet on the purely philosophic account, with his temperament being the most likely source of his downfall on a literal reading of the relevant verses.

Maimonides continues with a second example, quoting Lamentations, 2: 9: 'Yea, her [Israel's] prophets find no vision from the Lord' and explains that 'this was the case because they were in Exile' (*Guide*, II: 32, 362). But to what extent is this a case of God preventing prophecy? Maimonides' explanation later in the *Guide* for the inability to prophesy in exile again seems highly naturalistic:

> You know that every bodily faculty sometimes grows tired, is weakened, and is troubled, and at other times is in a healthy state. Now the imaginative faculty is indubitably a bodily faculty. Accordingly you will find that the prophecy of the prophets ceases when they are sad or angry, or in a mood similar to these two … This is indubitably the essential and proximate cause of the fact that prophecy was taken away during the time of the *Exile*. For what *languor* or *sadness* can befall a man in any state that would be stronger than that due to his being a thrall slave in bondage to the ignorant … (*Guide*, II: 36, 372–3)

The reason that prophecy was not possible in exile has an entirely naturalistic explanation – the prophets could not be in the state of perfection necessary for prophecy while under the physical and psychological cloud of exile. God did not need to prevent them from prophesying by a miraculous act of will; the prevention was a natural consequence of their depressed state.

Ultimately though, none of this falsifies Maimonides' claim that these individuals were prevented from reaching the rank of prophet by an act of divine will. But this is a perfect example of where we have to 'join the dots' in order to fully understand what Maimonides is saying. For what, in Maimonides' view, *is* an act of divine will? Tucked away at the very end of the chapters of the *Guide* devoted to prophecy, we find the following, which we may recall from 3.4:

> It is very clear that everything that is produced in time must necessarily have a proximate cause, which has produced it. In its turn that cause has a cause and so forth till finally one comes to the First Cause of all things, I mean God's will and free choice. For this reason all those intermediate causes are sometimes omitted in the dicta of the prophets, and an individual act produced in time is ascribed to God, it being said that he, may He be exalted,

has done it. All this is known. We and other men from among those who study true reality have spoken about it, and this is the opinion of all the people adhering to our Law. (*Guide*, II: 48, 409–1ĺ0)

Maimonides is telling us that when the *Tanakh* speaks of God doing something, it is not saying that God suddenly took a decision to act in a certain way. Rather, in what is cited here as the opinion of those 'adhering to our Law', this is simply shorthand for speaking of the entire causal chain for which he is ultimately responsible. God's will is actually just the First Cause of a lengthy causal chain. If we link this idea with the other 'opinion of our Law' regarding prophecy, we end up with the view that when Maimonides tells us that God prevents certain individuals from reaching the rank of prophet by an act of will, that is equivalent to saying that there is a natural causal process that prevents them from attaining this rank. The natural environment that exile creates so as to prevent prophecy, and the natural causal reasons that Baruch was simply not up to the job, can all ultimately be ascribed to God's will. But for Maimonides this does not mean that God suddenly decided to prevent the prophets from prophecy when they were in exile. Rather God, as the being responsible for the natural causal order, is ultimately responsible for the fact that prophets in exile are unable to prophesy because of the natural causal order.

As to the reference to the miraculous in God's withholding of prophecy, Maimonides has already written that 'miracles too are something that is, in a certain respect, nature' (*Guide*, II: 29, 345). Maimonides' point, not elaborated upon in great detail here, is that God implanted miracles in the nature of things in the original act of creation. Given the complications that we have discussed in understanding anything about what God does, understanding exactly what went on at this point in creation would take us too far from our topic. But this entire discussion shows us that there is plenty of material explicit in Maimonides' *Guide* that would lead us to naturalise even those elements of the prophetic process that he ascribes to the miraculous will of God, as long as one makes the necessary connections between the relevant discussions distributed throughout the work.

Given the above analysis, it is difficult to know the extent of the difference between Maimonides' purported view and that of the philosophers. It is certainly the case that Maimonides agrees with the philosophic idea of prophecy as a naturally acquired perfection, and also that in his subsequent discussion of the mechanics of prophecy, the ostensible difference between the views makes no further appearance. And though he uses the language of divine will to describe the prevention of prophecy, that same divine will is interpreted elsewhere as designating the workings of nature. For Maimonides, it is a deeply held belief that the natural order is not something that God has to supervise constantly and act upon at each and every second, but is an independently operating realm that God has put into action as a First Cause. It therefore has within it the necessary structures to enable those with the correct constitution to become prophets, and those who lack the necessary qualification to be 'prevented'. Whether God genuinely intervenes supernaturally to prevent prophecy, in a manner other than the naturalistic way we have described, is at the very least open to question.

3. THE MECHANICS OF PROPHECY

Regardless of whether God intervenes to *prevent* prophecy, the basically naturalistic view of how one *becomes* a prophet yields the following initial summary of the prophetic process:

> Know that the true quiddity of prophecy consists in it being an overflow overflowing from God, may He be cherished and honoured, through the intermediation of the Active Intellect, toward the rational faculty in the first place and thereafter toward the imaginative faculty. (*Guide*, II: 36, 369)

It is important to understand the various terms used here before we can understand how exactly prophecy works on this model.

Some of the ideas are familiar from what has gone before. Thus, we know that the idea of emanations from God was part of the Neoplatonic picture of the universe to which Maimonides subscribed (**2.1**). But up to this point we have used the idea of emanation as a way of accounting for the creation, and thus existence, of the corporeal world from its incorporeal beginnings in God. In this context we are looking at divine emanation as mediated by the Active Intellect so as to give us knowledge that amounts to prophecy. In order to understand this, we need to know more generally how the medieval Aristotelians understood the process by which human beings come to *know* things, or the process of human cognition.

We know that the Active Intellect is the final intellect in the chain of intellects that emanate from God, and that it in some way governs the sublunar world of which we are a part. But on the basis of commentaries on one of the most difficult chapters in Aristotle's entire canon – *De Anima*,

III. 5 – this intellect was given a further central role in the acquisition of human knowledge.

Let us begin with the following brief reminder of a central Aristotelian distinction – that between matter and form. We know from **2.4** that all substances can be analysed into these two components of matter and form, though these are not two physically separable components of things – in our world, matter cannot exist in isolation from its form. Rather, the matter and the form are two aspects of a single substance. But in addition to this, we also need to know that the form of something *actualises* its matter.

At a simple level, we could envisage a mass of bronze – the matter – that is being used as raw material for a statue, at which point the matter takes on a certain form. Originally the bronze had the *potential* to take on a certain shape and that has now been *actualised* in the bestowal of the form of the statue upon the matter. Taking the same thought to a more abstract level, the idea is that matter considered in isolation is pure potential. It can only become a substance when it accepts a certain form. Indeed, in all the substances we experience, we are seeing matter that has been actualised by a form. So in fact, as we have mentioned previously, seeing as it cannot exist as pure matter in this world, the matter of the bronze would already have been 'actualised', since before being shaped into the statue it would have the form of a 'pile' of bronze, but it is in the nature of matter to take on successive forms. In taking on a new form that actualises its potential, the further point to note is that there is an external cause of this change. This is simply an inevitable part of the Aristotelian scheme, since nothing can change from a state of potentiality to actuality without something external bringing about that event – really just an extension of the principle that every event must have a cause. So, for example, there has to be a sculptor who creates the statue out of the pile of bronze, who actualises its potential in this way by bestowing the form upon it.

Let us now return to the act of cognition. For Maimonides, man's intellect is, to begin with, 'merely a faculty consisting in preparedness' (*Guide*, I: 70, 174). Before a man knows anything, he is in a potential state to know things and has therefore what is variously called a potential, material or Hylic Intellect. It is like pure matter, pure potential, that is prepared to receive knowledge but that needs a form to actualise this potential so that it can actually know things. In order to gain knowledge, however, the intellect must abstract the forms from the images presented to it by sense experience.

As Maimonides puts it, in the simple act of cognising a piece of wood, the intellect 'has stripped its form from its matter, and has represented to himself the pure form' (*Guide*, I: 68, 164). In this act of knowing from perception, the medieval Aristotelians spoke of the mind becoming identical with this form that it has abstracted from its sense experience. One can also, of course, gain knowledge through demonstrating truths on the basis of forms, but in all of these cases what was once a Potential Intellect has now received a form and therefore become actual – or an intellect *in actu*. This actualised intellect was termed the Acquired Intellect by the Arabic Aristotelians.

As we have noted, if this Potential Intellect is *changing*, if it is moving from potential to actual, there has to be something that causes this to happen. Aristotle therefore speaks of some other agent that actualises our Potential Intellect to make it actual, i.e. to give us knowledge, just as 'light makes potential colours into actual colours' (*De Anima*, III. 5, 430a17). Just as without light, we are unable to perceive colour, without some analogous enabling element we could not have knowledge. Aristotle therefore posits a further Separate Intellect that 'shines' on our Potential Intellect to actualise it and give us knowledge. And for the medievals, it was the Active Intellect, as the final emanated intellect in the cosmological hierarchy that played this role. This Active Intellect somehow causes our intellects to pass from potential to actual as a result of our intellects being correctly prepared to receive that which emanates from it. And this gives us the basic concepts for understanding the nature of prophecy according to Maimonides.

With prophecy, what we have is an emanation from God that eventually yields the Active Intellect, and the emanation from this Active Intellect similarly reaches to the sublunar world. Those with a suitably perfected intellect can then pick up this emanation in order to receive a prophetic communication. If we envisage the Active Intellect as a radio transmitter and the Potential Intellects of human beings as radio receivers, then the point is that human beings, when appropriately trained, can pick up the signals that the Active Intellect is transmitting, and in this way their Potential Intellects are actualised – and the better the quality of the radio receiver, the clearer the reception.[7]

Among the Arabic Aristotelians who influenced Maimonides, the model of exactly how this relationship between the Active and Potential Intellect worked was a matter of some controversy. To pick up our analogy, the controversy centred on what exactly was being transmitted by the Active Intellect. Al-Farabi took the Aristotelian analogy of light as an 'enabler' literally. For him, the 'overflow' (or emanation) from the Active Intellect is the condition necessary for *us* to abstract the forms from the objects of our senses. So for al-Farabi, the Active Intellect does not itself transmit knowledge of the forms. Instead it transmits a signal that enables *us* to go through the process of retrieving the forms from the images that we sense. Avicenna, in contrast, believed that the Active Intellect actually bestows the knowledge of each and every particular form on the Potential Intellect at the moment that we gain knowledge. So the Active Intellect actively transmits the forms to us (though for Avicenna we also conjoin with the Active Intellect at this moment so the transmitter analogy is slightly inaccurate).

Whatever the precise nature of this process, we can clearly see that prophecy, up to this point, is simply a special case of the ordinary act of cognition, giving us a whole new outlook on the naturalism we have already seen at work in Maimonides. For on the Aristotelian model of cognition, it is not as if God is literally communicating messages to every person who gains an element of knowledge. Rather, God's emanation is responsible for the structure of the universe, and for the existence of the Active Intellect that governs our part of it. The emanation of the Active Intellect is, in a similar way, responsible for our ability to know. But all of this is simply written into the structure of nature, such that when we gain knowledge, we do so not because God is literally telling us something, but because we are tuned into the natural systems for which God is ultimately responsible. With the prophet, everything is in perfect working order, which means that far more of the knowledge potentially available to human beings is gained through the process. But ultimately prophecy becomes a natural species of knowing via the agency of the Active Intellect – God's possible preventative role apart.

In his earliest descriptions of prophecy in the *Commentary on the Mishnah*, this intellectual process is presented as if it is the whole of the story. Indeed, in the *Mishneh Torah* we are told that prophecy can in some cases begin and end with the personal intellectual development of the prophet:

> It is possible for a prophecy to be intended solely for the prophet himself, for the development of his mind and to increase his knowledge, so that he may know what he had not known previously concerning exalted themes. (*Mishneh Torah*, 'Laws of the Foundations of the Torah', VII: 7)

A similar idea is also mentioned at *Guide*, II: 37, though the person who is perfected without perfecting others is not there called a prophet. But while the *Guide* also writes of prophets gaining such intellectual perfection, there the intellectual process is only the first stage. Indeed, if the process were to end with the intellect, that person would be a 'man of science engaged in speculation' (*Guide*, II: 37, 374) – a philosopher. The rank of prophecy is only achieved by one whose intellect *and* imagination receive the intellectual emanation. For the prophet, the emanation must 'overflow' in turn to the imaginative faculty, which Maimonides identifies in a number of ways throughout his writings, and not always positively. At one point it is even characterised as 'in true reality the *evil impulse*' (*Guide*, II: 12, 280). This is mainly because the imaginative faculty deals in images, with its 'actions' being 'retaining things perceived by the senses, combining these things, and imitating them' (*Guide*, II: 36, 370). Thus, it is responsible for our characterising all existent things in material imagistic terms, including God, in which case it is the cause of a cardinal sin for Maimonides. But unlike our colloquial use of the term, imagination is not simply about flights of fancy. While it certainly *is* responsible for that aspect of thought, the prophet's perfected intellect and perfect moral habits that lead to an ascetic 'turning-away of thought from all bodily pleasures' (*Guide*, II: 36, 372), keep these wilder excesses of the imagination in check. Thus, the imaginative faculty for Maimonides was the faculty through which we 'think' more generally in images gained from our experience, in our use of memory for example, and as such it becomes an essential tool for our everyday lives as physical beings. Indeed, those for whom the emanation from the Active Intellect only reaches their imagination include 'the legislators' – or the politicians (though also included are 'the soothsayers, the augurs, and the dreamers of veridical dreams' (*Guide*, II: 37, 374)). The political elements of prophecy in particular are essential, and it is the imagination that translates the abstract intellectual emanation it receives into more concrete form for application to the real world.

Dreamers of veridical dreams, i.e. dreams that depict actual events, are also not to be entirely dismissed. Maimonides writes that between dreams and prophecy 'there is only a difference in degree, not in kind' (*Guide*, II: 36, 370). Indeed, on Maimonides' account, with the one notable exception of Mosaic prophecy, all prophecy is communicated through a dream or a vision – the former obviously while the prophet is asleep, the latter in 'a fearful terrifying state, which comes to a prophet when he is awake' (*Guide*,

II: 41, 385). Thus, the 'noblest action' of the imagination 'takes place when the senses rest and do not perform their actions' (*Guide*, II: 36, 370) and it is receptive to these dreams and visions. In this state the imaginative faculty can receive the emanation from the intellect that produces prophecy, and when it is being directed by reason, the imaginative faculty suddenly takes on a far more positive role. Indeed, it is central to the process of prophecy and Maimonides identifies it with the 'angel' that is the intermediary in all prophecy (*Guide*, II: 45, 403), other than that of Moses.

So according to Maimonides' naturalistic account, prophecy is the result of an emanation from God (acting, as ever, as the first remote cause) to the Active Intellect which emanates to the rational faculty (in the natural way that it does for ordinary cognition). In prophecy, this emanation also overflows towards the imaginative faculty. Indeed, 'it is from the rational faculty that that overflow comes to the imaginative faculty' (*Guide*, II: 38, 377). Here the prophetic message is presented in either a dream or a vision and in various guises depending on the rank of the prophet. But in all of its manifestations, it is an entirely natural process that takes place in the human mind, a process that *any* human mind with the appropriate constitution and training could potentially go through. We end up then with the view that with a perfect individual

> whenever … his imaginative faculty, which is as perfect as possible, acts and receives from the intellect an overflow corresponding to his speculative perfection, this individual will only apprehend divine and most extraordinary matters, will see only God and His angels, and will only be aware and achieve knowledge of matters that constitute true opinions and general directives for the well-being of men in their relations with one another. (*Guide*, II: 36, 372)

In summary then, without the emanation to the imagination one is merely a philosopher or man of science; with only the emanation to the imagination one is a legislator or soothsayer. But with an emanation that reaches both the rational and the imaginative faculties, one is a prophet who receives abstract knowledge that can be moulded by the imagination into a form that is communicable to the masses. The prophet's intellect directs the imaginative faculty so that the images produced are controlled to represent the truth that the intellect apprehends, but in a figurative form that can be applied to world events and that the masses can understand. And all of this without mention of God's miraculous withholding of prophecy.

4. WHAT IS GOD'S ROLE?

With the essentials of Maimonides' view before us, we can ask how it differs from the more traditional view of prophecy articulated by Halevi. One way of doing this is by asking exactly what God's role is in all of this.

On Halevi's view, God could decide at a particular time to tell someone that, for example, a particular city is going to be destroyed, as long of course as that person observes the Torah and is suitably located. Most importantly, this prophecy would be communicated directly by God in ordinary language. Indeed, at Sinai God communicated verbally with the entire nation, though the difficulty they had in coping with this phenomenon meant that only Moses would subsequently enjoy this direct form of communication. Halevi readily admits that given the incorporeality of God 'we do not know how the intention became corporealized and the speech evolved which struck our ear', but nonetheless he asserts that God 'does not lack the power' (*Kuzari*, I: 89, 62–3). Halevi does struggle a little with direct communications of corporeal prophetic visions of what is essentially an incorporeal divine realm. But with verbal communications, however exactly they occur, prophets who are fully awake and neither dreaming nor having visions can hear the actual words that God wishes to communicate to them. Though prophecy need not always involve the prophet actually hearing the words of God – at times a prophet is 'enwrapped by the Holy Spirit... directed by the Divine Influence, the prophet being powerless to alter one word' (*Kuzari*, V: 20, 284), – it is always God who directly delivers his message in the form in which it is to be delivered to the people. Of all those who were chosen, Moses was the most exalted since he was chosen for the most important revelation of all. But he received prophecy in the same way as any other prophet.

On Maimonides' model we find a very different picture. Firstly, the prophet receives information – 'God's message' – through his intellectual relationship with the Active Intellect. But God is therefore simply the remote cause of the 'message'. It comes from God only in the sense that God is ultimately responsible for the existence of the Active Intellect and the structure of nature that it governs. God does not directly tell anyone what is going to occur. Secondly, even the Active Intellect is not delivering an actual message to the prophet. Rather, the intellectual emanation the prophet receives is subsequently 'translated' into actual language and images by the imaginative faculty, which allows for the application of the intellectual emanation to events in the real world. This is particularly clear in Gersonides' description of the process where

> the Agent [or Active] Intellect imparts to him this emanation in a general way; it is not about the individual or nation as a definite person or as a definite nation. The imagination receives this emanation in a particular way by virtue of the existential factors previously discussed. (*Wars*, II, 6, 53)

Incidentally, it is worth noting that Gersonides appears to have no qualms whatsoever about endorsing a fully naturalistic view of prophecy, devoid of any mention of the possible preventative actions of God. For Gersonides, prophecy is simply the most excellent form of philosophy.

We can see then that rather than literally receiving a message, it is more like the prophet's faculties, due to their perfection, are able to work out both philosophical truths and the route that the natural world is going to take on the basis of their knowledge of the general structure of the universe. As a basic analogy we might think of our knowledge of the laws of gravity. As a result of that knowledge of an abstract physical truth, I know that if I were to pick up the pen next to me and let go of it, it will fall. To put it rather grandly, I am applying an abstract truth to my own existential situation. A prophet is doing the same thing but at a *far* more complicated level. The prophet grasps philosophical truths from the emanation received, which also overflows to the imagination, which can apply the abstract knowledge to actual events in the prophet's own environment, allowing the prophet to know the future. But only the prophet, with his superior perfection in all faculties is able to make all of the links, first through his superior relationship with the Active Intellect and thus his superior cognition, and subsequently by translating this abstract input into an actual message that refers to real events, as the following passage makes clear:

> For the very overflow that affects the imaginative faculty – with a result of rendering it perfect so that it brings about its giving information about what will happen and its apprehending those future events as if they were things that had been perceived by the senses and had reached the imaginative faculty from the senses – is also the overflow that renders perfect the act of the rational faculty, so that its act brings about its knowing things that are real in their existence, and it achieves this apprehension as if it had apprehended it by starting from speculative premises... For all things bear witness to one another and indicate one another. (*Guide*, II: 38, 377)

On this account then, receiving prophecy does not seem to be a case of God communicating words to a prophet at a particular time. Rather, we find the perfect physical, moral and intellectual person who has greater knowledge of the workings of the universe than ordinary mortals. But he gains this knowledge through a relationship with the Active Intellect that occurs when he tunes into the emanation that constantly emanates from it. This emanation extends to the rational and imaginative faculty of the prophet, where it takes shape as a message that can be communicated. It is also worth noting that given that all prophecy involves visions or dreams that are 'translations' from an intellectual emanation, Maimonides has no problem accounting for the fact that messages from and about God are couched in 'corporeal' visions. This is simply the way that the imagination works with its information.

This type of view has some interesting and possibly troubling implications. On the one hand, this view is radically universalistic and thus diametrically opposed to the view of Halevi. In principle at least, anyone could be a prophet. Coming from the opposite pole, however, it could also be highly limiting. Given the requirements for prophecy that Maimonides sets out and the non-verbal mode in which it is communicated, it is unlikely that the entire nation of Israel would have attained the rank of prophet at the Sinai revelation. And indeed, Maimonides denies that all of them did –

> though through a miracle all the people saw the great fire and heard the frightening and terrifying voices, only those who were fit for it achieved the rank of prophecy, and even those in various degrees. (*Guide*, II: 32, 363)

Further, given that prophecy does not occur as articulated speech for Maimonides, but is eventually translated into images and then speech by the prophet, it is notable that even the voice that they heard was merely a terrifying noise 'but not the articulations of speech... Moses being the one who heard words and reported them to them' (*Guide*, II: 33, 364).

Most troubling of all for the traditional reader of the *Guide*, though, the human input into prophecy becomes very pronounced on this picture. God's role in prophecy is mediated so many times for Maimonides that he is 'relegated' to the status of its First Cause rather than its direct source. And if that is the case, what does it mean for the revelation of the Torah at Sinai? To what extent does God directly communicate the Torah as 'divine dictation' at all? It is here that the supremacy of Mosaic prophecy becomes highly significant. For unlike Halevi, Maimonides makes a qualitative distinction between Mosaic prophecy and all other forms of prophecy. Though he writes that he will not speak of this difference in the *Guide* having already done so in his *Commentary on the Mishnah* (most notably in his thirteen principles of faith in the *Introduction to Perek Helek*) and in the *Mishneh Torah* (Laws of the Foundations of the Torah), he still manages to give us plenty of information about the distinction.

We know from Maimonides' earliest written statement on the issue that Moses prophesied 'without angelic mediation'.[8] The idea of angels as the intermediaries in prophecy is actually a rather complicated one. For example, angels appear 'only *in a vision of prophecy* or *in a dream* whether this is explicitly stated or not' (*Guide*, II: 42, 388). Leaving aside the can of worms this opens for the interpretation of all biblical passages that mention angels, there are at least three senses in which prophecy can be mediated by an angel. On the one hand, Maimonides tells us that the term 'angel' is simply a figurative way the rabbis used to designate 'individual natural and psychic forces' (*Guide*, II: 6, 264). Thus, he speaks of the term 'angel' as being a way of referring to both the Separate Intellects (*Guide*, II: 6, 262) and, as we have already mentioned, the imaginative faculty. On the other hand, when the imagination finally presents the prophet with the prophetic message, it does so in varying forms depending on the status of the prophet, and in some of these the prophecy is indeed addressed to the prophet in his dream or vision by an angel. Maimonides actually lists eleven ranks of prophet in the *Guide*, though the first two levels are in reality only 'steppingstones towards prophecy ... [and] even though he may sometimes be called a prophet, this term is applied to him in a general sort of way, because he is very close to the prophets' (*Guide*, II: 45, 395).

The unique nature of Mosaic prophecy, however, gives us a twelfth level and its most important distinguishing feature mentioned in the *Guide* is that Moses prophesied 'without action on the part of the imaginative faculty' (*Guide*, II: 45, 403). Thus the mediation of the angels mentioned in Maimonides' thirteen principles is explicitly identified with the mediation of the imagination here in the *Guide*. And the reason that Moses' prophecy did not involve any imaginative elements is that it was law – the Torah. All prophets other than Moses needed their imaginations to translate intellectual emanations into prophecies regarding future events in the world, since the subject of all prophecy other than that of Moses is restricted to world events, as Maimonides informs us in the *Mishneh Torah*:

> You have learnt that the only purpose of the prophet is to inform us of things that are going to occur in the world – plenty and famine, war and peace etc ...
> These are the sorts of matters the prophet imparts, but he does not establish

a new religion or add a commandment or annul one. (*Mishneh Torah*, 'Laws of the Foundations of the Torah', X: 3)

We know that for Maimonides prophets have the same standing on legal matters as any sage of later times and are subject to the same legal procedures as anyone else in a rabbinical court. They do not have the power to change the law, or indeed to establish law on the basis of their status as *prophets*. As Maimonides points out in his *Commentary on the Mishnah*, if rabbis outnumbered prophets on an interpretation of law, the rabbis would win.[9] But, Moses as the legislator par excellence, is unlike any other prophet, for Moses establishes the Torah. Unlike the political types who legislate using the imaginative faculty, Mosaic legislation, as the communication of divine law unmediated by the imagination, not only attends to society, but is a law that

takes pains to inculcate correct opinions with regard to God, ... and that desires to make a man wise, to give him understanding, and to awaken his attention, so that he should know the whole of that which exists in its true form. (*Guide*, II: 40, 384)

In arguing that the imagination does not play a role in Mosaic prophecy, we could read Maimonides as saying that the Torah was revelation that came from God directly, thus solving the problems of mediation and human input that we raised earlier. By privileging Mosaic prophecy, Maimonides is able to present a more traditional line on revelation at Sinai. In truth, however, at the burning bush mention is made of an angel appearing in Mosaic prophecy (see *Guide*, III: 45, 576), and the whole issue of mediation by angels in Mosaic prophecy is a very vexed one. Even if it is unmediated by the imagination, that hardly equates on the Maimonidean picture to a straightforward verbal presentation of the Torah to Moses directly. Any communication still has the Active Intellect and the rational faculty to negotiate and Maimonides does write that 'the *intellect* overflowed toward him without [the imagination's] intermediation' (*Guide*, II: 36, 373, emphasis added). So whether Moses received prophecy without the mediation of *any* of the Maimonidean candidates for angelic status – i.e. the imagination or the intellects – is highly questionable. And if he received prophecy through the Active Intellect, then it is still being mediated and one can still question whether this emanation would be immediately received as the words of the Torah. Again, as with the issue of God withholding prophecy, one's answer to this question of whether God directly delivered revelation *in words* to Moses will depend on one's view on the extent and nature of Maimonides' naturalism and esotericism.

5. CONCLUDING REMARKS: NATURALISM AND SUPERNATURALISM

We have before us two apparently diametrically opposed views of prophecy. On the one hand we have the view of Halevi which depends upon a special faculty that only Jews share. Generally, if they are in the right place – the land of Israel – and are doing the right things – the *mitzvot* – God might grant them a prophetic vision. But this is something that God miraculously chooses to do, or not. Indeed, as soon as one goes down this miraculous line, there is no *need* for any qualifications on the part of the prophet, as Abrabanel is keen to point out in his critique of Maimonides:

> [P]reparations are not necessary for the existence of prophecy as the philosophers, and those who follow them have maintained. For only if prophecy is [considered] a natural perfection can preparations be [deemed] necessary, but when it is [considered] a miraculous event, the work of the absolute will of God, then [it is clear] that preparations are not required.[10]

On the other hand we have Maimonides' view of prophecy as a natural process available to all humans who are morally, intellectually and 'imaginatively' perfect. It is something that people can achieve and regardless of how we answer the question of God's ability to prevent prophecy directly, it does not require that God make a special effort to contact the person in order to make him a prophet.

It is true that on both pictures a potential prophet must have certain qualifications. Both Maimonides and Halevi cite physical conditions that have to be fulfilled if one is to be a prophet. For Halevi these depend on one's Jewish inheritance of the *'amr ilahi* and one's physical location. For Maimonides it requires that one has a physically perfect imagination and the correct 'environment' in which to prophesy – one that is free of the burdens of exile. Yet Halevi's conditions are supernatural conditions for prophecy; Maimonides' are all part of the natural order. And therein lays all the difference in the world.

Halevi's view is predicated on the existence of an intangible yet real holiness that exists to make real ontological connections (detectable by our 'holiness counter') between the Jewish soul and God. For Maimonides the qualifications are naturalistically conceived. A prophet did not receive prophecy simply because he was in Israel, but because of the sovereignty and peace that Jews enjoyed there. Moreover, in stark contrast to Halevi, it is not only Jews that have the potential to be prophets. While it remains the case for Maimonides that not everyone is constituted in such a way that they could reach the requisite level of perfection, the presence or absence of such a constitution has nothing to do with ethnic divides and a supra-rational divine endowment. Nonetheless, Jews remain in a privileged position for attaining the moral and intellectual perfection necessary for prophecy even on Maimonides' model, for Maimonides believes that the *mitzvot* are the ideal route to the perfection necessary for prophecy. Thus observing the commandments plays a role in one's qualifying for prophecy for both Halevi and Maimonides, albeit in very different ways. And so it is to the nature of those commandments that we now turn.

NOTES

1   See Moshe Halbertal and Avishai Margalit, *Idolatry*, trans. Naomi Goldblum (Cambridge Mass: Harvard University Press, 1992), 60–1 and 158–9.

2   See Shlomo Pines, 'Shi'ite terms and Conceptions in Judah Halevi's Kuzari', repr. in *Studies in the History of Jewish Thought*, (ed.) Warren Zev Harvey and Moshe Idel (Jerusalem: Magnes Press, 1997), 219–305.

3   Menachem Kellner, *Maimonides' Confrontation with Mysticism* (Oxford: The Littman Library of Jewish Civilization, 2006), 43.

4   We will focus on the *Guide,* but there is plenty of material on prophecy in Maimonides' other works that a comprehensive study of his view would have to take into account. Those interested in taking their study of the topic further should refer to the readings listed at the end of the chapter.

5   See Maimonides' *Shemonah Perakim*, VII, translated as 'Eight Chapters' in *Ethical Writings of Maimonides*, (eds), Raymond L. Weiss and Charles Butterworth (New York: Dover, 1975), 59–104. Quotation from 81.

6   Translated in Alvin J. Reines, *Maimonides and Abrabanel on Prophecy* (Cincinnati: Hebrew Union College Press, 1970), 26.

7   I first heard this 'radio' analogy from Avram Stein in those first classes that led me into Jewish philosophy. But I have since found it in Norbert Samuelson, 'The Problem of Freewill in Maimonides, Gersonides, and Aquinas', *CCAR Journal* (1970), 2–20, 14.

8   *Introduction to Perek Helek*, translation taken from I. Twersky (ed.), *A Maimonides Reader* (New York: Behrman House, 1972), 419.

9   See Moses Maimonides, *Commentary on the Mishnah*, Arabic text with Hebrew translation by Joseph Kafih, 6 volumes (Jerusalem: Mossad Harav Kook, 1962–8). See vol. 1, 14.
10 Reines, *Maimonides and Abrabanel on Prophecy*, 26

FURTHER READING

For a detailed scholarly study of prophecy in medieval Jewish philosophy that will be an ideal next step for those interested in this topic, see Howard Kreisel, *Prophecy: The History of an Idea in Medieval Jewish Philosophy* (Dordrecht: Kluwer, 2001).

For discussion of Halevi's view centred around some interesting questions it raises in the context of the *Kuzari* see Robert Eisen, 'The Problem of the King's Dream and Non-Jewish Prophecy in Judah Halevi's Kuzari', *The Journal of Jewish Thought and Philosophy*, vol. 3, (1994), 231–47.

For Halevi's Shi'ite influences see Shlomo Pines, 'Shi'ite terms and Conceptions in Judah Halevi's Kuzari', repr. in *Studies in the History of Jewish Thought*, (ed.), Warren Zev Harvey and Moshe Idel (Jerusalem: Magnes Press, 1997), 219–305.

Discussion of Halevi and Maimonides can be found in Harry Austryn Wolfson 'Halevi and Maimonides on Prophecy', repr in I. Twersky and G. H. Williams (eds), *Studies in the History of Philosophy and Religion*, vol. 2, (Cambridge, Mass: Harvard University Press, 1977), 60–120.

For a different comparison between Maimonides' view of prophecy and a more supernatural approach, see Alexander Altmann, 'Maimonides and Thomas Aquinas: Natural or Divine Prophecy?' *AJS Review*, vol. 3, 1978 (1978), 1–19.

Menachem Kellner usefully compares and contrasts the naturalisms of Maimonides and Gersonides in, 'Maimonides and Gersonides on Mosaic Prophecy', *Speculum*, vol. 52, no. 1 (January, 1977), 62–79.

Much of Abrabanel's critique of Maimonides has been translated with commentary by Alvin J. Reines, *Maimonides and Abrabanel on Prophecy* (Cincinnati: Hebrew Union College Press, 1970).

5

Rationalising the Commandments

As we noted in our introduction, Judaism is a religion that emphasises the importance of very specific practices. Indeed, as famously summed up in Saadia Gaon's statement that the Jewish nation was 'a nation only by virtue of its laws' (*Emunot*, III: 7, 158), it appears that classically, practice was essential to Jewish self-definition. The 613 biblical *mitzvot* were the foundations of this practice that every Jew was expected to observe. The sphere of practical observance was subsequently extended well beyond this foundation in the rabbinic period, when through the Oral Torah it was developed into the vast and complex halakhic system.

All of this implies that God must care deeply, so to speak, about how we act. He has told us what we must do and as we have seen in the previous chapter, at least according to Judah Halevi (and many later mystical thinkers would follow him in this), when Jews perform God's commandments, this has real effects on the soul of the Jew and causes actual changes in divine realms of the universe. To put it in technical theological vocabulary, performing *mitzvot* is a theurgic activity – it leads to real changes in the heavenly spheres. Yet if we cast our minds back to the philosopher's worldview as expressed in the *Kuzari*, we will recall him saying that the particular acts that a person performs are of no intrinsic importance. As long as one 'has grasped the inward truths of all branches of science' one need not be 'concerned about the forms of thy humility or religion or worship, or the word or language or actions thou employest' (*Kuzari*, I: 1, 38). What matters is what one comes to know. How one acts in the service of this end is a matter that is of no concern to the God of the philosophers.

Given the centrality granted to practice in Judaism – to this day most forms of Judaism see its practical concerns as fundamental regardless of whether they recognise rabbinic *halakhah* as authoritative – and the opposing view presented by Halevi's philosopher, it becomes important for those working in Jewish philosophy to address the subject of Jewish practice. Many of our medieval thinkers did so by pursuing, whether implicitly or explicitly, the question of the reasons for the biblical commandments – *ta'amei ha-mitzvot*.

Within Judaism, the question of the *ta'am* – usually translated as reason – for the commandments had been discussed since Talmudic times. But the traditional rabbinic quest for a *ta'am* was a search for the scriptural basis of *mitzvot* and the subsequent derivation of halakhic decisions. The rabbis of the Talmud were concerned with whether the laws could be shown to derive from acceptable scriptural or rabbinic sources and methods. Questions of philosophical justification, however, do not concern whether laws can be shown to have legitimate sources within a particular system, in this case biblical-rabbinic. Proving conclusively that the commandment not to eat pork has a source in the Torah says nothing about the philosophical question of the rationality of such a demand. To put it in its most basic terms, the philosophical question is whether there is any good reason for keeping the commandments other than the plain fact that God has commanded them.

This question, however, was viewed with some scepticism in the rabbinic period, a scepticism that would continue to exert a marked influence, since revealing the reasons for commandments could have dire consequences:

> Rabbi Isaac said: why were the reasons of the Torah not revealed? Because in two verses reasons were revealed, and the greatest man in the world stumbled on them. It states 'He shall not take for himself many wives [lest they turn his heart away]' [Deut., 17:17]. Solomon said, 'I shall take many and I shall not be turned away.' Yet Scripture writes 'And at the time of Solomon's old age his wives turned his heart' [I Kings, 11: 4]. (*bSanhedrin* 21b)

As Rabbi Isaac is pointing out, if the reason for a commandment is revealed, certain people – King Solomon in the above case – might think that the reason does not apply to them. Studying the reasons for the commandments can therefore have antinomian consequences – it can lead people to think the laws do not bind them.

Nonetheless, a distinction also drawn in the Talmud does suggest the possibility of rational reflection on the law:

> Our Rabbis taught: 'Mine ordinances [*mishpatim*] shall ye do' [Lev., 18: 4], i.e. such commandments which, if they were not written [in Scripture], they should by right have been written and these are they: [the laws concerning] idolatry, immorality and bloodshed, robbery and blasphemy. 'And my statutes [*huqqim*] shall ye keep' [ibid.], i.e. such commandments to which Satan objects. (*b Yoma* 67b)

Here we find a fledgling effort to distinguish between different categories of commandment – *mishpatim* (judgements) and *huqqim* (statutes) – that has often been read as affirming that there is a category of commandment that lends itself to independent human understanding. Human reason would certainly be a prime candidate for providing us with the basis on which the laws termed *mishpatim* 'should by right have been written' in the absence of revelation. The *huqqim*, on the other hand, certainly do not fall into that category but are instead those to which Satan objects, meaning, according to the Talmudic commentator Rashi, that he can object to them on account of their being of no use – or irrational – and thus tempt Israel to transgress on the basis that a Torah containing such commandments cannot possibly be true. Here, incidentally, the *huqqim* only number five – eating pig, wearing *sha'atnez* (mixture of linen and wool), *halitzah* (removing the sandal in the levirate ritual), the purification of the leper (individual stricken with *tzara'at*), and the scapegoat.

Rabbinic attitudes apart, the question of whether or not God's commandments are merely dependent on his will or have some independent form of rationality is a question with important ramifications. It is also a question with a long history, given what probably remains its best-known formulation as early as Plato's *Euthyphro*. And the issues it raises affect our very conception of God and his relationship to humanity. If God's commandments simply depend on God's will, then we are unable to gain any rational understanding of them. We know we must obey God, but we cannot judge the justice of his commandments by any independent criteria. The very fact that God commands something makes it the right thing to do, regardless of our own judgement of its value. If, on the other hand, God's commandments can be rationally understood, then we are able to judge them against some independent criterion. So what is at stake is whether or not we can understand God as a being who has produced a 'legal' universe that human reason can understand.

The conception of God and his relationship to humanity that the two views bring with them differ radically, as Maimonides apparently recognises. When describing those who do not believe that reasons should be given for any law we can safely infer, without fear of overstatement, that Maimonides does not hold the opinion in high regard:

> There is a group of human beings who consider it a grievous thing that causes should be given for any law; what would please them most is that the intellect would not find a meaning for the commandments and prohibitions. What compels them to feel thus is a sickness that they find in their souls… For they think that if those laws were useful in this existence and had been given to us for this or that reason, it would be as if they derived from the reflection and the understanding of some intelligent being. If, however, there is a thing for which the intellect could not find any meaning at all and that does not lead to something useful, it indubitably derives from God; for the reflection of man would not lead to such a thing. It is as if, according to these people of weak intellects, man were more perfect than his Maker; for man speaks and acts in a manner that leads to some intended end, whereas the deity does not act thus, but commands us to do things that are not useful to us and forbids us to do things that are not harmful to us. (*Guide*, III: 31, 523–4)

Thus, against the background of a kalamic theological dispute, in which the Mut'azilites believed God was subject to an independent objective standard of justice and the Ash'arites argued that God must be the only source of value, the medieval Jewish philosophers addressed this issue of *ta'amei ha-mitzvot* (rationalising the commandments). In this chapter we will be dealing again with the thought of Maimonides, who presents the most systematic discussion of the issue, but we will begin with Saadia Gaon who first brought the topic to the fore with his introduction of a specific category of rational commandments.

1. SAADIA GAON: RATIONAL AND REVEALED COMMANDMENTS

Saadia's classic discussion can be found in the third treatise of *Emunot ve-De'ot* where, following his usual procedure, he first notes how the commandments were revealed miraculously by God's prophets, after which 'we discovered the rational basis for the necessity of these prescriptions' (*Emunot*, III: 1, 138). And it is that rational basis with which he is particularly concerned in this section of the book.

Saadia begins by setting out four general 'demands of reason' that for ease of reference I have numbered in the quotation below:

[1] Logic demands that whoever does something good be compensated either by means of a favour shown to him, if he is in need of it, or by means of thanks... [2] Reason also demands that he that is wise do not permit himself to be treated with contempt or to be insulted... [3] Furthermore reason demands that the creatures be prevented from wronging each other in all sorts of ways... [4] Reason also deems it proper for a wise man to give employment to an individual who performs a certain function and to pay him a wage for it... since this is something that redounds to the benefit of the worker without hurting the employer. (*Emunot*, III: 1, 139)

Saadia then argues that each of God's commandments fall under one or other of these so-called 'demands of reason'. But he distinguishes between those commandments that fall under the first three, and those that fall under the last of them. Thus, acts of 'humble submission' and 'standing before [God]', presumably in acts of worship such as praying, fall under [1] since they are acts of thanks or recompense for God's great acts of grace, which Saadia tells us at the very beginning of Treatise III include the act of creation and his giving his creatures 'the means whereby they might attain complete happiness and perfect bliss... the commandments and prohibitions' (*Emunot*, III: Exordium, 137). Under [2], Saadia includes such commandments as our not swearing falsely in God's name. Under demand [3], to prevent wrongdoing among his creatures, one could include any number of commandments that regulate our behaviour towards each other.

Saadia then goes on to group all of these commandments under a single category:

[T]he approval of each of these classes of acts that we have been commanded to carry out is implanted in our minds just as is the disapproval of each of the classes of acts we are forbidden to commit. Thus has Wisdom, which is identical with reason, said: *For my mouth shall utter truth, and wickedness is an abomination to my lips* [Prov., 8:7]. (*Emunot*, III: 1, 140)

These commandments, which he goes on to term the rational precepts of the Torah, or *mitzvot sikhliyyot* in the Hebrew equivalent, are evidently taken by Saadia to be understood by some innate sense of reason 'implanted in our minds'. They 'have important uses and great justification from the point of view of reason' (*Emunot*, III: 1, 141), which allows us to detect their inherent rationality.

What, though, of that class of commandment that falls under reason's demand concerning an employer and his worker? For Saadia, those commandments covered by demand [4] form a class apart that, 'from the standpoint of reason are optional' (*Emunot*, III: 2, 143). Thus, by way of contrast to the rational commandments, this division

> consists of things neither the approval nor disapproval of which is decreed by reason, on account of their own character, but in regard to which our Lord has imposed upon us a profusion of commandments and prohibitions in order thereby to increase our reward and happiness. (*Emunot*, III: 1, 140)

The point that Saadia is making is that we cannot understand these commandments as inherently rational as we could the earlier category of rational commandments. They are therefore termed 'revealed commandments' or *mitzvot shimiyyot*.

On the face of it then, Saadia presents us with a distinction between rational and revealed commandments, with the former, but not the latter, capable of being rationally understood. There are, however, ways of collapsing the distinction that Saadia himself intimates, which has led some scholars to question this straightforward reading. Saadia is willing, for example, to say that the 'non-rational' revealed commandments, like the rational commandments, could be characterised as showing submission towards God. So we can subsume both categories of commandment under demand of reason [1] – that whoever does something good be compensated – which might appear to make the revealed commandments as 'rational' as the rational commandments.

In order to understand Saadia correctly though, we need to distinguish between the following two statements:

> (a) There is a rational basis for the claim 'one ought to observe divine commandments'.
> (b) There is a rational basis for the content of each specific commandment considered individually.

Saadia begins Treatise III by noting that '[God's] messengers executed certain signs and wondrous miracles...[and] afterwards we discovered a rational basis for the necessity of their prescription' (*Emunot*, III: 1, 138).

In saying that there is a rational basis for prescribing the commandments, Saadia implies that he would affirm statement (a) – there is a basis for the general idea that it is rational for us to observe God's commandments. This could be based either on the requirement for our general submission to God in response to his grace towards us in creating us, or on the more self-interested basis that performing commandments brings increased reward (though that also ultimately traces back to God's grace). At this level, we simply characterise each commandment from the perspective of its *form* as a divine commandment. Since it is a divine commandment it is rational for me to perform it, inasmuch as it is rational for us to submit to God generally. Indeed, the commandments are 'good for us' – they 'leave their traces upon [our] souls, rendering them pure and unsullied' (*Emunot*, V: 1, 205). Nonetheless, when we look at the individual *content* of each commandment, rather than looking at them formally as instances of 'submission to God', we find that we can understand some of them as rational independently of such generalised appeals to God, but not others. In particular, we cannot understand the revealed commandments in this fashion. We trust that God knows how performing certain rituals is good for us, and we recognise that God would not require them of us were they not. But from a human perspective, we can only recognise the intrinsic rationality of the rational commandments. Thus Saadia would deny statement (b), since at the level of particular commandments, some do and some do not have a rational content that we can recognise independently of generalised appeal to God's grace. On this understanding, we can continue to uphold our original distinction between the two classes of commandment.

But if we look a little deeper into Saadia's discussion of particular commandments, we again find some surprising parallels between the categories. So, taking two examples of rational commandments to begin with:

> The divine Wisdom imposed a restraint upon bloodshed among men, because if license were to prevail in this matter, they would cause each other to disappear. The consequence would be, in addition to the pain experienced by the victims, a frustration of the purpose that the All-wise had in mind with regard to them...

> Theft was forbidden by [divine] Wisdom because, if it were permitted, some men would rely on stealing the others' wealth, and they would neither till the soil nor engage in any other lucrative occupation. And if all were to rely on this source of livelihood, even stealing would become impossible, because,

with the disappearance of all property, there would be absolutely nothing in existence that might be stolen. (*Emunot*, III: 2, 141–2)

Both of these explanations justify the prohibitions in question on the grounds of their consequences. In ethical theories this is known, for obvious reasons, as a consequentialist approach to ethics, which takes many different forms but is fundamentally based on the idea that the rightness or wrongness of actions is judged solely on their consequences, considered from an impersonal standpoint. Thus, murder and theft are here shown to be wrong not because they are wrong in themselves, but on account of their problematic consequences. This type of approach is usually contrasted with deontological approaches, which present us with moral principles or duties the violation of which is intrinsically wrong. On such approaches we have a duty not to murder, not on account of the consequences of murder, but simply because it is wrong. In rationalising the above commandments, however, Saadia can clearly be seen to side with the consequentialists.

Turning to the revealed commandments, we find that having said that they are 'optional' from the perspective of reason, Saadia in fact believes that 'most of them have as their basis *partially* useful purposes' (*Emunot*, III: 2, 143, emphasis added). So, for example:

> Among the benefits accruing from the consecration of certain seasons, by desisting from work on them, there is first of all that of obtaining relaxation from much exertion. Furthermore it presents the opportunity for the attainment of a little bit of knowledge and a little additional praying…

> Among the advantages, again, that result from the prohibition against the eating of [only] certain animals is the prevention of any comparison between them and the Creator. For it is inconceivable that God would permit anything resembling Him to be eaten or, on the other hand that [the eating of such a being] could cause defilement to man. This precept also serves to keep man from worshipping any of these animals, since it is unseemly for him to worship what has been given to him for food, nor what has been declared unclean to him. (*Emunot*, III: 2, 143–4)

Like the rational commandments, the revealed commandments are here given a form of consequentialist justification by Saadia. It is not that eating pork is wrong in itself, but that its prohibition has certain beneficial consequences. Given then that Saadia provides the same form of rationalisation for each type of commandment, we might again ask what becomes of the apparent distinction with which he began.

We will have more to say about means-end reasoning towards the end of the chapter, but it is worth noting here that Marvin Fox has argued that ultimately Saadia fails to establish the existence of a class of commandments that we can genuinely term rational, in part because of the weakness of consequentialist reasoning. For Fox, consequentialist justifications are not robust enough to ground a category of rational *commandments* – where commandments are divine absolutes – since such justifications are always relative to the ends that they posit. And in some cases, the ends might be better served by actions that transgress the commandments. In a classic example, if my committing a murder would prevent ten other murders, I *ought* to commit murder according to consequentialist reasoning. As much as sophisticated forms of consequentialism attempt to avoid this 'consequence', its critics match the development with subtler forms of the objection.

We can reinforce the problem from another direction, by looking at the second justification for the prohibition on theft quoted above: 'if all were to rely on this source of livelihood, even stealing would become impossible, because, with the disappearance of all property, there would be absolutely nothing in existence that might be stolen' (*Emunot*, III: 2, 141–2). What Saadia here envisages as an anarchic mess could be also be viewed as a Marxist dream – an end to private property. The serious point that emerges from the flippant remark is that when one justifies an act on account of its end or goal, one has only justified it for those who agree on the value of that goal. Allowing, for the sake of the argument, that stealing would indeed lead to the end of private property, many would see this as a justification of stealing, even from an impersonal perspective. Thus, you can justify the rationality of a commandment as a means to an end, but only if the end is one that is considered to be of value. Thus, Fox claims that if Saadia is looking to justify the existence of a set of rational commandments as absolute divine commands, consequentialist reasoning is not up to the task. On a consequentialist reading, the rationality of an act is always relative to its consequences. So Fox collapses the distinction by arguing that all the commandments must ultimately be considered as 'revealed' – none of them can be justified absolutely independently of appeals to revelation.

Fox's basic problem with consequentialism might have some philosophical merit. We may be uneasy with the idea that murder would be morally justified if its consequences were beneficial. But while Fox might have a point regarding the nature of consequentialist reasoning, it is less clear that it plays such a central role in Saadia's discussion. Without entering into detailed exegesis of the texts, it certainly seems as if Saadia does want to uphold a distinction between the rational and the revealed commandments based on the idea that the former have their own intrinsic rationality that, in his opinion, any rational person would recognise. His further discussion of them does attempt to flesh out some of the further discursive reasons we might give for them in consequentialist terms, but ultimately for Saadia, we *intuitively* know that those commandments are rational – their approval is after all 'implanted in us' in his opinion.

We can see that this is the case from the following discussion of what we should say to a purported prophet who announces the abrogation of certain rational laws such as that prohibiting adultery:

> Our reply to him should be the same as that of all of us would be to anyone who would show us miracles and marvels for the purpose of making us give up such rational convictions as that the truth is good and lying reprehensible and the like. He was thereupon compelled to take refuge in the theory that the disapproval of lying and the approval of the truth were not prompted by reason but were the result of the commandments and prohibitions of Scripture, and the same was true for the rejection of murder, adultery and stealing. When he had come to that, however, I felt that I needed no longer to concern myself with him and that I had my fill of discussion with him. (*Emunot*, III: 8, 164)

The point Saadia is making is that when discursive reasons for rejecting murder and stealing run out, one may have to fall back on the simple assertion that someone who thinks that these are acceptable is just wrong. And if someone cannot 'see' that, then Saadia would be forced to give up on reasoning with that person, for ultimately there is something wrong with their rationality if that recognition is not 'implanted' in them. Saadia is thus more of an 'intuitionist' than a consequentialist, to coin another term from modern moral philosophy (again, simply to clarify the sort of view he takes rather than to impute a fully worked out intuitionist theory to him). He believes that there are certain objective ethical truths that our minds ought to be able to intuit if they are in good working order.

While it is certainly true that appeals to moral intuition as justification for allegedly objective truths are no less problematic than consequentialist justifications – as becomes clear as soon as one begins to argue with someone who has very different moral 'intuitions' – Saadia, not to mention many subsequent thinkers, believed that such moral truths existed and that he could therefore base a theory of rational commandments on them. With the revealed commandments, on the other hand, this is not the case. They are not intrinsically rational in this way. There might be certain benefits that accrue to them, which Saadia is willing to set out, though even then the same end could no doubt have been reached in a different fashion – there are certainly other ways of resting than observing the Jewish Sabbath. But Saadia knows that in the end, he cannot fall back on the simple claim that these revealed commandments are intrinsically rational. We can appeal to God and his plan for humanity to account for the 'rationality' of the revealed commandments. But on a case-by-case basis, we cannot recognise them as rational independent of such appeal to God's grace and will. Thus, we end up with the classic understanding of Saadia as arguing for a distinction between rational commandments that are intrinsically rational and revealed commandments that are not.

2. MAIMONIDES' INTELLECTUALISM

As the first to recognise a category of commandments that we can understand as rational, Saadia had taken a significant philosophical step. It was not enough, however, for Maimonides. Against a background in which the Ash'arite view had become the theological orthodoxy in the Islamic world, Maimonides argues for a more thoroughgoing form of intellectualism that lays great stress on the idea that both the natural and the 'legal' expressions of God's will are subject to the same rational categories. Maimonides therefore begins the section of the *Guide* that deals with *ta'amei ha-mitzvot* (*Guide*, III: 25, 502–3), by looking at God's 'actions', i.e. nature, and dividing these 'actions' into four classes:

1) Futile actions – Those undertaken with no end in view.
2) Frivolous actions – Those that have low ends ('unnecessary and not very useful').
3) Vain actions – Those in which the end aimed at is not achieved.
4) Good and Excellent actions – Those which have noble ends ('necessary or useful').

A modicum of rational reflection leads one to conclude that God's actions obviously cannot be vain, futile or frivolous, and thus Maimonides argues that philosophically speaking, we have to say that all of God's actions must fall into the fourth class of being 'good and excellent' – there must be some rational purpose behind all of God's works in nature. Since commanding laws is simply another of God's actions, by simple application of the same reasoning Maimonides concludes that the laws too must all be 'good and excellent' with noble ends. How though are we to characterise these ends?

At this point we should recall our earlier discussions regarding the manner in which Maimonides treats statements telling us that God has done something (see **4.2**). When acts are ascribed to God in the Torah, we are not to understand this as implying some sort of divine intervention in the natural order, but rather as telling us that he is the First Cause of such 'actions', which in fact have perfectly natural scientific explanations. This naturalism is even applied to the idea of God's commands – 'The term "command" is figuratively used of God with reference to the coming to be of that which He has willed' (*Guide*, I: 65, 159). But this means that just as we look to natural causation to explain God's actions, we should be looking to the same scheme of natural causes in order to understand God's commands. So if we are looking to demonstrate the rationality of the laws, we are to turn to the causal structure of nature. But how, one might ask, can the study of nature rationalise the commandments? In order to understand this, we again need a little Aristotelian background.

For Aristotle, we can only gain deep understanding of something if we know 'the why' of it, the explanation that tells us what it is and how it has come to be such as it is, and Aristotle identifies understanding the 'why' of a thing with grasping its primary cause:

> Knowledge is the object of our inquiry, and men do not think they know a thing till they have grasped the 'why' of it (which is to grasp its primary cause). (*Physics*, II. 3, 194b18–19)

Aristotle famously defines four causes, which he terms the material, formal, efficient and final causes. But Aristotle's four 'causes' are not four different things. They are rather four different ways of referring to the two fundamental Aristotelian concepts with which we are already familiar: form and matter. The material cause refers to the matter and the other three causes refer to the notion of form in differing ways. They each act as different ways of answering the 'why' question that needs to be answered if we are to gain the sort of genuine understanding – scientific knowledge (*episteme*) – that he speaks of above. And for Aristotle this type of causal knowledge actually lays bare the structure of the universe.

For our purposes, it is the Aristotelian idea of the final cause that we have already encountered at **2.1** that is central. The example we used there was of someone who is walking in order to be healthy, the point being that we explain the action by reference to its purpose. Such explanations are also termed teleological explanations. So final causes or teleological explanations in Aristotle explain something by being that 'for the sake of which' something is done or exists, and even if we are rightly sceptical about the science involved, we can easily grasp and acknowledge the basic idea that by ascribing a certain purpose to something we can enquire what needs to be done to achieve it. However, having a teleological explanation for something is not in itself sufficient to produce the sort of understanding that Aristotle is after. In order for something to qualify as *episteme*, we must have a demonstration, which, as noted in earlier discussions (**1.1**), is the type of conclusive argument that begins from self-evidently true first intelligibles. For Aristotle, these first principles of science are definitions that state the form of something. Thus, form, as the fundamental explanatory concept in Aristotelian science, is the basic building block of scientific explanation. Forms are real and active constituents in nature to which we must appeal if we are to gain a genuine understanding of its causal structure.

How is all of this relevant to rationalising the commandments? Maimonides shares the general Aristotelian scientific picture, meaning that if he wants to know the reasons for the commandments, he will have to grasp their 'causes'. And since we know that the laws are good and excellent and that this means they serve noble or useful ends, we can presumably give a teleological explanation of the commandments that would appeal to this good and excellent purpose – or their final cause. That is why we see Maimonides using words like 'cause', 'meaning' and 'end' as virtual synonyms in his discussion of *ta'amei ha-mitzvot*:

> There are also people who say that every commandment and prohibition in these Laws is consequent upon *wisdom* and aims at some *end*, and that all Laws have *causes* and were given in view of some *utility*. (*Guide*, III: 26, 506–7, emphasis added)

Just as God has arranged nature so that created existents realise certain ends or structures, the laws that he has commanded are similarly to be explained in terms of what they are 'for the sake of'. So for Maimonides, revealing the wisdom of the commandments equates to understanding their final causes – or their form. Thus it is clear to Maimonides that the commandments, being addressed to human beings, were given in order to realise the form of humanity, or to bring about human perfection. So we rationalise the commandments by showing how they actualise the form of man by leading man to the fulfilment of his ultimate perfection.

While the precise nature of this final perfection is a hotly disputed topic in Maimonidean scholarship (see chapter 7), we can at least give some general idea of what it is that rationalises the commandments for Maimonides by considering the statements he makes during his discussion of *ta'amei ha-mitzvot*:

> The Law as a whole aims at two things: the welfare of the soul and the welfare of the body. As for the welfare of the soul, it consists in the multitude's acquiring correct opinions corresponding to their respective capacity... As for the welfare of the body, it comes about by the improvement of their ways of living one with another. (*Guide*, III: 27, 510)

It appears as if the welfare of the body is a function of social order while the welfare of the soul consists in the multitude gaining correct opinions in speculative matters – on God's existence and unity, for example. So the Law aims on the one hand at improving and maintaining the social and political order, while on the other hand it seeks the philosophical improvement of individuals. But these in turn are merely the necessary preconditions for two corresponding perfections:

> For it has already been demonstrated that man has two perfections: a first perfection, which is the perfection of the body, and an ultimate perfection, which is the perfection of the soul. The first perfection consists in being healthy and in the very best bodily state... His ultimate perfection is to become rational in actu, I mean to have an intellect in actu;... (*Guide*, III: 27, 510–11)

The perfections of body and soul consist respectively of the physical health of the individual and the acquisition of correct opinions 'that investigation has rendered compulsory'. This latter idea is importantly different from the idea of the welfare of the soul, which can be achieved by the simple acceptance of correct opinions on the basis of statements in the Torah. Intellectual perfection requires that such opinions actually be *demonstrated*, not just accepted on some other basis such as the authority of tradition.

Ultimately then, the commandments aim at these two perfections, but they do so by immediately establishing the two types of welfare. On the one hand, there are commandments that regulate society (welfare of the body) so as to allow for the health of the individual (perfection of the body) who does not have to worry about being harmed. On the other hand, there are commandments that teach correct opinions (welfare of the soul) as a precursor to further investigation in which these opinions, and others that might not be explicitly taught, could eventually be demonstrated (leading to the perfection of the soul):

> The True Law then…has come to bring us both perfections, I mean the welfare of the states of people in their relations with one another through the abolition of reciprocal wrongdoing and through the acquisition of a noble and excellent character. In this way the preservation of the population of the country and their permanent existence in the same order become possible, so that every one of them achieves his first perfection; I mean also the soundness of the beliefs and the giving of correct opinions through which the ultimate perfection is achieved. (*Guide*, III: 27, 511)

So the Torah is seen as an immediate means to achieving the preparatory stages of 'welfare' to the extent that is possible for all society, thus setting individuals within it on the road to perfection. Maimonides therefore rationalises the commandments by showing how they fit into an overall scientific theory that begins from the form of humanity. The intellectual religious task that remains is the reconstruction of this theory so that we can understand *how* the commandments relate to this final cause. But such a reconstruction is no easy task, especially when Maimonides appears to insist that all the laws have a cause.

> It is, however, the doctrine of all of us – both of the multitude and of the elite – that all the Laws have a cause, though we ignore the causes for some of them and we do not know the manner in which they conform to wisdom. (*Guide*, III: 26, 507)

Such a thoroughgoing intellectualism was evidently a departure from Saadia's distinction between the rational and the revealed, as well as the rabbinic distinction between the *mishpatim* and *huqqim*. Moreover, though the list of *huqqim* was very limited in the Talmud, Maimonides extended it to cover entire categories of law that had not previously been subsumed under that heading. Most notably, in the *Mishneh Torah* he identifies all the sacrificial laws and all the laws regarding purity and impurity as *huqqim*.[1]

Maimonides does admit that while all of the laws have reasons, 'we ignore the causes for some of them and we do not know the manner in which they conform to wisdom' (*Guide*, III: 26, 507). Indeed, he notes that while there is a reason for all the generalities of a commandment, there may not be a reason for all of its particular details. There may be no reason why a lamb rather than a ram had been specified for a given sacrifice, though there would be a reason for doing the sacrifice. But even with this slight qualification, by extending the category of *huqqim* as he does, Maimonides sets himself quite a challenge. For while we might be able to understand how the prohibitions against murder and idolatry relate to the final cause in a perfectly straightforward fashion, it is rather more difficult to understand how refraining from wearing a mixture of linen and wool would have quite the same effect. The type of teleological explanation that we have described might seem viable for the rational laws, but is far more problematic for the *huqqim*, which by Maimonides' calculation constitute far more than a few anomalies.

3. RATIONALISING *HUQQIM* AND HISTORICAL EXPLANATIONS

Apart from his earlier argument that none of God's laws can be anything other than 'good and excellent', Maimonides also cites scriptural support for his view:

> Keep them therefore and do them; for this is your wisdom and your understanding in the sight of the nations, who shall hear all these statutes, and say, Surely, this great nation is a wise and understanding people. (Deuteronomy, 4: 6)

How, the argument goes, could the nations appreciate the wisdom and understanding of the Jewish people through their statutes if they are in principle unintelligible? Rather, if this verse is to make sense, even the *huqqim* must have a rational explanation that could be universally appreciated. And despite the difficulties *huqqim* present, Maimonides does not deviate from the teleological model of explanation. He does, however, supplement the model with historical explanations.

Taking sacrifices as our example, Maimonides begins by subsuming them under the general category of laws of worship, a group of laws that contribute to the final intellectual perfection by realising what Maimonides terms God's 'first intention of the Law' (*Guide*, III: 29, 517). This first intention is 'the apprehension of Him, may He be exalted, and the rejection of *idolatry*' (*Guide*, III: 32, 527), a rejection that must 'wipe out its traces and all that is bound up with it' (*Guide*, III: 29, 517). Commandments that direct our attention towards God and away from these false opinions are therefore said to be of great utility, and the sacrificial laws are seen as instrumental in achieving this end. So we have a teleological explanation for these laws that parallels the explanation of the *mishpatim*.

However, the explanation as it stands is extremely problematic since it is difficult to understand *how* the ritual slaughter of a particular animal at a particular place and time will lead to true opinions about God. In fact, there is every reason to think that such practices will have the opposite effect, since according to Maimonides the sacrificial cult was a prominent part of the Sabian culture, an ancient polytheistic civilisation that he discusses at some length and uses as a subsequent point of reference throughout his discussion of *ta'amei ha-mitzvot*. This idolatrous culture with its belief in astrology, myth and magic in service of the stars was precisely what the Torah laws were supposed to be effacing. So how could laws that incorporate these idolatrous practices produce correct opinions?

In order to give a full rationalisation of these commandments Maimonides has to appeal to 'the second intention' of the law. Basically, in order to realise its first intention, the law cannot always take the most direct route. Instead, it sometimes has to take historical circumstance and human psychology into account. Under the rubric of this second intention, Maimonides therefore supplies us with the historical and psychological information that will allow us to understand how such practices can form part of our journey to intellectual perfection. Thus, in explaining sacrifices, Maimonides describes how the Sabian modes of worship were relevant to the evolution of the monotheistic biblical system of sacrifice:

> If you consider the divine actions – I mean to say the natural actions – the deity's wily graciousness and wisdom, as shown in the creation of living beings, in the gradation of the motions of the limbs, and the proximity of some of the latter to others, will through them become clear to you ... Many things in our Law are due to something similar to this very governance on the part of Him who governs ... For a sudden transition from one opposite to another is impossible. And therefore man, according to his nature, is not capable of abandoning suddenly all to which he was accustomed ... For just as it is not in the nature of man that, after having been brought up in a slavish service occupied with clay, bricks, and similar things, he should all of a sudden wash off from his hands the dirt deriving from them and proceed immediately to fight against *the children of Anak*, so it is also not in his nature that, after having been brought up upon very many modes of worship and of customary

practices, which the souls find so agreeable that they become as it were a primary notion, he should abandon them all of a sudden. (*Guide*, III: 32, 525–8)

Maimonides here combines psychological generalisations about human nature with historical information about the Sabian culture in order to show that the system of sacrifices were a kind of divine trick (termed 'wily graciousness' by Maimonides). The fundamental psychological fact to which he appeals is that people who become accustomed to certain ideas are unable to adopt a wholesale revision of them. And given the historical climate, at that time sacrificing animals was the accepted mode of divine worship to which even the Israelites had become accustomed given its prevalence in surrounding cultures. Had God, therefore, commanded the abolition of sacrifices at the historical moment of the revelation at Sinai, it would have seemed to the people as tantamount to forbidding their only mode of communication with God. Taking this into account, God prescribed a modified version of the Sabian sacrificial cult, but purified it of its idolatrous elements. In this way, God was able to safeguard the people's trust in the law by retaining enough of what they were used to, while at the same time modifying and purifying it from its most idolatrous elements to lead them to a more refined view of God. As Maimonides writes, God 'suffered the above-mentioned kinds of worship to remain, but transferred them from created or imaginary and unreal things to His own name' (*Guide*, II: 32, 526). The 'wily graciousness' therefore consisted of God using modified idolatrous practices in order to lead the people to belief in the existence of the one God of Judaism, and eventually to wean the people off idolatrous worship altogether.

Effectively therefore, while some *mitzvot*, such as prayer, 'come close' (though notably are not identified with) the direct realisation of the first intention of the Law, the sacrificial laws 'pertain to a second intention' (*Guide*, III: 32, 529). When faced with the *huqqim* we find a clash between the ideal of what worship of God should be, and the demands of human nature given the historical circumstances of the original Sinaitic legislation. These belong to the second intention of the Law in not requiring the abolition of all modes of worship that might originally have had idolatrous associations but rather accommodating some such practices as a concession to human nature. In the final analysis then, sacrifices are rational because given human nature they were a necessary means to the final end of intellectual perfection. Sacrifices do not lead one directly to this ultimate perfection. They certainly did not miraculously cause a demonstration of

God's existence and unity to pass before the minds of the Israelites. But their performance did wean the Israelites away from belief in the efficacy of idolatry and towards a more refined conception of God that could, given time, mature into the philosophical conception of Maimonides.

Not all of the *huqqim* were accommodatory in this fashion – many were more directly opposed to Sabian practices. Thus, *sha'atnez* was prohibited precisely because of its use in the garments of the Sabian priests (*Guide*, III: 37, 544); and the use of sheep, goat and oxen in the Jewish sacrificial services was dictated by the *prohibition* on killing such animals among different Sabian sects (*Guide*, III: 46, 581–2). The particular type of *hoq* presumably depended on the psychological needs of the people regarding each of the Sabian practices that a commandment was addressing. But the pattern of explanation for all such *mitzvot* remains historical and could possibly even account for those particulars that Maimonides originally said had no reason, such as the use of a ram rather than a lamb in a particular sacrifice. The use of historical information in the explanation of *huqqim* would certainly help to explain our ignorance of the reasons for certain commandments and when Maimonides speaks of the deficiency of our knowledge as one cause of this ignorance (*Guide*, III: 49 612), it is a deficiency in our knowledge of this very information to which he is presumably referring.

In the final analysis then, the historical explanations show us how, despite appearances to the contrary, the *huqqim* are rational commandments that can play a role in actualising human perfection. As a result, Maimonides recasts the distinction between *mishpatim* and *huqqim*. It is not that the *huqqim* have no rationale, but rather that the rationale of the *mishpatim* is clear to all, while that of the *huqqim* requires rather more background knowledge. For Maimonides then, the only difference between the categories is the transparency of their utility to the multitude. Most people would not have been able to see what role the *huqqim* could play in producing human perfection, but those who know enough about the history of idolatry can understand how it supplements the teleological explanations.

4. MEANS, ENDS AND *MITZVOT*

When discussing Saadia, we referred to the criticisms that can be levelled at consequentialist forms of justification. Though it is not clear that Saadia really does rely on his consequentialist musings to rationalise the commandments, there is a sense in which Maimonides does just that, since in his opinion the commandments are rational because they lead to the perfection of humanity, albeit via a circuitous route at times. But this leads to a number of philosophical problems with Maimonides' approach.

The most famous criticisms of Maimonides' rationalisation are usually directed at his use of historical explanations. Retaining sacrifices as our example, his view that they are based on idolatrous practices would be cause for concern in itself. However, the problem that most exercises Maimonides' critics is that the historical explanations imply that commandments like these have outlived their usefulness. The sacrificial laws are understood to be a means to human perfection, but only due to the historical circumstances. Though far from a perfect form of worship, the people needed sacrifices because of their idolatrous environment. Since we no longer live in an environment where idolatrous sacrifice is seen as the only way to worship God, and understand that we can worship in other ways, by praying for example, why not pray rather than sacrifice? Of course that was precisely what Jews had done ever since the destruction of the Temple, but this was seen as a temporary blip. The Temple would eventually be restored in a messianic age and sacrifices would be reinstated. The question one can ask following Maimonides' reasoning though, is why? The historical circumstances that necessitated the sacrificial system no longer apply, so would not prayer be a more rational and efficient means to the end of human perfection? Why continue with a form of worship that is basically idolatrous and that God only 'suffered' for historical reasons that are no longer relevant? Incidentally, in a nod to his preference for silence mentioned in chapter 3, Maimonides notes in his discussion of sacrifices that abandoning them at Sinai would have been equivalent to a prophet in his day calling for an end to prayer and substituting silent meditation. Some have argued that Maimonides is hinting that this would be no bad thing.

Maimonides' historical rationalisations actually raise all manner of further problems for the authority of the Law. Can the Law adapt in order to take historical changes into account? And if not, what obligates a person to continue to adhere to laws that appear to have passed their 'sell-by date'? Is there any reason now to perform these commandments given that the historical approach does not furnish us with a reason that we can use? Maimonides believed that the law was 'eternal and absolute' and does not draw such heterodox conclusions from his historical explanations:

The Law was not given with a view to things that are rare. For in everything that it wishes to bring about ... it is directed only toward the things that occur in the majority of cases and pays no attention to what happens rarely ... In view of this consideration, it also will not be possible that the laws be dependent on changes in the circumstances of the individuals and of the times, as is the case with regard to medical treatment which is particularised for every individual ... On the contrary, governance of the Law ought to be absolute and universal, including everyone, even if it is suitable only for certain individuals and not suitable for others. (*Guide*, III: 34, 534–5)

Nonetheless, philosophically speaking, this seems like a difficult position for him to justify. There are evidently problems with the idea of the absolute nature of divine laws once one accepts Maimonides' approach to rationalising them.

Maimonides is not unaware of these problems. In fact, they explain why the reasons for the *huqqim* had to be held back from the masses. If, as we saw in the Talmudic discussion, the rather wiser Solomon felt that he no longer had to observe certain commandments on account of their reasons being inapplicable to him, then knowledge of Maimonides' rationalisations would likely cause the less educated to presume that they no longer have to observe 'idolatrous' and 'outdated' commandments. That, for Maimonides, is precisely *why* the *huqqim* are commandments whose utility is not made clear to the multitude.

Interestingly, however, it is not actually the historical explanations that are at fault here. The real problem is the basic teleological structure. The reason that the commandments no longer appear to be rational is because they no longer serve the ends that Maimonides believes once rationalised them. Originally, these commandments served the end of perfecting humanity, since they weaned people away from their idolatrous beliefs towards the correct opinions. The historical explanations merely serve to make this clear; they show *how* these rituals served that end. But the problem now is that, given the changes in historical circumstances, they *no longer lead* to that end. So Maimonides rationalises the commandments in terms of a means-end relationship and the historical explanations make it clear that this relationship no longer holds. Basically, if sacrificing animals still led to human perfection, the commandments would still be perfectly rational. The fact that they do not is the real root of the problem. If the commandments cannot serve their purported ends they cease to be rational, and while this may not lessen their authority in Maimonides' eyes, it does mean that they have lost the philosophical cogency he thinks they have.

One could (and some do) argue that the commandments continue to serve the original ends. One might, for example, appeal to a constant human vulnerability to paganism that needs to be fought continuously. Josef Stern has argued that at least in Maimonides' time the threat of idolatry remained in the guise of false versions of Neoplatonism that were then popular (as opposed to the genuine version used by Maimonides himself). So the commandments had not outlived their usefulness and had to counteract the still very real threat of idolatrous forms of worship.[2]

But in truth, it might be that Maimonides is less concerned to rationalise our continued observance of the commandments than he is to show that the commandments 'reveal a God who acts by reasons that are intelligible to man,'[3] as David Hartman puts it. According to Hartman, Maimonides was not concerned with the meaning that the commandments might have for us as individuals. He was not 'attempting to inspire one to observe commandments, but to convince his reader that nature and Torah reveal the same God'.[4] For Hartman and others, Maimonides was primarily concerned to show how the commandments reflect a God whose laws are intelligible to man.

With this distinction in mind, we could admit that the historical explanations are not attempting to give people reasons that they can use to justify obeying the sacrificial laws. Indeed, and somewhat ironically, for God's ruse regarding sacrifices to be effective, the person to whom the commandment is addressed *cannot* be allowed to understand the reason, or he would realise that it was all a trick to wean him off such quasi-idolatrous practices. But do Maimonides' rationalisations achieve the alternative aim of revealing a God whose laws are intelligible to man? The problem is that according to Maimonides the commandments are part of an eternal and absolute law. But we cannot explain why it was rational for God to command the sacrificial cult as part of an *eternal* law. The teleological explanations only rationalise the commandments for as long as they serve the ends they were designed to serve, and that time has passed. So the teleological explanations show that the commandments that God has given are entirely mutable. In the final analysis, at a purely philosophical level, Maimonides' rationalisation makes it just as difficult to understand why it was rational for God to command these laws *for eternity* as it does to understand why one ought to perform them.

What all of this shows is that if we consider the commandments to be a means to a certain end, we can always ask whether or not they serve that end. If, as in the case of the *huqqim*, they no longer appear to do so, we are always left with the need for a more general justification of our obligation to the Law and for God's commanding it, the lack of which will still allow antinomian concerns to be raised. Of course, if it is the teleological approach that is the problem, the difficulties pervade Maimonides' entire approach. It is not simply a problem for the historical explanations of the *huqqim*. It is a problem for the whole idea that commandments are simply means to an end.

None of these problems would arise if the commandments could be shown to be intrinsically rational, as Saadia argued was the case for the rational commandments. In that case their rationality would cease to be dependent on whether or not they serve certain external ends. Making such a case is difficult enough for Saadia's rational commandments. Making it for the *huqqim* would multiply the factor of difficulty many times over. Yet the alternative teleological approach simply makes the commandments a slave to their philosophical ends. As Fox pointed out, we cannot retain the absolute nature of the commandments on such an approach.

One might of course ask whether this constitutes a genuine philosophical objection to the teleological approach. Ultimately the problems we have raised might be thought to be more theological than philosophical, for the only obstacle to a method that leads to changing one's practices is a *religious* belief that they are divine and eternal laws. The Maimonidean approach, it could be argued, gives us an Archimedean point from which to rationalise and constructively criticise Jewish practice, which is surely a good thing philosophically speaking. For our thinkers, however, what we are terming a religious belief in the perfection and immutability of God's law would have been a natural corollary of the philosophically demonstrated truth of God's perfection and immutability. The idea that the law is eternal (and thus eternally binding) turns out in their eyes to be as philosophically sound as it is religiously demanded. Thus, whether belief in the eternity of the law can be retained alongside a teleological approach to its rationality remains a pertinent *philosophical* question to ask. And the fact remains, as mentioned in our discussion of Saadia, that the value of teleological justifications can be questioned even for justifying secular ethical imperatives. Nonetheless, while their respective approaches might be problematic, the idea that God's commandments can be understood to be rational remained one to which Maimonides and to a lesser extent Saadia was committed. Their God was not an arbitrary legislator; that was a view for those suffering from 'a sickness of the soul'.

NOTES

1　See Maimonides, *Mishneh Torah*, 'Laws of Trespass', VIII: 8 and 'Laws of Immersion Pools', XI: 12.

2　See Josef Stern, *Problems and Parables of Law: Maimonides and Nahmanides on Reasons for the Commandments* (Ta'amei Ha-Mitzvot) (Albany, NY: SUNY Press, 1998), chapter 6

3　David Hartman, *Maimonides: Torah and Philosophic Quest* (Philadelphia, PA: Jewish Publication Society, 1976), 183.

4　*Ibid.*, 185.

FURTHER READING

An interesting discussion of the Talmudic approach to the commandments can be found in David Novak, 'The Talmud as a Source for Philosophical Reflection', in Daniel H. Frank and Oliver Leaman (eds), *History of Jewish Philosophy* (London: Routledge, 1997), 62–80.

For Marvin Fox's discussion of Saadia see 'On the Rational Commandments in Saadia's Philosophy', in *Proceedings of the Sixth World Congress of Jewish Studies*, vol. III (1977), 33–43.

For a reply by Lenn Goodman that takes an approach similar to my own, see his 'Rational Law/Revealed Law', in D.H. Frank (ed.), *A People Apart* (Albany: SUNY Press, 1993), 109–39.

Many books on Maimonides discuss his approach including:

David Hartman, *Maimonides: Torah and Philosophic Quest* (Philadelphia, PA: Jewish Publication Society, 1976), chapter 4; and Oliver Leaman, *Moses Maimonides* (Richmond: Curzon, 1997), chapter 9.

A more detailed philosophical analysis of Maimonides on *ta'amei ha-mitzvot* on which my discussion is based can be found in my *Two Models of Jewish Philosophy: Justifying One's Practices* (Oxford: Oxford University Press, 2005), chapter 1.

For an in-depth treatment of Maimonides' approach and a comparison with that of Nahmanides, see Josef Stern, *Problems and Parables of Law: Maimonides and Nahmanides on Reasons for the Commandments* (*Ta'amei Ha-Mitzvot*) (Albany, NY: SUNY Press, 1998). Stern also offers an alternative analysis of Maimonides, which yields a different answer to the antinomian concerns we have highlighted.

6

Freewill and Omniscience

We are by now well aware of the centrality of the commandments for Judaism in general, and for the medieval Jewish philosophers in particular. This focus on the commandments leads us into further important areas for philosophical reflection, none more so than that of freewill. As Hasdai Crescas noted:

> Choice is one of the foundations of religion ... since a commandment [cannot be given if] the person to whom the command is addressed is compelled and forced to do a fixed thing. On the contrary, it is necessary that his simple will be able to do any of the alternatives; then a commandment to him will be appropriate and relevant. (*Light*, II: 5, intro, 472)[1]

Crescas is drawing our attention to an important principle, much later enshrined in the phrase "'ought' implies 'can'", according to which it only makes sense to say that someone ought to do something if it is possible for the person in question to do it. I cannot sensibly command someone to do something that they simply cannot do, such as draw a square circle. More mundanely, if I tell someone that they have to get up and help with the housework having bound them to a post from which they cannot escape, then that would be similarly unfair since it is *physically* impossible. Of course one *could* issue these commands, but they would be unjust. If one is unable to do something, then it is surely unfair to command them to do it.

In the moral sphere, the idea that I am free to choose whether to act morally or not is absolutely fundamental to our commonsense concept of moral responsibility. If a malevolent scientist has programmed or hypnotised someone to act in an evil fashion and that person does so through no choice of their own, we would not hold *them* responsible for their actions; they could not be blamed for acting in the way that they do. Similarly, if someone were forced to act morally, that person would not be responsible for their good actions and would not be deemed praiseworthy. In neither of these cases can we say that the person in question is good or evil; their actions were beyond their control. The point is that we only hold people morally responsible, and thus morally judge them, if they have freely chosen to act in the way that they did. We would not make these judgements, it is argued, if the person committing the act had no choice and was acting under some form of compulsion. We need only think of the basis of pleas for mitigation in a court of law to see how these ideas have real application.

Crescas is making this very point for the divine commandments. If God is perfectly just, and he is going to command us to act in a certain way and hold us accountable for those actions, then surely we must be able conform to his commandments. The importance of this can be clearly illustrated if, for the sake of argument, we take a traditional stance on reward and punishment. It would be very difficult to justify either rewarding or punishing someone who was acting under compulsion and could not choose to do otherwise. And this notion of 'choosing to do otherwise' is the way that Crescas here sums up our intuitive sense of what human freedom is – it is our ability to 'do any of the alternatives', to say that we could have acted in a way other than we did at the time. We are free to act if we are free to choose among a number of alternatives. My sitting here writing at this moment is an act of free choice if I could genuinely have chosen to stay in bed instead.

But why would one think that we are *not* free in this way? The problem that most concerned the medievals was that of God's omniscience. The idea that God knows all that there is to know was central to the three main monotheistic faith traditions. Yet God's omniscience brings a number of problems in its wake. The very idea that God has many different discrete pieces of knowledge created difficulties for God's unity and simplicity. And the idea of God picking up knowledge as history progresses was seen as implying that God was changing as he continuously tracked this new information, only knowing things when they happened and thus having our actions causally affect him. But with God's immutability a recurrent theme for many of our thinkers, it was argued that he surely cannot change in this way. As, Maimonides notes, 'there is a general consensus ... that it is not true that new knowledge should come to Him, may He be exalted, so that he would know now what He did not know before' (*Guide*, III: 20, 480). But if he cannot change, how can he continually acquire new pieces of information? The problem is easily solved if we say that God knows everything, including what will occur in the future. God knows all that has been, is, and will be, so he is not tracking change as it happens and recording it from his experience as we would do. He has always known that things would be thus and so. This, however, brings us back to the problem of human freedom with which we began.

Let us take, as an example, the fact that I have freely chosen (pressure from my publisher notwithstanding) to sit and write this chapter at my computer today, Monday, 10 December 2007. For convenience we can refer to the proposition 'DR will be writing chapter 6 on the morning of Monday, 10 December 2007', as p. Let us also take an arbitrary time in the past, which we will call t_1. In philosophical terms, we would say that at t_1, p is a future contingent, a proposition concerning an event in the future that we believe to be a *possible* state of affairs, since it might or might not occur depending on what I freely decide to do on the morning in question. Now if God is omniscient, then on the most straightforward understanding of that term we would say that at t_1 God knows that p. But if God knew at t_1 that DR would be writing chapter 6 on the morning of Monday, 10 December, 2007, then we have a problem with the idea that this is truly a possible state of affairs, a free act such that I could have chosen to do something else. The basic problem can be stated relatively simply. If I know something, it has to be true, or else I couldn't possibly know it – that is simply part of the definition of knowledge and is why I can know that $2+2=4$, but I cannot know that the moon is made of cheese. But that means that if God *knows* something about the future, then it must also be true. So if God knows at t_1 that p, then p is true at t_1. But that means that at t_1 it was not contingent whether or not I would act in this manner. It was settled by the mere fact that God knew it. Indeed, God is infallible, so it becomes a cast iron certainty that whatever God knows regarding the future will occur. And if it is certain, it is no longer a contingent matter whether or not it will happen.

If we think about what this implies, we come up against a significant problem for human freewill. For I thought I had freely chosen to spend the day writing this at my computer screen. As a matter of fact, however, it has been settled since at least t_1 that this would be the case. Whatever I might subjectively feel about it, if God knew at t_1 that I would be doing this, then p was true at t_1 and I could not have chosen to do otherwise, for that would render God's infallible knowledge that p false. My subjective feelings of freedom are thus an illusion. It turns out that I was inevitably to be sat writing this chapter on Monday, 10 December, 2007. Indeed, if God is immutable, one would presume that he has always had this knowledge, and thus it had been determined since the beginning of time, so to speak, that I would now be typing these words (and, incidentally, that you would be reading them at this precise moment). But what then becomes of our freewill? If all future contingents are known by God, they cease to be contingent and human freewill seems to disappear.

One might object to this by asking what if I had changed my mind, or indeed what if circumstances had prevented me from writing this today due to a computer breakdown. But the reply would be that if I had changed my mind, God would have known *this* at t_1, i.e. God would *not* have known p at t_1. He would instead have known at t_1 that DR will intend to write chapter 6 on Monday, 10 December, 2007, but he will then change his mind/his computer is going to break down. So God would indeed not know that p, since p is not true. As Saadia Gaon tells us explicitly

> Should it be asked, therefore: 'But if God foreknows that a human being will speak, is it conceivable that he should remain silent?' We would answer simply that, if a human being decided instead of speaking to be silent, we would merely modify our original assumption by saying that God knows that that human being will be silent. (*Emunot*, V: 4, 191)

When we speak of God having knowledge of future contingents we are not talking about lucky guesses or predictions that happen to come true; we are talking about knowledge. He would always know the true variation on whatever course history will take. One cannot outwit God by suddenly changing one's mind at the last moment – he would have known that you were going to do that.

This, then, is the dilemma that we will be discussing in this chapter, focusing particularly on Gersonides and, for the first time in any detail, Hasdai Crescas. And with freewill – or more broadly the idea of future contingents – a fundamental of the Jewish faith, and the standard view of God's omniscience similarly well entrenched, one might expect them to have little room for manoeuvre. By the end of this chapter, that expectation might have to be revised.

1. COMPATIBILISM: SAADIA, HALEVI AND MAIMONIDES

The simplest solution to the dilemma religiously speaking would be to take a compatibilist approach. According to compatibilism, we can hold onto both an undiluted understanding of divine omniscience and the idea that we act freely despite it. Thus, according to the well-known saying attributed to Rabbi Akiva, 'everything is foreseen, but free choice is granted' (*Mishnah Avot* 3: 15). Of our medieval thinkers, Saadia, Halevi and Maimonides (exoterically at least) all support this contention.

In Treatise IV of *Emunot ve-De'ot*, Saadia sets out the parameters of the problem in precisely the manner that we have done above. Thus, he begins with the moral considerations we have discussed, writing that 'it is in keeping with the justice of the Creator ... that He gave [man] the power and ability to execute what He had commanded him and to refrain from what He had forbidden him' (*Emunot*, IV: 3, 186). Similarly, reason demands 'that the All-Wise do not charge anyone with aught that does not lie within his competence or which he is unable to do' (*ibid.*). And the freedom that man has is precisely that freedom 'either to act or desist from acting' (*ibid.*), a freedom of the will that precedes the act itself in Saadia's opinion. Freedom is not the mere lack of constraint at the time of acting for Saadia. That would not constitute the freedom of choice that he believes essential to genuine freedom, which requires in addition the prior ability to decide to act in one way or another. Freedom to perform the act requires this prior freedom of decision or else we do not truly have freewill.

Regarding our specific issue, Saadia tackles it head on in the fourth chapter of the Treatise. Saadia's central point is that God's foreknowledge of things is not 'the cause of their coming into being' (*Emunot*, IV: 4, 191). Halevi argues in virtually identical fashion that 'the knowledge of events to come is not the cause of their existence' (*Kuzari*, V: 20, 282). In relation to God's foreknowledge therefore, both Saadia and Halevi point to the fact that it does not *causally* necessitate my actions – and they could well be right. God's knowledge of *p* need not mean that he actually intervened to cause it to occur. Unfortunately though, this is beside the point. For the problems with freewill here are not generated by any claims about causation. They are generated by the mere fact of God's foreknowledge. Let us try to explain this distinction.

Freedom is contrasted with determinism. But things can be determined in different ways. The most popular forms of determinism in much contemporary philosophical discussion are often causal and we find Crescas formulating this version of determinism in his *Light of the Lord*:

> Firstly, since it has been demonstrated in the sciences that in the domain of generable and corruptible things four causes precede their occurrence and that by virtue of the existence of the causes the existence of the effects is necessary, the existence of the effects is accordingly necessary, not possible. Now when we examine the existence of the causes as well, other causes must exist prior to them whose existence necessarily leads to their existence, such that their existence is necessary, not possible. But if we look for the cause of the [second] set of causes, the same reasoning holds, so that we ultimately reach one necessarily existent being (may Hs name be blessed). Thus, the possible does not exist. (*Light*, II: V, 2, 475)

If we pass over the references to Aristotelian ideas such as the four causes, the basic scientific principle here is that every event is necessitated by some prior cause, which itself is necessitated by a further cause and so on until we come to a necessary First Cause. If human actions are as much a part of this physical causal network as any other physical event, then though we might feel as if we are free, every action of ours is the result of a prior cause, which is itself the result of a prior cause and so on. If so, and these causes necessitate their effects, then we would not be free to act in a manner other than we did, since our actions would have been causally determined.

From a medieval Jewish perspective, causal determinism became most troubling when seen as a by-product of the notion of God's providence. Traditional views of divine providence understand the universe to be under God's direct control. God exerts control over every facet of his creation. We will defer discussion of providence until chapter 8, but the obvious problem is how we preserve freewill in the face of this, and this is right at the forefront of Halevi's concerns. Ultimately, Halevi's compatibilist assertion that acts of human freewill 'are completely outside the control of Divine Providence, but are indirectly linked to it' (*Kuzari*, V: 20, 249), does not move us much further on from Rabbi Akiva's more enigmatic statement of the same. But the important point is that this problem of causal determinism is logically distinct from our question concerning divine omniscience.

Causal determinism is admittedly sometimes seen as the route to fore-knowledge. Human beings could have foreknowledge if they could predict the precise progress of the causal chain. I know that when ball A hits ball B, ball B will move off, not because I am psychic, but because of my knowledge of causation. But my foreknowledge is limited and fallible. God, on the other hand, would have perfect foreknowledge because of his perfect knowledge of every causal chain. But let us imagine that our actions were not causally determined and there was no causal chain for us to trace. That would leave human beings floundering when trying to predict anything, but presumably would not affect an omniscient and omnipotent God. One would imagine that an omnipotent being does not *need* to gain its foreknowledge by tracking a causal chain, even if we cannot fathom how else it might gain such knowledge. So let us imagine that there was no such thing as causal determinism, but that God still had foreknowledge. In that case, we could not speak of God causing me to act in any manner since there *is* no causal chain that leads to my action. But presumably God could still know what I am going to do and the problem is that this *in itself* is enough to generate our problems with freewill. This is because, as we have already mentioned, whichever statements about the future God knows must be true, and their very truth means that when the time comes, that is what is going to occur. So again, the fact that God knew I would now be sitting here writing this means that it has always been true that this would be the case. Regardless of any causal chains (or lack of them) it was inevitable that I would now be doing this. Even if I was not *causally* determined to act in this way, the fact remains that I could not, at this point in time, be doing anything other than what I am doing if God had foreknowledge of it. I could not be doing otherwise.

This *logical* determinism is generated by the very truth of God's foreknowledge and makes no reference to causality. Though it might be difficult for us to comprehend how I could be determined to act in a certain way without a causal chain behind it, the fact remains that we can generate what we are calling logical determinism independently of such ideas. Indeed, philosophers since Aristotle have formulated the problem of logical determinism without recourse to God, simply by asking whether statements made now about the future already have determinate truth-values – is a statement about what I am going to do tomorrow true (or false) before it actually occurs? If so, then we can immediately generate the problem for freewill.

The sort of determinism that troubled our thinkers has been referred to as *theological* determinism, since the truths that yield logical determinism are here contained in God's knowledge. It is theological determinism that is our concern, and thus Saadia and Halevi rather miss the point when they claim that since God's knowledge does not cause us to act, we can solve the problem of freewill. For we could agree that God is not causing us to act, yet the mere fact that he *knows* how we are going to act means that when it comes to it, we will not be able to do anything other than act in that way.

Saadia does offer further arguments for the idea that God does not 'interfere' with our freedom. Among them are arguments based on the senses – 'a human being feels conscious of his own ability either to speak or remain silent' (*Emunot*, IV: 4, 187) – and rational considerations including that 'if God were to exercise force upon his servant, there would be no sense to His command' (*ibid.*). As we have already mentioned, however, our feelings of freedom need not reflect objective reality – our subjective feelings of freedom could very easily be mistaken. And while it is difficult to understand the point of the commandments if we are not free to obey them, that does not help us to explain *how* this freedom could co-exist with God's foreknowledge.

If we turn, very briefly this time, to Maimonides' exoteric view, we are able to reinforce some of the points we have made so far. Maimonides deals with the issue of freedom and foreknowledge by appealing to his theory of divine attributes (see chapter 3). Maimonides claims, correctly, that the apparent opposition between freewill and foreknowledge is generated by our assertion that God knows certain things. But if we do not know what we mean by the phrase 'God knows', specifically if the word 'knows' in that phrase has nothing at all in common with our ordinary understanding of that word, then the problem cannot be generated in the first place. So Maimonides' argument is that our concept of knowledge generates the problem, but on his theory of attributes, that concept is absolutely inapplicable to God. God's knowledge does not conflict with human freedom anymore than his goodness does, since ultimately we have no grasp at all on what these words mean when applied to God.

In a way this approach can help us understand the distinction between causal and theological determinism, since our point was that God's knowledge is a problem for our freewill, even if we cannot understand *how* he could gain such knowledge in a way that was not causal. And for Maimonides, since God's knowledge is so far removed from our own, there is every reason to think it possible for God to know about our actions even in the absence of any causal path. It is, however, worth noting that we have already seen much talk of God as the First Cause of a lengthy causal chain in Maimonides. Moreover, there is a sense in which some form of causal determinism is *necessary* for rationalists like Maimonides and Gersonides, for without it prophecy becomes rather difficult. In their view the prophet could work out what was going to occur by applying knowledge of principles of nature to particular situations. But this type of prediction would not be possible unless there were some form of causal chain that the prophet was able to trace. So even if God does not gain his knowledge in this manner, causal determinism might yet be a problem for Maimonides.

Leaving aside these questions, Maimonides' solution to the theological problem leaves us with as many questions as it does answers. Indeed, if all we need to generate the problem with freewill is the notion that God's knowledge is true, it seems difficult to avoid the problem even if we appeal to the most radical reading of Maimonides' negative theology. We need not claim to understand *anything* about what God knows or how he knows it. But surely, the most minimal requirement would be that his knowledge is true. And if it is true, then the problem for freewill remains. If Maimonides wishes to deny even that God's knowledge is true in order to solve the problem, then we really have lost all ability to speak sensibly about God. While Maimonides might refer us to his advice to be silent at this point, even those willing to follow Maimonidean negative theology might think this a step too far. Ultimately then, one might well feel that none of the compatibilists have actually managed to articulate how freewill and foreknowledge can be reconciled.

2. WHAT DOES GOD KNOW? THE VIEW OF GERSONIDES

The question that Gersonides sets himself in the third book of the *Wars of the Lord* is simple enough: 'whether or not God knows particular contingent things in the sublunar world, and if He does know them ... how He knows them' (*Wars*, III: 1, 89). Like Maimonides before him therefore, Gersonides is concerned generally with God's knowledge of contingent particulars of which the problem of future human action is just one element. And given what we already know about Gersonides' view of Maimonides' theory of divine attributes, it will come as no surprise that he is less than satisfied with the Maimonidean response to this problem. Indeed, Gersonides seems to accept that the freedom/foreknowledge dilemma cannot be resolved in the compatibilist manner of his predecessors and he instead takes a view that is striking in the context of traditional rabbinic thought.

He begins as usual with the views of his predecessors, in this case that of the sages – Maimonides included – who believe that God knows all particulars, and that of Aristotle, according to whom God does not know particular things in the sublunar world. This latter view however, divides into two camps: 1) the view that God does not know anything about the sublunar world – neither universals nor particulars; and 2) the view that God 'knows the things in the sublunar world with respect to their general natures, i.e. their essences, but not insofar as they are particulars i.e., contingents' (*Wars*, III: 1, 90).

This particular/universal distinction has been used in many different though interrelated ways throughout the history of philosophy. For our purposes, a particular, as the word suggests, is a single object or event. But if we take the example of a particular triangle, there are, of course, many other triangles and what is significant about them is that they all share a 'universal' nature. Thus the 'universal' is what is common to many things – many particulars are designated by a common universal. In the medieval discussion, the concept of universals is generally related to the idea of essences that we have encountered previously, since the essence of a substance is the 'universal' or shared characteristic that identifies it as that type of substance. The question for the Aristotelians then was whether God knows both universals and particulars, or only has knowledge of the former.

In *Wars*, III: 2 Gersonides presents eight arguments for denying that God has knowledge of various different categories of particular. If we are speaking of particular material objects, for example, then there is the argument that knowledge of such objects, including the book you are holding in your hands, is gained by sense perception, but God does not have the physical apparatus necessary for sense perception so he cannot know them. There is also the argument that particulars exist in time, while Gersonides' God is beyond time and thus cannot know them. This argument could be applied to particular objects and also to particular events in time, such as what you will do tomorrow, and this leads us back to our main focus – the freedom/foreknowledge dilemma.

For Gersonides, if God has foreknowledge yet human action is genuinely contingent, then God would have to know these actions *as* contingent. But that would mean knowing that one of two outcomes is possible, and thus not knowing which possibility was eventually to occur. That is what it is to know these things as *contingent* things. The problem here is that once the time came, however, and one of the alternatives was acted upon, God's knowledge would change, since he would now know which of the possible outcomes was true. But to say that God changes in this way in response to human action 'is utterly absurd' (*Wars*, III: 2, 94) according to Gersonides. If, on the other hand, he knows *which* of the two alternatives are going to occur, then God's knowledge of particulars would immediately remove all contingency from the world in the manner that we have previously discussed. So we end up having to deny God's knowledge of particulars in order to preserve our ability 'to do otherwise'.

Gersonides does go on to present the arguments in favour of preserving God's omniscience in the face of this. So, for example, as the most perfect being, God surely cannot be ignorant of anything for ignorance is the greatest defect. Moreover, God, as creator of the universe,

> has a complete knowledge of what shall happen to that which He has made…
> For he knows in one cognition everything that will happen with respect to the
> world according to the nature with which He has endowed it. (*Wars*, III: 2, 97)

Probably the most significant rejoinder to the first of these arguments for omniscience is that God's 'ignorance' of particulars would not actually constitute a defect in him. In the same way that many thinkers of the time did not believe that God could bring about an impossible state of affairs such as making a square circle, or creating a second omnipotent being – for these are not in the realm of the possible – it is not a defect if he does not know particulars. The reason for this is that particulars are not the sort of thing that *can* be known. Though this might sound strange to us, many of the ancients believed that only unchanging things were objects of knowledge. The everyday particulars that we claim to know are not actually objects of knowledge, and God cannot know something that is, by its very nature, unknowable just as he cannot do what is, by its very nature, not 'do–able'. The idea that God cannot know particulars since they are unknowable, however, is a little more difficult to accept than the idea that there are limits to what God can do, as we would assume that particulars are perfectly knowable. After all, surely *we* all know many particulars things. This idea that particulars are fundamentally unknowable requires, therefore, a little further explanation.

In our chapter on prophecy we discussed the knowledge gained from sense perception as Maimonides presents it. We noted that when Maimonides speaks of cognising a piece of wood, he tells us that the intellect 'has stripped its form from its matter, and has represented to himself the pure form' (*Guide*, I: 68, 164). In sense perception, therefore, the intellect abstracts the forms from the images presented to it, which means that our act of perception itself is not a form of knowing. It is the knowledge of the form – or the universal nature of the piece of wood – that we abstract from this perception that constitutes our knowledge. This classic Aristotelian view endorsed as much by Gersonides as by Maimonides, is what lies behind the view that God cannot know particulars. But it implies that particulars *cannot* be known qua particulars. It is a statement about the nature of knowledge *per se*. So to say that God does not know particulars as such is not a statement about limits on God's knowledge, for on this view humans cannot know particulars qua particulars any more than God can – they are fundamentally unknowable.

Gersonides therefore is convinced by the philosophical arguments against God having knowledge of particulars qua particulars, citing the argument that 'in claiming that God does not know particulars, no imperfection in Him results, only perfection; for His knowledge concerns superior things, not these trivial matters' (*ibid.*, 97). And when he cites the argument that God as creator must know everything regarding his creation and that 'he knows in one cognition everything that will happen with respect to the world according to the nature with which He has endowed it' (*ibid.*), it is the latter clause, the 'according to the nature with which He has endowed it' that is significant. For God does not know particulars qua particulars, but qua this 'nature', which leads Gersonides down a similar, though not identical path to the second Aristotelian view that he presents at the beginning of his discussion.

What then does God know according to Gersonides? After presenting the various arguments he concludes that 'there is no alternative but to say that God knows particulars in one respect but does not know them in another respect. But what these respects are, would that I knew!' (*Wars*, III: 4, 117). He does manage, however, to explain his view further, bringing together a number of the points made so far:

> It is evident that the sense in which God knows these particulars is the sense in which they are ordered and determinate, as is the case with the Agent Intellect ... For from this aspect it is possible to have knowledge of them. On the other hand, the sense in which God does not know particulars is the sense in which they are not ordered, i.e., the sense in which they are contingent ... He does not know which of the contradictory outcomes will be realised insofar as they are [genuinely] contingent affairs; for if He did, there would not be any contingency at all. [Nevertheless,] the fact that God does not have knowledge of which possible outcome will be realised does not imply any defect in God (may He be blessed). For perfect knowledge of something is the knowledge

of what that thing is in reality... Hence, God knows these things in
the best manner possible, for He knows them insofar as they are ordered
in a determinate and certain way, and He knows in addition that these
events are contingent, insofar as they fall in the domain of human choice. (*Wars*,
III: 4, 118)

What we see from this is that God does not have knowledge of
particulars insofar as they are contingent according to Gersonides. We can
grasp this idea most easily by considering future contingents. For example,
my writing at this point in time is an entirely contingent matter. If we accept,
as Gersonides does, that contingency really exists and that we are genuinely
free to choose between different alternatives, then perfect knowledge of a
contingent particular would mean knowing that it *might or might not* occur.
So if, for the sake of argument, God could know future contingents, he
would know them *as* contingent. But that means knowing that they might
or might not occur. And this is as true for human knowledge as it is for God's
knowledge. Basically, to put this in the logical terms we have used earlier,
any statement I now make about a future human act simply has no truth-
value. Statements about future actions are neither true nor false until the
time comes and we see the outcome of the free choice of the individual in
question. The future is genuinely open, and that is *not* a function of our
ignorance. There is a genuine asymmetry between the past and the future.
Statements about the past have truth-values. Statements about the future do
not. That is simply the way that reality has been constructed.

Gersonides does indeed believe this to be the case, but we have now
seen that the issue of future contingents is merely a special case, for in his
view God does not know particulars as such, regardless of where they are
located 'in time'. He does not know, for example, that I am here writing these
words at this moment, and never has done. But that is not a limit on his
knowledge, God can only know what is knowable and particulars do not fall
into that category. The particular problem of contingent human action is
just a special case of this.

There are other more technical reasons why Gersonides does not
believe that God can know particulars that trace back to the Aristotelian
definition of knowledge. For Aristotle, as we have seen, genuine knowledge
– *episteme* – is demonstrative knowledge that proceeds deductively from first
principles that state the form of something. In describing such knowledge,
Aristotle writes that 'it is not possible for it to be otherwise' (*Posterior
Analytics*, I. 2, 71b12). Such knowledge therefore is described as 'necessary'.

In other words, it begins from 'necessary' premises about the essences of things, and then proceeds deductively, i.e. in a necessity preserving fashion, to what will be 'necessary' conclusions. So just as God cannot have knowledge of particulars qua particulars, for they are unknowable as such, he cannot have knowledge of contingent things for they too cannot be 'known' in the pure Aristotelian sense of the term.

God does, however, know particulars insofar as they are ordered and determinate. The idea of particulars being ordered and determinate has already been explained by Gersonides in his discussion of prophecy and alluded to in our earlier discussion of causal determinism. To put it in the simplest possible terms, a prophet could only foresee the future if that future is ordered and predictable, i.e. if the sublunar world is governed by natural causal laws such that we can predict what is going to happen. A prophet is able to predict this course with far greater precision than most human beings, but ultimately the prophet is just working out how the principles that he gains from divine emanations govern the sublunar realm and apply to his immediate environment.

For Gersonides, much of this knowledge is actually gained through knowledge of astrology. While Maimonides dismissed astrology as 'stupidity'[2] and distinguished it from scientific ideas concerning the control exerted by the spheres and the Separate Intellects over the natural world, Gersonides believed that 'Human affairs are indeed ordered by the heavenly bodies' (*Wars*, II: 2, 34). Thus:

> It follows that when the heavenly bodies are in one particular position amongst their [various] positions, they guide a person toward a specific disposition, whereas when they are in a position contrary to the former one they guide the individual toward the opposite disposition. And this is the case with all the various events that are ordered by them... [S]ome heavenly bodies guide a person toward one [kind of] event and other persons towards its opposite. (*Wars*, II: 2, 35)

We are, however, able to subvert this order through our freewill – contingency must be preserved as noted above – though Gersonides believes that these subversive powers are only in the gift of the intellect, and thus such action is not a regular occurrence. Many scholars believe that these actions, whereby a human can escape the causal influence of the heavenly bodies, are the only genuinely contingent elements of the universe that remain unknown to Gersonides' God, thereby preserving only a limited form of contingency in the universe.

So what, in the end, does God know? God knows, through his perfect knowledge of his own essence from which the universe proceeds, the structure of the universe in its entirety and the intelligible plan that it follows. He knows for example, that a human has a certain essence and that one born when the sun is in a certain region of the Zodiac will be disposed to act in certain ways in certain situations. He will therefore know that given an immensely complex nexus of causal factors, someone born with my constellation of stars will be writing a book on Monday, 10 December, 2007. But he also knows that as a human being other factors can cause me to have chosen not to act in this way. Indeed, at best he knows all the possible decisions that a person of my type could take in any given situation. But ultimately, he does not know how I have actually decided to act, since he does not know me as a particular. He knows the various – indeed infinite – possible routes that history can take. What he is usually taken not to know, however, is which route has or will be instantiated. Notably of course, any prophetic prediction would be subject to the same limitations.

In conclusion then, Gersonides seems to take a view that bears similarities to the second Aristotelian route, though for Gersonides God does not only know universals or essences since he also knows hypothetical information regarding particulars through his knowledge of the aforementioned infinite causal possibilities. This allows Gersonides to dismiss the *rhetoric* of God not knowing particulars and therefore insist that God does know particulars 'in one respect'. Nonetheless, the view that he ends up with is certainly a controversial one within traditional Judaism for it remains the case that God does not know what is actually happening or going to happen in the sublunar world. He knows all the infinite possibilities given his knowledge of the scientific and astral determinants of the course the world can take. But according to Gersonides, his God would not know of an act should a human go against his astrological destiny. Moreover, he does not know that *I* have chosen to act a certain way. Indeed, he does not know which of the 'world histories' that he holds as possibilities is being instantiated.

3. FREEDOM OR FOREKNOWLEDGE? HASDAI CRESCAS' VIEW

For Gersonides, the freedom/foreknowledge dilemma was a real one, but since neither God, nor indeed anyone else *can* know particulars as particulars, and it is 'a fundamental and pivotal belief of the Torah that there are contingent events in the world' (*Wars*, III: 6, 135), the correct choice to make within this dilemma was clearly for freedom at the expense of foreknowledge. For Hasdai Crescas, however, God's omniscience is non-negotiable. Indeed, Gersonides was criticised for heresy by later authorities, and much of Crescas' discussion of omniscience is a thinly veiled attack on Gersonides himself. Crescas' concerns with a Gersonidean view thus led him down a very different, though ultimately no less troubling path.

Crescas begins Book II of *Light of the Lord* by setting out three 'roots of the law' regarding divine omniscience, the third of which is most significant for our discussion: 'His knowledge, may He be exalted, extends over the [disjunctive] parts of the possible, without changing the nature of the possible' (*Light*, II: I, 1, 466). This suggests the type of compatibilism that we have encountered in our pre-Gersonidean thinkers. Crescas is stating that God does have knowledge of contingent particulars ('the possible'), without thereby removing it from the realm of contingency ('the nature of the possible'). And his view of God's knowledge is the more straightforward view that makes no concessions to the type of Aristotelian epistemology that so influenced Gersonides – Crescas is well known for his critique of Aristotelian philosophy. Like Saadia and Maimonides before him, therefore, he appears to be saying that divine foreknowledge does not render future human action necessary but on the contrary, the nature of the possible is preserved and therefore human action is free.

How, though, does Crescas explain this apparent compatibilism? After arguing why the nature of the possible must exist, on both philosophical and biblical grounds, Crescas presents the arguments against the existence of the possible, including arguments from causal determinism and arguments from theological determinism, to the effect that 'if God knows which one of the two possible alternatives will occur, it follows necessarily that it will occur' (*Light*, II: V, 2, 476). Though it is clear in the Torah that God's knowledge does encompass all particulars according to Crescas, his problem is that he is actually convinced by many of the causal arguments that he puts forward and thus, much like Gersonides, ends up with a compromise position whereby 'the possible exists in one sense but does not exist in another sense' (*Light*, II: V, 3, 478). In order to understand this, he draws some further important distinctions.

If we study the arguments for the existence of the possible, in Crescas' opinion they 'entail only the existence of the possible in itself' (*Light*, II: V, 3, 479). The arguments against the existence of the possible, on the other hand 'imply [its non-existence] only in the sense of the possible in terms of its cause' (*ibid.*, 480). What, though, are 'the possible in itself', and 'the possible in terms of its cause'? Let us take our tried and trusted example of DR writing chapter 6 on the morning of Monday, 10 December, 2007. This event, p, is possible in itself, to use Crescas' term, which means that considered in isolation one can perfectly well conceive of the history of the universe without this particular event taking place – it is a possible, and not a necessary, event and thus p considered in itself is contingent – it is 'possible in itself'. It is certainly not necessary in the sense that a triangle having three sides is necessary. This latter, we would say, is 'necessary in itself', or in more contemporary terms it is logically necessary, since we cannot conceive of the alternative.

However, the fact remains that I did sit down and write this today, and Crescas believes that this event is necessitated by God's foreknowledge:

> The arguments based upon God's foreknowledge and prophetic predictions, even if choice is made a condition [of such knowledge], clearly does not imply the annulment of possibility in itself. Rather, the phenomena are possible in themselves yet necessary in terms of their causes; and in so far as they are necessary there is knowledge prior to their necessary [occurrence]. (*Light*, I: V, 3, 480)

My actions are not necessary when considered in and of themselves in the manner that logical necessities would be. I might or might not have decided to write today. The event is therefore possible in itself. My actions are, however, necessitated by their causes according to Crescas, which in this case is understood broadly and includes God's foreknowledge. The point again is that if God knows that p, then p must be true. So given that God knows what I will do, it simply must happen. In Crescas' terms, this renders such events 'possible in themselves yet necessary in terms of their causes'. God's foreknowledge does not change p considered in itself from being logically possible to being logically necessary. It does, however, render p necessary *given his foreknowledge* – his knowing p it makes it inevitable that it will have to occur. Thus p is necessary 'by virtue of God's foreknowledge, but it is possible in itself' (*Light*, II: V, 3, 481).

On this view then, we hold onto the more traditional conception of omniscience, but we seem to have done so at the expense of human freedom, for it does indeed turn out that while it is logically possible to conceive of a world in which p is not true, given that God knows p, it did indeed have to occur and I could not have acted otherwise. God's foreknowledge did therefore determine my action. So much for compatibilism.

There is a further interesting element to Crescas' presentation however, that at first glance suggests that a more compatibilist reading of his view is possible:

> [Moreover], since God's knowledge does not fall under time, His knowledge of the future is like his knowledge of existent things, in which there is no necessity nor compulsion in the things themselves. (*Light*, II: V, 3, 481)

The idea here is that God is eternal. This is sometimes understood in the sense that God is everlasting, i.e. he has no beginning and no end. But it is also understood by philosophers to imply that God is beyond time. Time is simply not a category that applies to God. Thus God knows everything timelessly. Gersonides and Maimonides, incidentally, seem to share this conception of divine cognition according to which God, as the creator of the universe, knows everything that he knows through a single, comprehensive and eternal (timeless) act of cognition.

Though the idea of a timeless God is not uncontroversial, accepting it for the sake of argument adds an extra dimension to our discussion, for if God's knowledge is eternal in this sense, how can God genuinely have *fore*knowledge of anything? Having foreknowledge means knowing it *before* it happens, but the very concept of 'before' cannot be applied to God if he is beyond the category of time. On the one hand, this has sometimes been offered as a solution to the freewill/foreknowledge dilemma, since it seems to dissolve it – God's eternity allows us to deny the problematic premise that God knows something *before* it occurs. God does not know anything *before* it occurs since he is not a being who exists in time and the very concept of 'before' that we use to generate the problem cannot be applied to him.

Despite initial appearances, however, this does not actually solve the problems we have raised for freewill. The dilemma, remember, is generated by the truth (and infallibility) of God's knowledge. But if we remove God from the equation and 'translate' into the language of whether statements about so-called future contingents have truth-values, then we can still generate the problem. For if it is simply a truth about the universe that DR will be writing chapter 6 on the morning of Monday, 10 December 2007, then given its truth, it was always going to happen. And if statements about the future are true in this way, then they are true regardless of whether or not anyone knows them, just as 2+2=4 is true regardless of whether anyone discovers this – it is simply a timeless truth. So if 'DR will be writing chapter 6 on the morning of Monday, 10 December 2007' is true at t_1, then it is going to have to happen and I cannot choose to do otherwise whatever I might think and regardless of whether or not anyone knows this truth. God, in the problem of divine foreknowledge, is simply the 'embodiment' of these truths – he knows them all. So monotheists have a convenient way of presenting the problem. But the problem of theological determinism is actually just the problem of logical determinism with the added bonus that there is a God who actually *knows* all of these truths. When Gersonides denies foreknowledge to God, one of his points is that statements about the future do not have truth-values and thus cannot be known, even by God. That is the essence of a future contingent. But for Crescas, God does have knowledge of these future contingents so these statements must be knowable and thus must have truth-values. But as soon as we say that they are in principle knowable and thus have truth-values, that is enough to generate the dilemma concerning human freedom.

If so, then Crescas, despite holding onto the nature of the possible, has only done so in a very attenuated manner. Thus, it might be that p is not a logical truth about the nature of the universe. But the fact that it is a truth, and in this context one that is known by God, means that it is necessitated by that very truth and there is no sense in which I could have done otherwise. So there seems to be little left to the idea that I exercise freedom of will in acting as I do.

In the final analysis then, we seem to be faced with a stark choice according to Gersonides and Crescas. The former allows us to hold onto human freedom at the expense of traditional understandings of divine omniscience; the latter allows us the traditional view of divine omniscience but has ultimately done away with human freedom. It is not the case that, for any of my future actions, or indeed any of my actions *per se*, I can choose (or could have chosen) to act in a manner that contradicts the true statements that cover the actions in question. Rabbi Akiva's statement, that 'everything is foreseen, but free choice is granted', suddenly seems rather less secure. One or other of the clauses might be true. But neither Crescas nor Gersonides manages to hold onto both of them unequivocally.

4. CONCLUDING REMARKS: THE NATURE
OF FREEDOM AND THE NATURE OF GOD

Neither Gersonides nor Crescas resolve the freedom/foreknowledge problem with which we began. Indeed, neither of them thinks that we can – it is a real dilemma in which one of the horns has to give, and though there are various attempts to resolve the dilemma in the history of philosophy, they are beyond the parameters of our discussion. The only method suggested for holding onto a compatibilist position that we have encountered was that of Maimonides, but his 'solution' entails accepting in full his theory of attributes, and one imagines that those who are concerned to hold onto both freedom and omniscience in the fullest traditional sense will be loathe to pay that price. Indeed accepting the Maimonidean solution would entail, as mentioned earlier, having to give up speaking of the truth of God's knowledge.

Before concluding though, it is worth noting the serious philosophical questions raised by the incompatibilist approaches that we have discussed, beginning with an important distinction that we find in Crescas. The text of *Light of the Lord* as it stands is ambiguous in indicating whether Crescas accepts causal determinism. There are those who believe that he does, and much of what he writes seems to reflect this. However, even if he does not, he certainly believes that events are necessitated as we have seen and he is not unaware of the problems that attach to this. He asks therefore, among other things, how we are to differentiate between the 'necessity by virtue of causality in which there is no feeling of force or compulsion and the necessity in which there is such a feeling' (*Light*, II: V, 3, 483). The distinction between causation and compulsion is one that is much used by compatibilists and Crescas uses it here to explain the justice of reward and punishment. Rewards are earned by those who act as a result of causal necessity, but not by those who act as a result of compulsion. What differentiates between the two on his account is that the one whose acts are caused takes joy in his actions and thus is deserving of reward, while the one who is compelled does not take joy in his action since it is done, as we might say, against his will.

Crescas is pointing us towards a potentially important distinction. We understand acts done under compulsion to be acts that are not free. If someone holds a gun to my head and forces me to act in a certain way, then we would accept that my act was not a free act but was compelled and

Crescas too accepts this. Yet for Crescas, this is to be distinguished from acts that are *causally* necessitated. The difference, at least subjectively, is that in the absence of compulsion, even if my acts follow a certain causal route, I can still say that I have acted in the manner that I have chosen – I wanted to act in a certain manner and was able to do so. So there is a sense in which my act remains a voluntary act even if it was caused, as long as it was not compelled.

It is argued in response that my so-called voluntary act is not really a free act if it was causally necessitated, since I could not have acted otherwise. The question that this raises, however, is whether or not the ability to do otherwise is really an appropriate characterisation of freewill. Consider the following: when we reflect upon our actions, we would want them to be actions that we do for reasons. We want to be able to say that we have acted as a result of considering the reasons for action and have taken a decision based on those reasons, which cause us to act. But if that is so, then it appears as if we *want* to have causal reasons for our actions. It is part of what makes us rational and responsible human beings.

It might be argued, however, that if reasons *necessitated* our actions we would still not be free, for we would be unable to act otherwise. Let us imagine the alternative then. Imagine that at each juncture of my decision-making process where I follow a set of reasons in order to make a decision, there is a moment of 'pure' freedom where I can decide one way or another. Let us say that at that moment I am genuinely 'free to decide otherwise' and my decision is uncaused. Is that really a valuable form of freedom? Do we really want our decisions to be uncaused in this way? Surely if each decision is an arbitrary and totally free decision, most of us would feel that our decisions were 'out of our control' and that we were not following a rational decision-making process. We want to think that we take decisions for reasons. We want our actions to follow a rational decision-making process, and not be the products of some unfounded and arbitrary decision. Similarly, once we have our reasons, surely we want them to cause us to act. Again, imagine that there is no causal link between our reasons and our actions. So at the last moment, I am totally free, regardless of any rational decision that I have made, and can do other than what I have rationally decided. Again – is that the sort of freedom that we would really value? Remembering that our original considerations regarding the value of freedom were its links to moral responsibility, is that the sort of freedom that brings with it moral responsibility? Surely we are only morally responsible for our actions if we decide upon them and do them because of those decisions. If I decide and intend to do something but a mental aberration suddenly makes me act otherwise, we would usually say that I was 'not in my right mind' at the time and probably plead mitigation. It is only when I act on the basis of my reasoned decisions that we would ascribe blame in that way. Moral responsibility, it seems, might *require* that our actions have causes.

If all of this is true though, we end up with an interesting question regarding freewill – do we really want to be 'free to do otherwise'? Can we give this idea any meaning that would really allow us to understand ourselves as rational and morally responsible agents? Surely we prefer to be acting within a causal chain. What we certainly do not want, as Crescas notes, is to be compelled to act in a certain way. But as long as we are acting in the manner that we decide, even if those decisions are the result of causal necessitation, might that be enough? Must freedom be understood as the freedom to do otherwise, or might it rather be the freedom to do as I choose, even if that choice is causally determined? As long as I am not acting under compulsion, Crescas might be correct to be at ease with the idea of causal necessitation. The concern of course is that if our decisions are all causally determined, we are still not free. But as yet, it seems difficult to come up with an alternative that would yield the type of freedom that we would actually value.

What this shows us is that when we actually analyse our ideal of freedom we begin to realise that matters are not as simple as we thought. If we dismiss the notion of causation, we seem to have little left of our notion of rational human action. When we crave the freedom 'to do otherwise', however, what is it that we actually crave? While we seem sure that we do not want to be at the mercy of some causally necessary chain, we surely do not want the genuine ability to freely choose to do anything at every juncture of our lives.

While all of the above has been couched in terms of causal determinism, the central point can be transferred to our discussion of theological determinism. For our concern with God's foreknowledge was that it removed our ability 'to do otherwise' and we have seen that this definition of freewill can be seriously questioned. If we instead define freewill as the freedom to act without compulsion and in accordance with one's will, it is not clear that God's foreknowledge is a problem. The important point that emerges from the above is that it is difficult to articulate a form of freewill that we would value as rational and moral agents but that also answers to an intuitive notion of freedom as acting without necessitation. None of this suggests any easy solutions, but it does allow us to begin to understand why someone like Crescas might be happy to countenance the idea of determinism. Even if we are unable to spell out exactly how we can retain our intuitive notion of freewill in the face God's foreknowledge, we would surely do well to come to some understanding of what sort of freewill we *are* seeking before dismissing Crescas' approach altogether.

On the other side of the issue, the fact that Gersonides is willing to sacrifice the most traditional notion of omniscience might cause us to ask how important that notion is. Why are many theists so insistent on this notion of omniscience? One reason might be the control it affords God over his universe. But is knowledge of the future necessary for this? As long as God retains the right to intervene should things start going wrong, surely he can fix his world even if he has no knowledge of the future. He would, on that view, still need to have knowledge of the present and of course even this is questioned by Gersonides. Yet, the naturalism that we have seen at work in thinkers like Maimonides and Gersonides suggests that the notion of an intervening God might not be quite as indispensable as theists think. Thus Maimonides dismisses in one of his well-known letters, those who

> like nothing better, and, in their silliness, enjoy nothing more, than to set the Law and reason at opposite ends, and to move everything far from the explicable. So they claim it to be a miracle, and they shrink from identifying it as a natural incident... But I try to reconcile the Law and reason, and wherever possible consider all things as of the natural order. Only when something is explicitly identified as a miracle, and reinterpretation of it cannot be accommodated, only then I feel forced to grant that this is a miracle.[3]

Different religious sensibilities call for different forms of religious belief. Some people need to believe in the interventionist God for whom, no doubt, traditional divine omniscience has a role to play, as only then will God know what you are doing and be able to react accordingly. For such people certain beliefs will be necessary, as Maimonides also notes:

> [T]he Law also makes a call to adopt certain beliefs, belief in which is necessary for the sake of political welfare. Such, for instance, is our belief that He, may He be exalted, is violently angry with those who disobey Him and that it is therefore necessary to fear Him and dread Him and to take care not to disobey. (*Guide*, III: 28, 512)

We already know what Maimonides thinks of those who would attribute anger to God. So it is clear that this type of belief is only necessary for people of a certain religious sensibility, but perhaps not for a Maimonides or a Gersonides, for whom the idea of God knowing every detail of every act of man might be less pressing. Eliminating such 'knowledge' from God does of course raise questions regarding providence, and we will have to examine how a thinker like Gersonides manages to reconcile his view with related concepts such as providence. This we will endeavour to do in our discussion of the problem of evil. Before looking at how things can go wrong though, we will discuss the nature of 'the good life'.

NOTES

1   All Crescas quotes in this chapter are taken from Bleich, *WPF*.
2   See Moses Maimonides, 'Letter on Astrology', translated in I. Twersky (ed.), *A Maimonides Reader* (New York: Behrman House, 1972), 464–73. Quotation from 466.
3   Moses Maimonides, 'The Essay on Resurrection', trans. A. Halkin, in A. Halkin, and D. Hartman, *Crisis and Leadership* (Philadelphia, PA: Jewish Publication Society, 1985), 209–45. Quotation from 223.

FURTHER READING

For an account of Saadia's compatibilism (and a more esoteric reading of Maimonides) see Alexander Altmann 'Free Will and Predestination in Saadia, Bahya, and Maimonides', repr. in *Essays in Jewish Intellectual History* (Hanover, NH: University Press of New England, 1981), 35–64.

In addition to Feldman's translation of Gersonides' *Wars of the Lord*, the third book has been translated with detailed commentary and a useful introduction as Norbert M. Samuelson, *Gersonides on God's Knowledge* (Toronto: Pontifical Institute of Medieval Studies, 1977).

Other close readings of Gersonides can be found in:

Norbert Samuelson, 'Gersonides' Account of God's Knowledge of Particulars', *Journal of the History of Philosophy*, vol. 10, (1972), 399–416.

Charles Manekin, 'On the Limited-Omniscience Interpretation of Gersonides' Theory of Divine Knowledge', in A. Ivry, E. Wolfson and A. Arkush (eds), *Perspectives on Jewish Thought and Mysticism* (Amsterdam: Harwood Academic Publishers, 1997), 135–70; and 'Freedom Within Reason? Gersonides on

Human Choice', in C. Manekin and M. Kellner (eds), *Freedom and Moral Responsibility: General and Jewish Perspectives* (College Park, 1997), 165–204. Manekin's careful reading is reflected in many elements of my discussion here.

The relevant texts in Crescas are analysed in Warren Zev Harvey, *Physics and Metaphysics in Hasdai Crescas* (Amsterdam: J. C. Gieben, 1998), Part Two. The philosophical import of Crescas' views are usefully discussed in the context of medieval and contemporary philosophical discourse in Seymour Feldman, 'Crescas' Theological Determinism', *Daat*, vol. 9, (1982), 3–28.

Tamar Rudavsky discusses all of our thinkers in *Time Matters: Time Creation and Cosmology in Medieval Jewish Philosophy* (Albany: SUNY Press, 2000), chapter 4.

7

The Good Life

While discussing rationalising the commandments in chapter 5, we had cause to mention Saadia's statement that the Jewish nation was 'a nation only by virtue of its laws' (*Emunot*, III: 7, 158). This was not simply an empirical observation about the behaviour of the Jewish nation. To most Jews up until the modern era, it was a statement with important normative implications. The laws of the Torah – the *mitzvot* – and their subsequent rabbinic elaboration through the Oral Torah, governed how a Jew ought to behave. If one were to ask 'what is the best life for a Jew to lead?', the answer one would expect to hear would be 'the life of performing *mitzvot*'. So the definition of 'the good life' for a Jewish individual was a life of Jewish practice; a life lived in accordance with the God-given practical prescriptions of the Torah.

Even outside of this specifically religious context, the question of the best life for man had concerned philosophers from ancient times. One of the most vexed questions concerning Aristotle's great ethical work the *Nichomachean Ethics* (which, following convention we will refer to as the *Ethics*), concerns where he truly stood on this question of defining 'the good life'. While Aristotelian philosophy was mediated to our Jewish thinkers through his Muslim interpreters, yielding such things as 'Aristotelian' theories of prophecy that will not be found explicitly in Aristotle himself, we know that the *Ethics* was a direct influence on these Muslim thinkers, and was known and quoted by Maimonides. In this case therefore, the conceptual alternatives are set out by Aristotle himself and while Plato's views are also influential in this discussion, the theories with which we will be dealing can, broadly speaking, be placed into one of two Aristotelian categories. For while Aristotle spends nine books discussing what we would recognise as a life of ethical practice, where moral virtues such as courage, truthfulness and temperance all appear, in Book X of the *Ethics* we find a statement that flies in the face of all that has gone before: 'For man, therefore, the life according to the intellect is best and pleasantest, since intellect more than anything else is man. This life therefore is also the happiest' (*Ethics*, X. 7, 1178a6–8).

We will investigate further the reasons for Aristotle's about-turn later on in this chapter. But you might immediately recognise this intellectualist strand from our Introduction as the view reflected in the opening statement of the philosopher's creed in the *Kuzari*. There we found that the perfect person is one who has reached the degree of the Active Intellect, and is told not to be 'concerned about the forms of thy humility or religion or worship, or the word or language or actions thou employest' (*Kuzari*, I: 1, 38). Applying this reasoning to Judaism specifically, the perfect Jew, it seems, need not worry about the practice of *mitzvot* since he has attained a more noble form of life – the contemplative life of intellectual perfection.

While Aristotle did not have a personal religious worldview with which to contend, it may come as more of a shock – though now that we are this far in the book, we may have lost the element of surprise – to see Maimonides apparently making claims that place him squarely within this intellectualist camp:

> The fourth species is the true human perfection; it consists in the acquisition of the rational virtues – I refer to the conception of intelligibles, which teach the true opinions concerning the divine things. *This is in true reality the ultimate end; this is what gives the individual true perfection,* a perfection belonging to him alone; and it gives him permanent perdurance; through it man is man. (*Guide*, III: 54, 635, emphasis added)

On such a view the life lived according to practical virtue need not become worthless. Aristotle notes that the contemplative individual who lives this intellectualist version of the good life will need 'external equipment' (*Ethics*, X. 8, 1178a24) and 'insofar as he is a man and lives with a number of people, he chooses to do excellent acts; he will therefore need such aids to living a human life' (*ibid.*, 1178b5–7). But the practical life does now seem to be classified as happiness 'in a secondary degree' (*ibid.*,

1178a9). In fact, Maimonides spells out the nature of the relationship between practical and intellectual perfection possibly even more explicitly than Aristotle had done in the *Ethics*:

> For it has been explained, or rather demonstrated, that the moral virtues are a preparation for the rational virtues, it being impossible to achieve true, rational acts – I mean perfect rationality – unless it be by a man thoroughly trained with respect to his morals and endowed with the qualities of tranquillity and quiet. (*Guide*, I: 34, 76–7)

Maimonides clearly states that practical perfection, both at an individual level – one must be 'thoroughly trained' – and politically – to provide 'tranquillity and quiet' – is necessary to provide a person with a suitable environment for contemplation. But there is a straightforwardly hierarchical relationship between the two perfections. Moral perfection is a necessary preparation for intellectual perfection. It is clearly not the ultimate perfection of man. That honour is reserved for the activity of contemplation (or *theoria*).

Is the life of *mitzvot* therefore second best? What of the many faithful Jews who observed the *mitzvot* meticulously yet had never in their lives encountered a demonstrative proof? Devoid of intellectual perfection, such believers could not enjoy the good life. Indeed, there is a sense in which they have been duped, since the centrality of Jewish practice seems evident from the texts to which they are devoted. None of those texts seem to speak of the good life as being one of contemplative bliss. They discuss and argue over the details of a life of practice.

As it stands, we are left with the question of whether it is the theoretical life or the practical life – the *bios theôrêtikos* or the *bios praktikos* – that is the best life for man. And while we will later have to ask why the ultimate perfection could not be composed of the two working in tandem, for the moment we appear to be presented with a straight fight for the title, with intellectual perfection apparently in the ascendant, at least for Maimonides. Hasdai Crescas certainly has him in mind, among others, when noting that the intellectualist view was one upon which 'have stumbled the feet of some of the savants of our nation' (*Light*, II· VI, 1, 425).[1] So the obvious question is whether such a view can be seriously considered from the perspective of medieval Jewish philosophy. In this chapter, we will mainly focus on the presentation of the two main conceptions of the good life that we find in Saadia and Maimonides.

The Good Life

1. SAADIA GAON: THE LIFE OF 'PROPORTIONAL REPRESENTATION'

We have seen already that Saadia Gaon believes sense experience to be one of four sources of knowledge (**1.3**). This empiricism – the view that sense experience can indeed furnish us with knowledge – is at the very basis of his views on the best life for man. For Saadia's discussion of the good life in Book X of *Emunot* is an elaboration of the view that given human nature, 'man's conduct in the course of his lifetime cannot logically be based on just a single trait' (*Emunot*, X: 1, 358). Though Saadia does not give us the precise definition of human nature on which he bases this analysis, the central idea is that man is a being with many 'tendencies... a liking for many things and a dislike for others' (*ibid.*), and as such man would not naturally be given to focusing his life on the cultivation of any one single trait, but should instead give expression to a whole host of them. Saadia's empiricism here seems to extend to the realm of value – since man has these different motivations and finds value in them, this seems for Saadia to be a sufficient foundation for supposing that they do indeed *have* some value.

From the point of view of method, this again has interesting echoes of Aristotle, who believed that in giving a philosophical account of a topic, one ought to begin with the *phainomena* – the opinions of the majority or of the wise – for 'men have a sufficient natural instinct for what is true, and usually do arrive at the truth' (*Rhetoric*, I. 1, 1355a15). For Aristotle, the opinions of the majority invariably contain some kernel of truth that, suitably refined, can be transformed into a more sophisticated philosophical theory. Saadia has even greater reason to trust the judgements of the wise, since the ultimate foundation of his 'empiricism' is the fact that it is God who created man with these tendencies, and were they not of value, God 'would not have implanted the love for these... things' (*Emunot*, X: 1, 359). Yet like Aristotle, Saadia is not simply saying that man should accept these tendencies as they are. Rather than be a slave to the various motivating factors that he believes, at first glance, to have value – what we will call *prima facie* value – man achieves the correct balance between them by 'giving his cognitive faculty dominion over his appetites and impulses' (*Emunot*, X: 3, 361).

Saadia sets forth a tripartite classification of the soul into the cognitive, appetitive and impulsive faculties, following the structure set out by Plato in his classic work the *Republic*. Saadia's division approximates that of Plato in assigning to the appetitive faculty our basic desires for food, drink and sex, together with our aesthetic needs, while the impulsive faculty is what 'renders a person courageous and bold, and endows him with zeal for leadership' though of course, when uncontrolled it can make him 'vindictive and vainglorious' (*Emunot*, X: 2, 360–1). But in the ideal case, reason is always in control of these faculties. We can initially state, therefore, that Saadia is looking at a life governed by *practical* reason, the form of reason that is associated with action rather than intellectual contemplation.

Saadia goes on in chapter IV to discuss this life of practice in detail, first listing the thirteen tendencies that man needs to balance in his pursuit of the good life as:

> 1) abstinence; 2) eating and drinking; 3) sexual intercourse; 4) eroticism (romantic love/passion); 5) accumulating money; 6) having children; 7) material development of the land (building, agriculture etc.); 8) longevity; 9) dominion (eminence and occupying positions of leadership); 10) satisfying one's thirst for revenge; 11) acquiring wisdom; 12) worship; and 13) rest.

Though we cannot dwell on the details here, his discussions of each principle are rich in psychological and social insights. But what makes this philosophically interesting is that it shows us that for Saadia, the good life is not simply to be equated with the moral life or indeed the religious life (narrowly understood). Rather like Aristotle in much of his *Ethics*, the ideal life for Saadia is more comprehensive than that, requiring that we balance these very different types of value in one life.

Saadia proceeds to devote a section to each principle, considering with each the argument for making that tendency the sole pursuit of one's life and then showing that such a one-eyed pursuit would be entirely misguided. Yet his advice regarding the good life cannot simply be reduced to the old adage 'everything in moderation' for

> it is not right to select [equal] parts from each of the above-mentioned thirteen categories: one should rather take from each type of activity the suitable proportion, as dictated by science and religious law. (*Emunot*, X: 17, 399)

Now of course for Saadia, it is God who arranged human nature in this manner and prescribed the best way for it to be fulfilled. Thus, it should not surprise us that the best way to balance the various tendencies is through religious law – in other words, *mitzvot* conduce to the best life for man. The reference in the quote above to science – though 'wisdom' is probably a better translation of the Arabic – implies, however, that there is also a contribution to be made by our own wisdom in blending the principles. Yet, while each principle is to be represented in correct proportion, we are not given any specific formula for working out the measure with which each is to be represented. No overriding general principle is given that ranks each of the motivations in a manner that would allow us to effect this balance independently.

In a sense this is a direct result of Saadia's starting point. The weight given to the *prima facie* value that each tendency has for human beings means that their value cannot be denied. But we therefore end up with a pluralistic set of such values, each with a role to play in the good life, and that sort of pluralism is often tied to the view that we cannot set out some form of systematic ordering principle that would allow us to know exactly how to balance the sometimes competing requirements of each value in every situation.

To illustrate this point, we can take one of the most famous ethical theories – utilitarianism. According to a utilitarian, the right action in any situation is that which produces the greatest happiness for the greatest number. So in its simplest form, utilitarianism will 'convert' all acts to a single scale of happiness in order to adjudge each situation. Whichever act converts to the greatest measure of happiness will be the right one. But Saadia's very starting point is that there is no such single 'ultimate' value and we cannot therefore measure the different values against a common scale to see which will yield more of the value in question. More importantly, it is likely that there will be situations in which two of the tendencies he discusses will conflict, so that acting in one way will privilege one of them over the other. This is not necessarily a problem and Saadia lists some examples of such conflicts and how one ought to act in those situations. But he does not specify hard and fast rules to govern every such situation. And many pluralists about value concede that one cannot produce such a ranking system that would yield the solution to all conflicts of value. Saadia certainly does not give us a system and given his pluralism, it is not all that surprising. He does, however, have a fallback position, since the prescriptions of the Torah can play this role for us. But reason, as we noted, also has a role to play for Saadia.

That there must be a substantive role for reason to play is indicated by the manner in which Saadia began, telling us that in pursuing the best life, the faculties of our soul must be directed by reason. Indeed, Saadia tells us that 'man acts as though he were a judge to whom the disposal of the different tendencies is submitted for decision' (*Emunot*, X: 1, 358). At the same time, it is God who 'indicated to us the manner of our procedure with them' (*Emunot*, X: 3, 361), so God, presumably through the prescriptions of the Torah, does not simply drop out of the picture. But what exactly are the roles assigned to the Torah and to reason in working out the best way to proceed? One thing we know is that Saadia is talking about practical reason, and we can turn to Aristotle's account to reconstruct the ideas that might fill in the gaps in Saadia's own presentation. While not presented thus by Saadia himself, this is an attempt to fill in a philosophically cogent background to the material that he does present.[2]

Aristotle is aware that in the practical sphere we cannot necessarily formulate absolute principles that would govern all situations. So, much as Saadia seems to incline towards the view that no system of principles will give us a recipe for mixing our various motivations in the correct proportions, Aristotle warns us that

> we must be content then, in speaking of such subjects and with such premises to indicate the truth roughly and in outline and in speaking about things which are only for the most part true. (*Ethics*, I. 3, 1094b19–21)

Yet this is far from ruling out the use of reason in our practical endeavours. It is just to note that practical reason is not the same as theoretical reason.

What then, is the nature of this practical reason? In Aristotle's account, we can reconstruct the practical reasoning of a virtuous person by appeal to what he called the practical syllogism. While the precise structure and status of this syllogism is a matter of dispute among scholars, and detailed analysis is well beyond our scope here, for the purposes of illustration we will present one version of it.

The practical syllogism contains a major premise that specifies a general conception of the good – for example, that courage is a good – and a minor premise stating one's perception of this particular situation as one that calls for an act of courage. The 'conclusion' of this so-called 'practical syllogism' is then the courageous act. Thus we have:

Major Premise: In a situation of type S one must act courageously
Minor Premise: This is a situation of type S
Conclusion: I must act courageously

Regardless of whether this is the precise form of reasoning that Aristotle has in mind, it makes it clear that moral decisions involve *rational* deliberation through practical reason, whose job it is to deliver both the conception of the good life and the judgements as to what it requires in particular situations. And while Saadia does not present any such detailed account, what concerns Saadia throughout the entire discussion, is that in action, the 'cognitive' faculty of the soul should govern the appetitive and impulsive faculties, and it is practical reason that governs right action in this way. Thus for Saadia, it seems that practical reason certainly has a role to play in the good life. It cannot, it is true, work out general principles in advance for balancing the different traits of the good life in every situation, but in any given situation, one can use one's practical reason to decide how to act in that particular case, given a conception of the good life that is also delivered by practical reason. So when we encounter a situation that requires us to act, the very recognition that it calls for a specific action is an exercise of practical reason. It is just that it is not the form of reason one cultivates in devoting one's life to the contemplative ideal.

The role of practical reason here does not run contrary to Saadia's claim that the Torah is necessary to allow us to balance the different elements of the good life. Since Aristotle too believes that we cannot simply formulate general principles against which to check our judgements, we need to develop some other form of sensitivity to practical situations that allows us to judge how we are to act. What we need to do is enable people to judge each situation as it comes along, and this can only be done by inculcating dispositions in people so that they become 'such as to act virtuously'. According to Aristotle, one becomes a morally virtuous individual through training rather than instruction, that is, one becomes virtuous by actually doing virtuous things. So it is only by doing just acts, for example, that we become just, by doing generous acts that we become generous. The central factor in acquiring moral virtues for Aristotle is training and habituation rather than formal instruction. Through such habituation, people over time can develop a rational ability that enables them to continue their ethical journey independently of such instruction, as one begins to understand how to act and why.

This Aristotelian account of virtue formation seems true to the experience many of us have in gaining our ethical 'sensitivities'. As children we do not learn what to do in classrooms or lecture theatres but are actually told what to do, usually by parents, with reference to particular situations. The hope is that with effective training we will eventually develop the ability to go on making these judgements on our own. So this habituation is not just a case of installing a blind habit, but is rather a method of installing a cognitive process by which we can make the correct discriminations in practical cases. And if we reconstruct Saadia's approach in similar fashion, we would find that it is through habituation to the *mitzvot* of the Torah that we are furnished with this training. The Torah teaches us how to act in all manner of situations, with the expectation that this will train us effectively so that we know in what proportion each of our natural motivational factors ought to be manifested. Our cognitive faculty will be able to control the other faculties of the soul appropriately if we have followed the prescriptions of the Torah so as to develop our practical reasoning abilities.

The truth is that regardless of whether or not Saadia takes this specific line, it is clear that he comes down on the side of the life of practical activity as the best life for man, as opposed to the life of *theoria*. Indeed, Saadia explicitly states that a life devoted exclusively to the intellect – or as he puts it 'the exclusive devotion to wisdom to the neglect to all other objects' (*Emunot*, X: 3, 362) is futile. The reasoning he uses – as one gains greater wisdom, one becomes aware of the flaws in those things one studies – is not entirely convincing, especially as applied to the sort of intellectualism that we find in Aristotle, since Aristotle's contemplative ideal is not concerned with acquiring knowledge of imperfect things. On the contrary, the life of *theoria* would be a life devoted to contemplating the eternal truths to which one's philosophical reasoning has led.

Nonetheless, this is not Saadia's only criticism of the life exclusively devoted to knowledge. When discussing the value of acquiring knowledge, Saadia notes that exclusive devotion to this quest is not possible for human beings:

> For if, while engaged in acquiring knowledge, a person failed to concern himself about his sustenance, shelter, and clothing, his knowledge would be nullified, since his existence depends on these things. (*Emunot*, X: 14, 393)

Moreover, he notes that relying on other people to supply such necessities would lead to enmity. This does not, however, relegate such actions to the sort of secondary status we saw given to them by Aristotle and Maimonides. Having already argued for the value of these pursuits in the general economy of the good life, there is certainly more to Saadia's evaluation of practical activities than their mere instrumentality in serving some intellectual end. Life more widely conceived has value for Saadia, and the pursuit of knowledge is simply one piece of this puzzle.

2. MAIMONIDES ON HUMAN PERFECTION

It is clear that for Saadia the best life for man as a form of practical perfection fits very well with a traditional Jewish approach. Once we come to Maimonides, however, we are closer to explicit Aristotelian territory both in content and form, and as with Aristotle, the question of what for Maimonides constitutes man's perfection continues to be an area of vigorous debate.

As noted already, the primary thrust of the *Guide* – and incidentally also of his more popular works – seems to be in favour of a life devoted to the intellect. While we quoted earlier from the final chapter of the *Guide*, the idea of intellectual perfection as man's 'natural form' or essence is first introduced in its opening chapter. And as mentioned in chapter 5, the commandments lead to the 'welfare of the body' and the 'welfare of the soul', which are a mere precursor to the two perfections of man which are:

> the perfection of the body, and an ultimate perfection, which is the perfection of the soul. The first perfection consists in being healthy and in the very best bodily state ... His ultimate perfection is to become rational in actu, I mean to have an intellect in actu; ... (*Guide*, III: 27, 511)

So even there, the ultimate perfection was intellectual. However, in order to delay the difficult questions until now, we cut that quote off before its completion. For in his description of this ultimate intellectual perfection, Maimonides tells us that it is a perfection to which 'there do not belong either actions or moral qualities ... it consists only of ideas towards which speculation has led and that investigation has rendered compulsory' (*Guide*, III: 27, 511).

This would appear to be a view as radically opposed to that of Saadia as possible. Not only is intellectual perfection the highest form of perfection, but action and moral qualities have *no place at all* in this perfection. And not only do they have no place in the activity of man; it also turns out that practical considerations are not fit objects for contemplation within that final perfection.

To explain: in a discussion of the fall of man that has long exercised scholars, Maimonides tells us that Adam was created in a state of intellectual perfection, through which he was able to distinguish truth from falsity. After his sin though, Adam was 'punished' by being diverted away from the contemplative ideal by his passions and captivated instead by the faculty for apprehending 'fine and bad', a distinction that belongs to the category of 'things generally accepted as known, not to those cognised by the intellect' (*Guide*, I: 2, 24). Adam was therefore 'deprived of that intellectual apprehension' (*Guide*, I: 2, 25), and instead acquired the 'faculty of apprehending generally accepted things' (*ibid.*), the main example here being his realisation that his nakedness was 'bad'. Though not to be taken as literal history for Maimonides, the implication of all of this is that Adam was originally in a state of intellectual perfection – an ideal state – that deals with the realm of truth. To be concerned instead with value judgements regarding 'fine and bad' – the sorts of judgements we make in the practical sphere – is to be concerned with a lesser realm not belonging to the ultimate intellectual perfection. If this is correct, then not only can actions not belong to the ultimate perfection, but the perfect individual is not even thinking about them.

The point being made here can be illustrated by turning to an important debate in moral philosophy between cognitivists and non-cognitivists. What is at issue in this debate is whether or not we can speak of truth and knowledge in the sphere of moral judgement. So, for example, we know that the statement '2+2=4' is true. Moreover, its truth does not depend on our opinion. It is a matter of fact that holds true independent of our own beliefs. If I happen to believe that '2+2=5', I am simply wrong. The point is that there are mathematical truths that are independent of my mathematical beliefs and that determine whether my beliefs are true or false. There are other fields though where this is not the case. I might, for example, think that a particular brand of chocolate tastes wonderful. Others might disagree. But I cannot tell them that they are wrong. I cannot say that the statement 'Chocolate X is good' reflects an objective matter of fact. It is all a matter of taste. There is no fact of the matter that my belief describes.

The question at issue between moral cognitivists and non-cognitivists is where moral judgements fall within this spectrum. Moral cognitivists believe that moral judgements are reflections of an independent moral reality and thus can be known to be true or false. Non-cognitivists believe that such judgements are, in the most literal sense, a matter of opinion concerning which there simply is no 'truth'. Moral judgements, in their view, reflect our own moral attitudes rather than an independent reality. To use a famous example from the literature, if I judge the setting on fire of a cat by some children to be wrong, it is not because I somehow saw a moral property of 'wrongness' mysteriously hovering above the burning cat and the children setting it alight. While we must appeal to physical facts to explain scientific observations, we do not need to appeal to any moral facts in order to explain my observation that this act is wrong. We simply need appeal to my emotional reaction to the physical facts that I have witnessed. The negative ethical value that I describe is not something that I discover in the world. It is something that originates in my attitudes, to which I give expression. Such is the view of a moral non-cognitivist in its most basic form.

With all of this in mind, we can now understand what Maimonides means in *Guide*, I: 2, when he writes that issues to do with 'fine and bad' do not have truth-values and are not objects of intellectual apprehension. He is aligning himself with those we would today call moral non-cognitivists and saying that we cannot have moral knowledge. And this means that the ultimate intellectual perfection, which aims at truth, is not going to involve contemplating moral truths – for there are none. At this point therefore, it seems as if Maimonides believes that the best life for man is the life of contemplation, not practice, and the objects of contemplation do not even include truths associated with the moral sphere since there are no such truths.

There are, however, those who argue that far from disparaging the value of practice in favour of a life of contemplation, Maimonides in fact believed that *practical* perfection is the ultimate perfection. The practical interpretation of this ultimate perfection comes in a number of variations, but all of them point to the 'twist' that comes right at the very end of the *Guide* as their textual basis:

> It is clear that the perfection of man that may truly be gloried in is the one acquired by him who has achieved, in a measure corresponding to his capacity, apprehension of Him, may He be exalted, and who knows His providence extending over his creatures as manifested in the act of bringing them into being and their governance as it is. The way of life of such an individual, after he has achieved this apprehension, will always have in view, loving-kindness, righteousness and judgement, through assimilation to His actions, may he be exalted, just as we have explained several times in this Treatise. (*Guide*, III: 54, 638)

Maimonides seems here to undermine all that he has said concerning the primacy of intellectual perfection by concluding the *Guide* with the view that the true perfection is practical assimilation to and imitation of God's attributes of action. According to this quote, assimilation to God's actions *follows* the intellectual apprehension that we had taken to be final. Thus we are thrown back to a life of practice rather than one spent in the intellectual apprehension of primary intelligibles.

Other than this textual evidence, there is also philosophical reason to suggest that Maimonides might after all have believed that the ultimate perfection for man is practical, stemming from what we learned in chapter 3. For we saw there that we cannot gain any positive knowledge regarding the nature of God. All we can do is speak of negative attributes, or remain silent. But if we cannot say or know anything about God's nature, how can the ultimate perfection be the apprehension of God? Following this type of line, Kenneth Seeskin argues that the intellectual perfection to which Maimonides refers throughout the *Guide* is in fact the Socratic ideal of being aware of the limits of our intellectual capacities. Socrates' claim to wisdom was based on his awareness of his ignorance – at least he *knew* that he knew nothing. For Maimonides, similarly, the wise person would know of his inability to know anything positive about God. What we can do though, is speak of God's actions in terms of their moral consequences (though not, of course, in terms of the moral 'characteristics' they ordinarily entail). Thus there is a sense in which we can imitate God's moral acts, even if we cannot know anything about God's nature, and we are led then to the imitation of God's ethical actions through recognising the limits of our intellectual faculties. For Seeskin, therefore, the Socratic critical form of knowledge leads us 'to contemplation of God's moral attributes and thus to the 613 commandments'.[3]

Other scholars, such as Shlomo Pines and Lawrence Berman, prefer a more political reading of the ultimate perfection that follows the Arabic interpretations of Plato. On their reading, our apprehension of God's 'governance' 'leads and ought to lead to a sort of political activity which is the highest perfection of man'.[4] The limits on our apprehension of God here lead to political action rather than a moral end; to the governance of the state in the manner of what Plato called the philosopher-king, rather than to the moral perfection of the individual. But again, on this reading the ultimate perfection is practical rather than theoretical.

Our discussion so far leaves us then with three questions. 1) As we saw in Saadia, it is at least reasonable *prima facie* to believe in the primacy of practical perfection. But why would one think that intellectual perfection is the ultimate perfection for man? 2) Why are we treating these two perfections as mutually exclusive alternatives? Why could man's perfection not be a hybrid of the two? 3) Given the ambiguity in his writings, what *does* Maimonides believe to be the ultimate perfection for man? The rest of the chapter will be constructed around the answers to these questions.

3. WHY INTELLECTUAL PERFECTION?

We can gain some clues as to why anyone would think that intellectual perfection was the ultimate perfection by returning to *Guide*, III: 54, quoted earlier. There, Maimonides has already introduced three forms of human perfection – material (or economic) perfection, physical perfection and moral perfection – before telling us that intellectual perfection is the true human perfection. He goes on to say:

> This is in true reality the ultimate end; this is what gives the individual true perfection, a perfection belonging to him alone; and it gives him permanent perdurance; through it man is man. If you consider each of the three perfections mentioned before, you will find that they pertain to others than you, not to you, even though, according to the generally accepted opinion, they inevitably pertain both to you and to others. This ultimate perfection, however, pertains to you alone, no one else being associated in it with you in any way... Therefore, you ought to desire to achieve this thing, which will remain permanently with you, and not weary and trouble yourself for the sake of other things... (*Guide*, III: 54, 635)

The central points here are that 1) through intellectual perfection man is man; 2) it belongs to the individual man alone; and 3) it gives man permanence. We will work through these ideas in order, beginning with the idea that through intellect 'man is man', or as we saw Aristotle put it, 'intellect more than anything else is man' (*Ethics*, X. 7, 1178a7). In order to explain this point, we should look at Aristotle's so-called *ergon* argument, presented in the first book of the *Ethics*.

The *ergon*, of something is usually translated as its 'function' or 'characteristic activity'. The highest good for something is going to be performing this *ergon* well. So, for example, the *ergon* of an eye is to see, and the definition of a good eye is one that sees well. As far as humanity is concerned, we have already encountered the idea that rationality is the essence of humanity – or its 'form'. This distinguishes human beings from all other life forms and as such is their defining characteristic or *ergon*.

Thus we can determine the *ergon* of something by discovering its form. And the best life for human beings is therefore going to be the performance of this rational *ergon* with excellence. Even allowing for the fact that the Aristotelian concept of form is hardly scientific by today's standards, one might nonetheless agree that it is reason that sets man apart from other creatures, thus making him 'man'. And for Maimonides similarly, it is specifically intellectual perfection that is the human *ergon*, as opposed to any form of practical perfection. But we need to dig a little deeper to see what leads him to *exclude* actions and moral qualities.

We can immediately point out that even if intellect is the faculty that is unique to us, it is just one part of what makes us human. Without our other faculties we would not *be* human. As Aristotle admits

> such a life would be too high for man; for it is not in so far as he is man that he will live so, but in so far as something divine is present in him... If intellect is divine, then, in comparison with man, the life according to it is divine in comparison with human life. (*Ethics*, X. 7, 1177b27–31)

Contemplation is 'the activity of God' (*Ethics*, X. 8, 1178b22) for Aristotle and, at least in certain passages, it appears to be the same for Maimonides, for whom

> God is an intellect in actu... He is not by way of sometimes apprehending and sometimes not apprehending but is always an intellect in actu... He and the thing apprehended are one thing, which is His essence... Accordingly, He is always the intellect as well as the intellectually cognising subject and the intellectually cognised object. (*Guide*, I: 68, 165)

We have seen previously (**4.3**) how knowledge is a matter of the intellect becoming identical with the object it knows. With God, the 'object' known is himself and thus God is eternally contemplating himself – his is an activity of 'self-intellection'. While we already know how problematic it is to speak of God for Maimonides, and many therefore struggle to reconcile these statements about God with his negative theology, we will have to gloss over that here, noting, however, that since it could be said that we are speaking of one of God's actions, that might somewhat alleviate the discomfort, given Maimonides' concession on talking of God's actions.

All of the above, however, shows us that reason is not unique to humanity as the *ergon* argument would have had us believe, for it is also the activity of God. Indeed, what is unique appears to be that human beings are intellect *together* with all the other faculties that render us human. And if that is the case, why should the *ergon* of man not be a combination of the faculties of the soul so that our characteristic activity would be the exercise of our various faculties along with, or governed by reason, rather than the activity of reason alone? If other animals also have perception and locomotion, for example, but we have both of these along with reason, why could our *ergon* not be the combination of the three, albeit in hierarchical order? Some form of Saadian pluralism would be perfectly consistent with the idea that man's *ergon* is his reason, but that as man, this reason has both practical and theoretical elements, with the latter in control of, rather than excluding, the former. We seem to have little problem with the idea of a hierarchy of faculties with reason at the top, despite the fact that reason is used in the service of our other 'lower' faculties – in order, for example, to get food to eat. But we are still left wondering why it is that Maimonides puts theoretical reason on such a high pedestal. Surely the life of practical reason, with a measure of contemplative activity, is more characteristic of man than the life of pure contemplation, which is divine, but not necessarily human.

Notably, Crescas makes this very point in his critique of the idea that intellectual perfection constitutes the best life for man. The point, as he sums it up, is that on this view 'the purpose of the law – i.e., to bring about the survival of the intellect – for man, is for something other than him!' (*Light*, II: VI, 1, 433). Crescas' point is that this so-called form of man, partaking as it does of the nature of the divine, is an entirely different species to the man who is commanded to perform the commandments. *That* man is a man of flesh and blood, related to the animal kingdom, though elevated above it through his reason. It is this 'elevation' through reason that interests Maimonides and Aristotle to the exclusion of all else. But as soon as one does exclude all else, this 'form' of man is no longer the form of man *qua* man. That merely physical man turns out to have no purpose at all on the intellectualist reading. He is to be left behind in the intellectual transformation that takes place as 'man' gains intellectual perfection. While Maimonides would simply accept that this is indeed the case and that man ought to transcend his animal nature, in our attempt to understand why, we need to turn to the second point Maimonides makes in *Guide*, III: 54: that intellectual perfection 'pertains to you alone'. What does this mean and how does it lead us to the idea that it is *the* ultimate perfection?

Again, the source of this idea is Aristotle. For Aristotle, the best life is the life of *Eudaimonia*, usually translated as happiness, but meaning something far broader than what that word might suggest to us. The life of *Eudaimonia* is a life of well-being, the generally flourishing life. And *Eudaimonia*, if it is indeed the highest good for man, has to be the final end and self-sufficient. The idea of being the final end is that the life of *Eudaimonia* is not to be pursued as a means to some further end. It is not pursued for the sake of anything else, but is simply desired for itself. So whatever *Eudaimonia* turns out to be, it has to fulfil this condition of being desired for its own sake, and not for the sake of anything else. But while the concept of an end in itself is certainly present in Maimonides' writings elsewhere, it is the notion of self-sufficiency that is explicit in Maimonides' presentation at *Guide*, III: 54, and he understands it in a very particular way. Maimonides seems to be saying that self-sufficiency is concerned with whether this perfection pertains to you alone, and thus could presumably be enjoyed without the need for anything or *anyone* else. And it would appear that only the life of contemplation fulfils such a condition. The life of contemplation can be, indeed is best pursued in isolation according to Maimonides:

> Total devotion to [God] and the employment of intellectual thought in constantly loving Him should be aimed at. Mostly this is achieved in solitude and isolation. Hence every excellent man stays frequently in solitude and does not meet anyone unless it is necessary. (*Guide*, III: 51, 621)

Intellectual perfection is entirely confined to the self and no one else. In that sense it is self-sufficient. It is notable, however, that Aristotle rules out this meaning of self-sufficiency in saying that 'by self-sufficient we do not mean that which is sufficient for a man by himself, for one who loves a solitary life, but also for parents, children, wife...' (*Ethics*, I. 7, 1097b8–10). Of course, Maimonides might not have followed Aristotle here. But even allowing for that, Maimonides admits that a perfected society is a necessary condition for intellectual perfection, since one does not have the peace and leisure to contemplate in a society run amok. Thus, even allowing for disagreement with Aristotle, it is not the case for *Maimonides* that no one else is associated with the ultimate intellectual perfection. We need other people to behave in a certain way in order to enable the philosophers to engage in contemplation. It is true, however, that once one has these necessities, the life of practical perfection still requires a societal setting, whereas the life of contemplation does not. Practical perfection, once 'reached' remains a perfection that is to be maintained with other people. Indeed, the very idea that it can be reached as an end point is misleading.

It needs to be constantly maintained and as such is more an ongoing societal process than a final end state. Intellectual perfection, on the other hand, while also a continuous process rather than some static end state, is something that can be engaged upon in isolation, given the fulfilment of these necessary conditions. Thus, the life of contemplation is something that can be engaged in alone and achieved alone, as long as these conditions are in place.

Relating the two ideas of being a final end and being self-sufficient, the idea would be that if the ultimate perfection is not self-sufficient, we would still be pursuing the further good that would improve upon it. But that would mean that this state would also not be the final end, since we would be pursuing it for the sake of the additional value that would complete it and render it self-sufficient. So the central idea in Aristotle appears to be that in defining *Eudaimonia*, we are looking for the ultimate and self-sufficient form of life which 'when isolated makes life desirable and lacking in nothing' (*Ethics*, I. 7, 1097b15–16). The idea is that the ideal life that we are pursuing could not be defined in such a way that the addition of something else would improve upon it.

It is not clear that Maimonides puts these claims together in this way, but if we take this more strictly Aristotelian understanding of final ends and self-sufficiency, does the life of *theoria* turn out to the best life? We can begin by approaching the question from the opposite direction and asking whether the life of practical perfection in isolation would satisfy these conditions. The answer would presumably be negative, since even according to Saadia, such a life would be improved by the addition of intellectual elements. Thus a life of practical perfection is certainly not self-sufficient, and if we accept the interpretation above regarding the link between the two conditions, it is not a final end either since we would be pursuing a further end – that of the combined life of practical and intellectual perfection.

While a life of practical perfection could arguably be improved upon by the addition of intellectual perfection, what of the life of *theoria* taken in isolation? Intellectual perfection is certainly an end in itself, especially when we understand its nature correctly. For the life of intellectual perfection is not a life spent demonstrating the ultimate truths that Maimonides calls first intelligibles. While the demonstrations of truths might themselves be in the service of a further end – the knowledge of the conclusions – the point about *theoria* is that it is not *that* life. It is the life spent contemplating those truths that one has already demonstrated and 'nothing arises from it apart from the contemplating' (*Ethics*, X. 7, 1177b2). Such an activity is therefore without doubt an end in itself, not undertaken for any further end. Moreover, for Maimonides and Aristotle it is indeed self-sufficient. The life of pure contemplation cannot possibly be improved upon by the addition of the life of practical virtue. If it were, then our lives would presumably be superior to that of God, who at least on the conception of God as pure intellect would *lack* this practical perfection.

The foregoing observations return us again to what ultimately appears to be the underlying reason for the heightened evaluation given to contemplation – that contemplation is a divine activity whereas the life of practice is only human. As Aristotle states:

> So if among excellent actions political and military actions are distinguished by nobility and greatness, and these are unleisurely and aim at an end and are not desirable for their own sake, but the activity of intellect, which is contemplative, seems both to be superior in worth and to aim at no end beyond itself, and to have its pleasure proper to itself (and this augments the activity), and the self-sufficiency, leisureliness, unweariedness (so far as this is possible for man), and all the other attributes ascribed to the blessed man are evidently those connected with this activity, it follows that this will be the complete happiness of man… (*Ethics*, X. 7, 1177b15–25)

We already know that the best life for man must be self-sufficient and 'desirable for its own sake'. But the additional issue identified in this passage is very simply that the activity of the intellect is 'superior in worth'. When all is said and done, 'it would be strange to think that the art of politics, or practical wisdom, is the best, since man is not the best thing in the world' (*Ethics*, VI. 6, 1441a21–23). This is the ultimate reason that the life of contemplation is of greater, indeed absolute value – it is a life more divine than human. For Maimonides this is precisely why we extol its virtues. For Crescas it is reason to say that it cannot be the ideal life for *man*.

There are thinkers who seem to think that one can argue for the superiority of the life of contemplation independently of theological considerations. Thomas Nagel, for example, has pointed out that 'reason has a use beyond the ordering of practical life'.[5] Reason, in his opinion, renders man capable of transcending his own existence for some higher goal. Nonetheless, the divinity of the intellect appears to drive Maimonides towards this contemplative end to the exclusion of all others, at least to the point that exclusion is possible for a human being. And that is why the ideal for Maimonides is to become like Moses and the biblical patriarchs who achieved that state whereby a person 'talks with people and is occupied with his bodily necessities while his intellect is wholly turned toward Him, may He be exalted, while outwardly he is with people...' (*Guide*, III: 51, 623). It is notable that unlike Aristotle, Maimonides *does* give us this recipe for achieving the perfect state and mixing the intellectual and practical modes of life, however unrealistic such a final state might seem to us.

What this entire dispute ultimately comes down to is a tension first made explicit in Plato's famous allegory of the cave in his *Republic*. The parable Plato tells there is of a journey to intellectual enlightenment in the guise of a parable about a prisoner who escapes the cave where he has been captive since birth, fed a diet of shadows and illusions that he believes to be reality. Once he escapes and eventually reaches the level of true enlightenment – and the life of intellectual contemplation – the question is posed of why he would wish to descend back into the cave, which in the parable represents our world of political activity. Plato himself admits that it will take a degree of compulsion to return the prisoner to a life of political activity.

The problem here is that there is a basic incompatibility between the practical and intellectual perfections. Even if not entirely incompatible, these two forms of life do generally detract one from the other. As Maimonides notes, the life of contemplation is best sought in seclusion and Aristotle believes that other than necessary concessions to natural human fatigue, one could potentially contemplate continuously (*Ethics*, X. 7, 1177a22). The life of moral or civic virtue in contrast is obviously a social life - man, after all, is a social animal according to Aristotle. And despite the biblical exceptions that Maimonides mentions, most ordinary mortals occupied with a life of civic virtue simply cannot at the same time be continuously contemplating eternal truths. The fact is that both Aristotle and Maimonides speak of the divinity of the life of pure reason and acknowledge that we can only approach it to the extent that is possible for human beings. But it appears as if the two forms of life are in competition and that Maimonides wishes to encourage us to cultivate the intellectual life to the extent that is possible, with the practical life a means to this rather than an end in itself.

In a sense, given that it is a divine value that is being privileged here, Maimonides' more thoroughgoing religious commitments give him greater motivation than Aristotle to take this intellectualist stance. One might see it therefore as a direct result of his theological commitments. But the highly naturalistic reading that is at the basis of his reasoning nonetheless renders it very discomforting for his more traditionalist co-religionists, which brings us to the final point made by Maimonides in *Guide*, III: 54: that through intellectual perfection, man achieves permanence.

What Maimonides means by this is that through one's intellectual achievements one gains immortality, the life of *Olam ha-ba* – 'The world to come'. We will have more to say about this at the end of the next chapter. But it suffices for the moment to note that according to Maimonides, it seems as if man's form – his rationality – is actualised throughout his life to a greater or lesser degree and it is this intellect that will continue to survive for eternity. Ironically then, what clinches the superiority of contemplation over ethical practice for Maimonides is the fact that such activity is somehow linked to religious ideas – those of 'divinity activity and immortality'. Yet what these religious commitments yield is what, 'Jewishly' speaking, would have been an unorthodox position on human perfection, together with what appears to be (indeed, as we shall see in the next chapter, *is*) a rather unorthodox position on human immortality as dependent on intellectual achievement. Together, they form an intellectualist package that seems to allow little to our humanity and thus little room for the life of practical perfection.

4. THE ROLE OF PRACTICE

It seems from our discussion that for Maimonides the best life for man is a life of *theoria*. What then, are we to make of the end of the *Guide* that appears to return us to a more practical conception of the best life? Having told us that the ultimate perfection for man is intellectual, and that to such intellectual perfection no 'actions or moral qualities' can belong, how can practice fit into the ideal life? There are those who will appeal to Maimonides' esotericism to solve this problem. Yet it seems as if everything that one needs is actually there on the surface.

To begin with, even if the final end is theoretical, that does not mean that practice has *no* role in the best life for man. We have already seen that to be pure intellect is to be God. A human *qua* human is essentially embodied and as such, in order to maintain his qualitatively inferior degree of intellectual perfection, man must maintain, both as an individual and within society at large, the necessary material conditions that are a function of practical perfection. Thus, practical perfection remains a necessary constituent of the perfect *human* life, even though it is not its final end.

The problem arising out of this is that one might believe that the life of *mitzvot* is therefore expendable. As we saw in our discussion of rationalising the *mitzvot*, if they are simply a means to some external end, then a more efficient means would surely be preferable. And it is notable that Crescas and others believed that a philosophical system that relegates the *mitzvot* to a mere means to intellectual perfection was a danger in times of persecution. Why should a persecuted Jew not decide to convert to the religion of the land? Surely if peace and tranquillity are conditions of the final end, it will be a lot more forthcoming if one opted out of Judaism for the religion of the majority. Intellectual perfection cannot fail to be easier to attain if one is not following a form of life that leads to anything but peace and tranquillity. And in Crescas' time, this was not merely an academic argument, as he tried to rebuild Jewish communities in Spain in the wake of the persecutions of 1391.

While Maimonides would never have acknowledged that the *mitzvot* were anything other than absolute and eternal as we have seen, he cannot rule this argument out in principle. Yet in practice he does seem to argue that only the *mitzvot* can serve the ultimate end. Indeed, it seems that this practical component of the final perfection is not simply ethical or political, but religious – in this case adherence to the Torah. The actions one undertakes or promotes in one's intellectually perfect state are divine *mitzvot*, since only a divine system can achieve the state about which Maimonides is writing.

This is clear from Maimonides' distinction between the system of the commandments and the moral realm of 'generally accepted opinions', or between divine law and other non-divine systems. The latter are

> directed exclusively toward the ordering of the city and of its circumstances and the abolition in it of injustice and oppression; ... no heed is given to the perfecting of the rational faculty, and no regard is accorded to opinions being correct or faulty. (*Guide*, II: 40, 383)

Divine law, on the other hand, is different. As we have seen, the *mitzvot* are directed towards both practical and intellectual ends,

> to the soundness of the circumstances pertaining to the body and also to the soundness of belief – a Law that takes pains to inculcate correct opinions

with regard to God...and that desires to make man wise, to give him understanding, and to awaken his attention, so that he should know the whole of that which exists in its true form. (*Guide*, II: 40, 384)

The divine law is ultimately connected to the final contemplative perfection of man. Maimonides therefore distinguishes between 'the Law in general' and 'divine law' by virtue of the ends at which they aim, and only divine law can vouchsafe us both the practical and intellectual elements involved in the life of the perfect individual. This perfect individual, such as Moses, is one who achieves perfect intellectual apprehension and as a result 'always has in view' assimilation to God's actions.

But what exactly does he have in view? We are told that we ought to have in view 'loving-kindness, righteousness and judgement, through assimilation to His actions, may he be exalted, just as we have explained several times in this Treatise' (*Guide*, III: 54, 638). What would assimilation to God's actions as 'explained several times in this Treatise' be? One thing we know from the *Guide* about God's actions is that while we can speak of the actions as being acts of moral virtue, we cannot as a result impute that virtue to God. We cannot say that God has any such virtues – we can only describe the actions that come from God in these moral terms. But if that is what we are supposed to be imitating, then that is precisely what Moses and the patriarchs are described as doing. They do indeed perform and teach acts that constitute practical perfection, but in so doing are not actually thinking about or concentrating on the cultivation of virtue. They remain devoted to the cultivation of their intellectual connection with God. Practical perfection is, so to speak, the last thing on their *minds*. Just as God performs actions but does not do so with the usual internal corollaries, so does the perfect man on this model. It is as if man's perfection 'overflows' much as God's perfection does, and this is manifest in his ability to continue to deal with society without this actually detracting from his continuous intellectual contemplation. While such 'perfection' might still leave much to be desired for many, there is little doubt that Maimonides can – and has – been understood as placing great emphasis on intellectual perfection to the detriment of the life of action. But on this view, a form of practice remains an element of life after intellectual perfection. While it is not itself part of the perfection of the individual, which is entirely intellectual, we might, however, characterise it as an 'emanation' from that individual.

Just as God emanates his perfection to the world of nature without being affected or changed, so the perfect individual's knowledge would emanate to society without him being affected and thus drawn away from the world of contemplation. His actions would be a form of practical activity consequent upon (or 'emanating' from) his understanding of the manner in which God 'acts', i.e. consequent upon the contemplative activity of theoretical reason. Such an individual need never cease contemplating, but the result of such contemplation would be the type of practical activity of the highest prophets. If we are trying to define the ideal life for man as a form of *imitatio dei*, there could be no better model than this. Whether it is a model to which most of us mere mortals can genuinely aspire is a rather different question.

NOTES

1   All quotes from Crescas in this chapter are taken from Harvey, *HCC*.
2   It should be noted that some believe the conception of the ethical presented in Book X to be inconsistent with earlier references to ethics in Book III. I believe that one can find a consistent view of ethics in Saadia and our reconstruction of Book X is, I believe, compatible with what he writes elsewhere.
3   Kenneth Seeskin, *Jewish Philosophy in a Secular Age* (Albany, NY: SUNY Press, 1990), 49.
4   Shlomo Pines, 'The Limitations of Human Knowledge According to Al-Farabi, ibn Bajja, and Maimonides', in Isadore Twersky, *Studies in Medieval Jewish History and Literature* (Cambridge, Mass: Harvard University Press, 1979), 82–109. Quotation from 100
5   Thomas Nagel, 'Aristotle on Eudaimonia', in Amelie Oksenberg Rorty (ed.), *Essays on Aristotle's Ethics* (Berkeley, CA: University of California Press, 1980), 7–14. Quotation from 12.

FURTHER READING

For a similar account of Saadia's view to that given here see Lenn E. Goodman, 'Saadiah's Ethical Pluralism', *Journal of the American Oriental Society*, vol. 100, no. 4 (1980), 407–19.

An excellent survey of the debate surrounding Maimonides' views on human perfection together with many relevant bibliographical references can be found in Menachem Kellner, *Maimonides on Human Perfection* (Atlanta, GA: Scholars Press, 1990). There are also interesting chapters by Lawrence V. Berman, Ralph Lerner and Steven Harvey in Joel L. Kraemer (ed.), *Perspectives on Maimonides* (Oxford: Littman Library of Jewish Civilization, 1991).

For discussion of Maimonides' interpretation of 'the fall' see Lawrence V. Berman, 'Maimonides on the Fall of Man', *AJS Review*, vol. 5, (1980), 1–15; and Shlomo Pines, 'Truth and Falsehood Versus Good and Evil: A Study in Jewish and General Philosophy in Connection with the *Guide* of the Perplexed, I, 2', in Isadore Twersky (ed.), *Studies in Maimonides* (Cambridge, Mass: Harvard University Press, 1991), 95–157.

For discussion of Aristotle on human perfection, see the essays by Thomas Nagel, J.L. Ackrill, Katherine Wilkes, John McDowell and Amelie Oksenberg Rorty in, Amelie Oksenberg Rorty (ed.), *Essays on Aristotle's Ethics* (Berkeley, CA: University of California Press, 1980).

A detailed account of Crescas' critique can be found in Warren Zev Harvey, 'Hasdai Crescas's Critique of the Theory of the Acquired Intellect', PhD dissertation, Columbia University, 1973. Much of the discussion in this work relates directly to the links between such intellectualism and views of immortality, to be discussed in the next chapter.

For an excellent introduction to moral cognitivism and non-cognitivism see David McNaughton, *Moral Vision* (Oxford: Blackwell, 1996). The rather unsavoury 'cat' example can be found in the first chapter of Gilbert Harman, *The Nature of Morality* (New York: Oxford University Press, 1977). And for an argument that despite appearances Maimonides in fact subscribes to a form of cognitivism (albeit not straightforwardly moral), see my 'Good and Evil, Truth and Falsity: Maimonides and Moral Cognitivism', *Trumah*, vol. 12 (2002), 163–82.

8

The Bad Life

Having spent the last chapter looking at the good life for man, it is natural to ask about how things can go wrong. For much as we might strive to gain human perfection, experience tells us that its achievement might in the end be out of our hands. Everyone can probably point to examples of good people – whether we understand that goodness practically or intellectually – who have suffered. And the injustice of much of the suffering that we witness is bound to raise the question that philosophers have formulated as the problem of evil. This question has come into sharp focus since the twentieth century, for philosophers of religion in general and Jewish thinkers in particular, as a consequence of the radical evil embodied in the holocaust, which elicited responses from across religious divides. But the problem of evil is one that at some point many people formulate, whether in a technical philosophical fashion or not, and it has evidently troubled people since biblical times. Indeed, it is the only philosophical question to which an entire biblical book dedicated.

While, to our eyes, not written in the form of a technical philosophical treatise – though with dialogue being the preferred mode of presentation for Plato, its dialogue form might have encouraged a philosophical reading – the book of Job is clearly an attempt to deal with this problem, and it contains elements that continue to resonate with philosophers and theologians to this day. Needless to say, it was the starting point for the philosophical discussion among medieval Jewish thinkers who would indeed have read it as a philosophical treatise. And though we are not here dealing with the book of Job specifically we will certainly have cause to refer to it. But first, we should pay some attention to the problem itself.

It has become the norm in modern analytic philosophy to distinguish between two forms of the problem. The first formulation focuses on the evidential relation between the existence of evil on the one hand and that of God on the other. In this evidential problem of evil, the apparent pointlessness of actual evil is presented as decisive evidence against God's existence. So in contemporary times the evidential form of the problem is often used as an argument against the existence of God. Now we know that the existence of God is non-negotiable for all of our thinkers who, when confronting this problem, are not worried that God might not exist. What they are doing therefore is attempting to work out a place for evil within their more general theology, which leads us onto the second formulation of the problem, as one of logical consistency.

The logical problem of evil takes the claim that evil exists, and argues that it cannot be consistent with the claim that God exists and is omnipotent, omniscient and perfectly good. To illustrate this version of the problem by taking one of those attributes as our starting point (one can run analogous arguments for the other two), an all-powerful God presumably has the power to prevent evil. Since God does not do so, we can only conclude that either He did not care enough to want to (and is thus not perfectly good) or was unaware that it was happening (and is thus not, in the most straightforward sense, omniscient). Gersonides, for example, appeals to the problem of evil as 'the strongest argument in the eyes of those who deny divine knowledge of particulars' (*Wars*, II: 2, 95). If God had knowledge of all particulars he would surely guide them, and thus the world, perfectly. The fact that he apparently fails to do so indicates that he cannot have knowledge of particulars. Essentially, the existence of evil means that one of the traditional attributes must be jettisoned, or at the very least interpreted in such a way as to solve the problem. In defence of divine justice, these responses to the logical problem of evil are called 'theodicies' and involve ever more subtle attempts to make consistent the traditional theistic view of God and the existence of evil.

The Gersonides example is useful since it immediately raises two related matters. The first is that it relates the problem of evil to that of providence. The extent to which God exercises guardianship over his creatures is deeply implicated in this whole problem. If we say that God extends his providence to his creatures, then the question of how they can suffer is exacerbated. If he does not, then the problem is 'solved', but leaving another in its wake concerning the nature of a God who does not care for his creation. As Gersonides puts it

> If we posit that he does extend his providence to human individuals, it would follow that we may attribute injustice to God, on account of the imperfect order of events in matters of good and evil accruing to men, since it often occurs that the righteous suffer and the wicked prosper.[1]

In this connection, discussions of the book of Job took the various protagonists to be presenting different views of providence, and thus all of our thinkers dealt with the question of providence together with the problem of evil. The two went hand in hand.

The second point is that the formulation of the problem assumes that God is at least omniscient, omnipotent and perfectly good. Now in the course of our study we have actually seen reason to doubt that all of our thinkers would accept these terms in their ordinary sense. Maimonides would certainly not be willing to accept this list at face value, and whether Gersonides' view of omniscience would be inconsistent with the existence of evil is at best questionable. We will need to bear this in mind as we attempt to understand the views of the medievals in this chapter, mainly focusing on the contrasting perspectives of Saadia and Gersonides, though also bringing Maimonides into the discussion at various points.

1. THE PROBLEM OF EVIL IN SAADIA

Saadia sets out the basic principles of his approach in *Emunot ve-De'ot*, V: 3, but also treats the problem in more depth in his commentary to the book of Job, and we will utilise both in order to understand his views. At the very basis of his view is the idea of the Mut'azilite school of *kalam*, that God's acts conform to an objective standard of justice that human beings are able to understand, at least up to a point. Yet the suffering of the virtuous constitutes *prima facie* evidence against God's justice. Setting his discussion in *Emunot* within the book on 'Merits and Demerits', against the background of an account whereby God keeps a record of a person's acts, Saadia is primarily concerned to reconcile the evils that befall the virtuous with some account of the justice of this divine book-keeping.

In *Emunot*, Saadia divides the sufferings of the righteous into two categories. The first is the category of punishment, though the manner of the divine book-keeping here needs some explanation. According to Saadia, a virtuous person might be punished in this world for his failings in order to get it all out of the way now, so to speak, so that in the next world this person will attain a constant status within the available levels of reward. Basically, God 'instituted recompense in this world only for the lesser [portion of man's conduct]' (*Emunot*, V: 2, 210). So a person, who overall falls into the category of the virtuous, will receive punishment in this world for his misdeeds so that he can be rewarded in the next. And a person who overall is classified as a bad person might therefore fare well in this world, but will be in for something of a shock come the next.

Saadia has a second category for understanding the sufferings of the righteous however, and that is as 'incipient trials with which God tests them, when He knows that they are able to endure them, only in order to compensate them for these trials later on with good' (*Emunot*, V: 3, 213). The first point to make about this is that such a person is only chosen if God knows he can bear the trials, and specifically for the reason that 'the whole purpose of the suffering of the upright is that the rest of God's creatures might know that He has not chosen the former for nothing' (*ibid.*). Thus the suffering has the purpose of educating the public in some way – but how? On the one hand, Saadia tells us that while a person is informed if he is being punished, he is not informed that he is undergoing a trial, as this would defeat the object of

> making certain that the patience of the virtuous person be not lightly esteemed by men, who might [otherwise] say that the only reason for his patience is that he knows that he will be amply rewarded. (*Emunot*, V: 3, 214)

It appears from the concern that the sufferer might be 'lightly esteemed', that there is an element of using this person as a public paradigm of faith, as an educational example. And indeed we see this made explicit in the case of Job who due to his riches 'had many envious detractors' and was chosen in order 'to demonstrate to Job's detractors how righteous he really was and how splendid was his forbearance'.[2] Job's ability to withstand the trials to which he is subjected vindicates God's choosing him for such rewards in the first place. So he is indeed chosen as a paradigm of faith, and this must be made clear to people so that they can understand why he had fared so well – at least up to this point. The public nature of this suffering and its educative purpose for the masses, both as a model of faith and a vindication of God's justice, is a significant element of the divine plan in meting out this treatment.

The further element that emerges from the above quote is the idea of compensating the sufferer later. So it appears as if the suffering adds value to the eventual reward that the sufferer will enjoy in the next world. Saadia does bring up the obvious objection here – why subject this person to the pain in the first place, only in order to give them increased reward? Surely God could either have given them the reward that they would have received anyway, without the added value of the suffering, or he could have just given them the extra reward in the first place. If they were really deserving of this extra reward - and unless God's justice were arbitrary we have to assume that they were - then surely he could have given it to them without making them suffer. To this, Saadia replies that 'the favors conferred upon man by way of compensation are more highly prized than those conferred upon him purely as an act of divine grace' (*Emunot*, V: 3, 215). According to this 'no pain no gain' theology, the good achieved through effort or struggle is better than one received effortlessly as a result of God's kindness. Thus, we are actually better off for suffering when we take a long-term view, for having passed this test of faith, our recompense in the afterlife will be immeasurably greater. Saadia explicitly tells us that suffering is a gift from God, developing the rabbinic idea of *yissurin shel ahavah* (afflictions of love), the most developed discussion of which is at *bBerakhot* 5a–b.

Ultimately then, suffering serves either to punish, or test and educate, but with these two explanations before us, we can ask why Saadia takes this dual route at all. One imagines that there is no such thing as a purely righteous individual. Thus, surely any person who suffers could be automatically placed in the first category – as someone who is receiving all his punishment now to give him a free run in the next world. The second category would still be required, however, for cases in which the 'punishment' was disproportionate and could not be accounted for in this manner. In such a case, we would be in the realm of trials for later compensation (and the public good). In fact Saadia does seem to think that there are 'completely guiltless individuals' (*Emunot*, V: 3, 214). Such individuals, he tells us, are 'subjected to trials in order to be compensated for them afterwards' (*ibid.*). It is not clear whether this is simply the same as the second explanation of suffering, or is distinguished from it by being solely concerned with compensation for that individual and not having any element of being for the education of the public.

Saadia does mention a further form of suffering in his commentary on Job: as 'discipline and instruction', as a parent might (in a different age) 'discipline his child with raps and cuffs and many pains to make him behave and act responsibly' (*BT*, 125). It is not entirely clear whether this is a separate category not mentioned in *Emunot*, or a sub-category of one of the others. On the one hand it could be a form of punishment – discipline often has such connections. Or, if understood as instruction, it could fall under the educative category – though more for the sufferer than those who are witness to it.[3] Either way, we will leave this further category aside and concentrate on the two main forms of suffering that he discusses.

It is undeniable that the reward and punishment approach to suffering has plenty of textual antecedents in the Jewish literature that preceded Saadia, both biblical and rabbinic, and it even persists in the post-holocaust world. But the first thing to note is that any such approach assumes a whole set of other religious ideas, such as that there is a next life in which compensation for apparent injustices can be recompensed. We will have more to say about this at the end of the chapter. For the moment we should note that while such ideas would be accepted parts of Saadia's medieval worldview, his approach would have less value for those who cannot work with such notions. Yet this punishment approach as a whole is far from necessary in any case. Indeed, God is portrayed as reprimanding Job's companions for suggesting that he somehow deserved his suffering as a punishment. In that specific case, Saadia explicitly rejects the idea that Job's travails are down to his own failings, and subsumes his fate under the category of trial, the purpose of which was 'so that when he steadfastly bears them, his Lord may reward him and bless him' (*BT*, 125–6). This is the solution offered by Elihu according to Saadia, whom he has saying

> God has caused you to suffer solely in order to take you away and transpose you from this realm of constraint to one of breadth and scope in which there is no straitness, there to bless you bountifully and set your table with rich viands. (*BT*, 369)

Importantly, while the notion that this was somehow a deserved punishment is dismissed in Job's case, it remains a *possible* explanation of suffering in other cases for Saadia. But whether understood from the perspective of reward and punishment, or from the alternate perspective of trial and education, the general approach that Saadia takes is to find a theologically sufficient reason for evil and suffering.

What can we say at this point about such an approach from a philosophical perspective? We should note, initially, that this is an important form of response to the problem of evil. The claim of the logical problem is that the existence of evil cannot be reconciled with the notion of an omnipotent and omniscient God who is also perfectly good. Saadia seems to accept that God is omnipotent and omniscient in a relatively straightforward sense, yet he argues that he can still be perfectly good if he has a sufficient reason for allowing suffering – which in Saadia's view he does. Given that the framework for Saadia's approach is that of God's justice, and his conception of it certainly seems to share something in common with our own moral notions, we might presume that Saadia believes that the reasons he gives for suffering are *morally* sufficient reasons.

The foregoing discussion reveals that the original statement of the problem of evil must implicitly rule out the possibility of God having a sufficient reason for inflicting suffering. For the claim of inconsistency made in the logical problem of evil has to assume that an omnipotent and omniscient God could not *possibly* have a sufficient reason for allowing suffering. If he does, then suffering need not be inconsistent with the existence of the traditional conception of God. While ruling such reasons out in principle must on the one hand appear difficult, the problem with giving such a reason has been starkly presented by the contemporary philosopher D.Z. Phillips, who has written with reference to a child dying from cancer, 'If this has been *done* to anyone, it is bad enough, but to be done for a purpose, to be planned from eternity – that is the deepest evil. If God is this kind of agent, He cannot justify His actions, and His evil nature is revealed.'[4] In this manner, we might find it distasteful, to say the least, that Job was victimised to educate the public, though we should also remember that this was not the only purpose of his suffering.

In answer to this, we might argue that God's justice is an absolute for Saadia, such that even if we are unable to fathom how it works, we can take it for granted that it is operative. But in that case we are falling back on God having a sufficient moral reason only accessible to himself – what we might term a theologically sufficient reason for suffering – though this ultimately leads us back to the idea that God's ways are mysterious to us and we must trust that everything he does is for a greater good that is beyond our understanding. If the point of Jewish philosophy, however, is to try to make these matters somehow accessible to human reason, then Phillips' point is one that is difficult to answer. One way to avoid it would be to move away from a Saadian conception of God that models his attributes on our human understanding of them. And if we want to move away from such an approach, we need to turn to our more Aristotelian thinkers, for whom God is simply not that sort of agent.

2. GERSONIDES ON PROVIDENCE

We can introduce the approaches of Maimonides and Gersonides via a discussion of providence. While we have not looked in detail at Saadia's view of providence, it is pretty clear that in his view God is literally watching our every move so as to reward or punish us accordingly, whether now or in the next world. With both Maimonides and Gersonides, it is immediately obvious that we are dealing with a very different animal. While Maimonides is the template for Gersonides' view, Gersonides' presentation, while far lengthier, simplifies his predecessor's presentation from a structural perspective, so we will look to his account, which of course also means that we do not have to deal with problems of Maimonidean esotericism.

Gersonides devoted Book IV of *Wars of the Lord* to providence, though he, like Saadia, also composed a separate commentary on the book of Job. Beginning though with his discussion as presented in *Wars*. Gersonides presents three possible views on providence:

> (1) The theory of Aristotle asserts that divine providence does not reach individual members of the human species but only the species itself, just as in other species. (2) The theory of most of the followers of the Torah maintains that divine providence reaches each and every individual human being as an individual... (3) The theory of the outstanding scholars of our Torah, who assert that divine providence reaches only some individuals, but not all men. (*Wars*, IV: 1, 155)

As noted earlier, one can argue for the first view on the basis of the problem of evil itself. If we can point to examples of undeserved suffering, we can use them as evidence that God does not exert providence over individuals. There is general providence according to this view, which is that measure of protection afforded by the manner in which God has set up the world, which in Gersonides' view is actually an effect of the motions in the heavenly spheres as we explained at 6.2. As we saw there, unlike Maimonides, Gersonides believed the science of astrology to be genuine rather than spurious and though human freewill can subvert the influence of the stars, much of what occurs in the world is due to the heavenly constellations. But the general providence this effects cannot protect individuals from particular evils that might befall them. We are all 'protected' by the earth being positioned and continuing to move in its orbit, by the force of gravity, and the predictable causal laws that allow us to get on with our everyday lives. But this is simply a matter of the impersonal and natural manner in which we are affected by the world around us. And while Gersonides accepts this mechanism of general providence, for him it cannot be the whole of providence.

In support of the second view – that individual providence is extended over everyone – Gersonides writes that 'it is obvious that a perfect master does not ignore the actions performed by those who are directed by him, and that he is able to reward each of them according to his deeds' (*Wars*, VI: 2, 158). Other than the fact that unless he wishes to align himself with mere 'followers' of the Torah rather than its 'outstanding scholars', Gersonides has immediately indicated that he will be taking the third view, it should be clear anyway from our earlier discussion that Gersonides cannot take this straightforward view of providence. As we know, according to Gersonides God does not know what is actually happening in the sublunar world, but only, at best, the infinite possibilities that the course of the world can take. So God cannot know every individual *as an individual* and thus cannot simply distribute justice according to each one's deserts. On his own view of omniscience, however, what more can he make of the third option that divine providence reaches *some* individuals? Surely that is even more problematic, since if providence is to extend over certain individuals, God will have to make choices between the people he doesn't know. So how can his view of providence be consistent with his view of divine knowledge?

Gersonides' explanation of the nature of providence takes the following form:

> Since man exhibits different levels of proximity and remoteness from the Agent Intellect by virtue of his individual character, those that are more strongly attached to it receive divine providence individually. And since some men never go beyond the disposition with which they are endowed as members of the human species and do not try to attain perfection so that they could become close to the Agent Intellect...such people are not within the scope of divine providence except in a general way as members of the human species, for they have no individual [perfections] that warrant [individual] providence. (*Wars*, IV: 4, 174)

Immediately, we see that individual providence for Gersonides is proportional to one's proximity to the Agent Intellect (synonymous with what we have previously referred to as the Active Intellect). Thus, returning to our discussion of the previous chapter, it seems that the greater one's intellectual perfection, the greater the degree of one's providence. On the one hand, one might understand this as meaning that God literally responds to individuals in proportion to their intellectual attainments – God looks after the clever people. This alone would be a highly controversial view, since the traditionalist would argue that God surely proportions his attention to those who perform *mitzvot*, not those who 'perform' philosophical demonstrations. But given his view of God's knowledge, Gersonides cannot even believe that God literally responds to people in accordance with their intellectual attainments. Thus, as he goes on to explain, the relationship between an individual and God's providence is to be understood far more naturalistically:

> For man is endowed with a practical intellect from which many kinds of useful arts are derived for his preservation. He is also given an intellect from which are derived the tendencies to flee from harmful things and to obtain advantageous things. In some men this providence is even more developed, for it communicates to them through prophecy impending evil or good, *so that they can protect themselves* against evil and obtain good. (*Wars*, VI: 5, 176–7, emphasis added)

Central here is the fact that God's role in providing providence is not an active one requiring his constant attention to affairs in the sublunar world. Instead, he has created us with certain capacities that, if used well, will lead to our own self-preservation. Thus, to take a simple example from Gersonides, birds do not migrate south in the winter because God is watching and makes the bird fly that way. Rather, birds have a natural instinct to do this (of which of course God is the First Cause), and that constitutes their general providential care. With human beings, the extent of providence is far more developed and individualised, since man has intelligence with which to direct his life in the correct way. Putting all the information together, we end up with a picture whereby man, through his own intellectual attainments, can achieve a greater or lesser degree of providence, not because God is watching and rewarding him for being 'clever', but because God provided man with a Potential Intellect, and the more that man actualises it, the more he will be able to look after himself.

In its most developed form, this intellectual attainment reaches the levels of prophecy, allowing a person to navigate his way through life by applying the universal knowledge gained from the Active Intellect to his particular environment. The basic mechanism of providence is therefore identical with that involved in the naturalistic view of prophecy discussed in chapter 4. Like prophecy, providence becomes something that man achieves through naturalistic means rather than something that God provides in response to particular circumstances. God is not a being who constantly manages human affairs. He has set up a world such that humans can, through their intellectual abilities (which *are* utterly dependent on God as First Cause), navigate their own way. Thus individual providence for humanity is found in God's 'informing them of the good and evil that is to come upon them', but the 'communication varies according to the different degrees of proximation to the Agent Intellect exhibited by these men' (*Wars*, IV: 5, 178), and the manner in which the individual can 'translate' the emanations received into representations of future events depends on the perfection of the intellect.

Gersonides' total picture is not quite as straightforward as this. Miracles are also a form of providence, to which Gersonides dedicates a whole separate discussion that we do not have space to discuss here. And Gersonides also writes of the good man who is planning to travel on a ship but gets a thorn stuck in his foot, thus missing the boat – which ends up shipwrecked. Thus, an instance of suffering saves this person from drowning and is understood as providential. Such a view, according to which people 'suffer pains providentially' (*Wars*, VI: 5, 179), appears far from the naturalism espoused up to this point and closer to a more traditional idea of God watching over us and intervening at specific points so as to protect us. Given what we know about Gersonides' view of God's knowledge of particulars, this cannot be the correct reading of providential suffering, which, Gersonides insists, 'is compatible with God's not knowing the individual as an individual' (*Wars*, IV: 6, 181). And precisely how providential suffering – an 'inferior kind of communication' (*Wars*, IV: 6, 181) – fits into the big picture is very difficult to determine. Some believe that it is in truth just a part of general providence, i.e. it is a result of the natural laws governed by the heavenly spheres, and is not really a form of individual providence at all, even if we subjectively give it such an interpretation after the fact. So it is simply part of the natural order that we retrospectively class as providential. Robert Eisen, however, noting that unlike Maimonides, Gersonides is not one to conceal his views even when they do not accord with more traditional ideas, insists that we must take Gersonides at his word. He has argued that providential suffering is a mechanism whereby natural providential laws are somehow activated by a person's intellectual level, though quite how this would fit into Gersonides' naturalistic metaphysics remains a problem. Interested readers can pursue this through the further reading, but with the background we do have, we can return to the problem of evil.

3. THE PROBLEM OF EVIL

Let us begin with an account of the origins of evil and bring Maimonides into the discussion. For Maimonides, God does not produce evil 'in an essential act' (*Guide*, III: 10, 440) since all divine acts are absolutely good. Evil instead is a 'privation', the absence of something rather than a positive existent, much as darkness is an absence of light rather than an existent thing. Indeed, both Maimonides and Gersonides share the view that ultimately evil is just a side effect of the creation of matter.

We introduced the distinction between matter and form, the physically inseparable but conceptually distinct elements that make up all physical entities some chapters ago (**2.4**). We have discussed the notion of form extensively over the course of this book, but have said less about matter, the basic 'stuff' that individuates forms so that there exist, for example, human individuals that can share that same form. But we have had cause to mention that matter has a defective nature (**2.6**) and is generally denigrated by the Aristotelians as a source of deficiency. It is inherently unstable since it takes on different forms over time. It is always in a state of privation, lacking the forms it does not currently have, and thus is always in a state of potential – the potential to take on forms other than the one it currently has. As a result, it is always unstable, and this instability is the source of evil.

At *Guide*, III: 12, Maimonides distinguishes between three different types of evil consequent on this instability. The first is a direct consequence of matter, whether our material nature, which makes us susceptible to illness and other physical threats, or the material nature of the world, which as a result of its instability is the cause of such things as earthquakes or drought. The second type of evil that Maimonides lists is down to the mistreatment of human beings by other human beings 'such as tyrannical domination of some of them over others' (*Guide*, III: 12, 444). The third type of evil we inflict upon ourselves as a result of our vices that cause us suffering and again illness. Gersonides simplifies Maimonides' three categories into two that are distinguished by whether their source is external or internal to the person. The first category, that he terms 'chance' events include natural events such as earthquakes, though in truth these are not what we would call chance events at all. In Aristotelian thought, 'chance' events were those that looked as if they occurred for a certain purpose but in fact did not. Aristotle uses the example of going to the market to buy something and meeting a debtor there. An observer might have thought that this person went to the market to meet the debtor – but this was not the 'causal' chain that was in fact operative. This would be called a chance event by Aristotle. The point here is that chance events are not events without natural causes. Rather, they are events that, as Gersonides says occur 'infrequently and only in a few things' (*Wars*, II: 1, 27), since they do not follow the general teleological patterns that we expect. The second category of evil for Gersonides places all moral evils, whether caused by ourselves (Maimonides' third category) or others (Maimonides' second category), under a single rubric, along with such physical frailties as ill health (a subset of Maimonides' first category).

However we divide them, what these causes of evil have in common for both thinkers is that that they all ultimately stem from the nature of matter. The instabilities of nature are explicitly down to matter in Maimonides, and while Gersonides puts them down to chance, given the understanding of chance with which he was working, we can clearly see that such events are the fault of the material constitution of nature. Moreover, Gersonides explicitly puts moral evils down to matter: 'they are attributable to matter, for the evil decision that arouses man to harm someone else does not derive from reason' (*Wars*, IV: 3, 168). Similarly for Maimonides all moral evils trace back to our material constitution, since 'all of them derive from ignorance' (*Guide*, III: 11, 440). When not fully under the control of our intellects (our form), the material aspect of our nature can lead to such things as greed and unreason, that in turn lead us to commit moral evils. Moral evil, therefore, is a result of ignorance, or at least not giving the intellect its due, since our pursuit of immoral ends is a result of falling under the spell of our non-rational faculties, most specifically the imagination, which leads us to place a heightened value on material goods and overindulge, leading us to sin.

With the origins of evil and theories of providence now in our armoury, we can begin to understand how Maimonides and Gersonides would treat the problem of evil. Let us begin with the simpler question. Why do the wicked prosper? The answer to this becomes very simple on their Aristotelian views, though it is only Gersonides who spells this out explicitly – Maimonides, as we will see in the next section, might ultimately have an alternative response at his disposal. As Gersonides notes, since general providence is determined by nature which is the same for everyone, the wicked will be affected as anyone else might be – whether positively or negatively. Thus, on Gersonides' understanding 'it does not follow that it is impossible for the sinners to receive benefits that are determined by the heavenly constellations' (*Wars*, IV: 6, 181). The evil can take advantage of nature much as anyone else can in order to gain material advantages. They will lack any individual providence, but will not lack the general providence that is quite literally a force of nature, and which on the whole is beneficial such that 'it is inappropriate for God ... to refrain from dispensing these marvellous benefits through the heavenly bodies just because of the infrequent evil that indirectly derives from them ...' (*Wars*, IV: 6, 185).

This raises the interesting point of why God should have created matter at all given its defective nature. Maimonides would have great difficulty accounting for this if he indeed believes in creation *ex nihilo*, but Gersonides, as we have seen, does not have to deal with this issue. Recalling our discussion of creation, according to Gersonides creation *ex nihilo* is impossible (**2.4**). Matter therefore existed and we do not have to account for God's creation of it. This does not necessarily solve all problems of course, since God's relationship to this eternal matter remains an issue – is he, for example, unable to sort out its deficiencies? Thus the attempt to absolve God of responsibility for matter's failings does not quite come off, giving us an indication of how answers to the problem of evil often suppress the problem, only for it to emerge elsewhere. But Gersonides can at least say that this is the best way the *material* world could be. Occasional misfortunes cannot be avoided.

In truth, this is not an easy position to defend, for one could surely make tiny adjustments to the natural material order that would alleviate all kinds of apparently unnecessary suffering. For example, could God not have created a world with one less fault line thus reducing earthquakes? If one argues that a *material* world could not have been created thus, then we would appear to be *really* limiting God's power. To argue that creation *ex nihilo* is logically impossible is one thing, but to argue that the conditions that God could impose on this formless matter are so limited seems far more problematic. So while we might argue that this is the best possible world given the existence of matter, in order to accept this we again have to fall back on there being certain unfathomable elements in God's ordering of the universe such that it is never going to be obvious to human reason that this is indeed the best possible world. So we again return to the idea, that the perfection of the world 'cannot be completely fathomed by the human mind' (*Wars*, IV: 6, 183), as Gersonides admits.

What of the sufferings of the righteous? Firstly, in his analysis of the book of Job, Gersonides notes how Job's afflictions fall into the two categories he has listed. Job is first afflicted by external evils affecting his family and possessions, through 'chance' events that are caused by matter. Subsequently, Job's own physical illness falls under the second category as coming from his own material failing, and given the description of Job as 'blameless and upright' in the opening verse of the book, we would assume that it is his physical rather than moral failings that are to blame. All of this leads Job to deny individual providence. But as Elihu points out to him, 'the Providence that is extended to the intellectual man is primarily because of his individual capacity to bring his potential power of conception into a state of actuality' (*CJ*, 232). Thus, while Job was morally upright, he was intellectually deficient, since he did not understand that God had given man the ability to gain providence through his intellect:

> He has given man an instrument whereby these evils can be avoided – reason. For man can avoid these evils either by right choice or by [being worthy of] providence in any of the forms previously mentioned. Anybody who does not endeavour to perfect his intellect according to its proper mode so that this providence will be connected with him should not complain if these evils fall upon him, for it is his fault that they have occurred. (*Wars*, IV: 6, 184)

Presumably, if Job had understood the nature of matter and the structure of the universe, he would have understood the nature of his suffering and might even have been able to avoid some of it. Moreover, Elihu reprimands him for not understanding that some of his suffering could have fallen under the category of providential suffering 'in order to turn him away from the path of rebellion towards which he was inclining', (*CJ*, 233), presumably as a result of his scepticism regarding individual providence. Correct understanding is therefore at the root of avoiding evil, or at times coming to terms with it by understanding its place in the grand divine scheme.

Yet while knowledge can clearly prevent our committing moral evil, and possibly even our avoiding predictable natural evils, how can it prevent the suffering that occurs as a result of factors beyond our control? How can it be that, as Maimonides writes,

> If a man's thought is free from distraction, if he apprehends Him, may He be exalted, in the right way and rejoices in what he apprehends, that individual can never be affected with evil of any kind... (*Guide*, III: 51, 625)

Losing one's child to a congenital disease, for example, can hardly be a result of one's ignorance.

Both Maimonides and Gersonides write how the pursuit of sensuous pleasures is a distraction that can sever the intellectual connection that constitutes providence and temporarily cut one off from this providential protection (which also, incidentally, accounts for the objection that the wicked would be able to profit if they are intellectually perfect – if they are sinning then by definition they are not intellectually connected with God). But we must recall that Job is righteous. One imagines that he cannot be accused of pursuing sensuous pleasures to the detriment of himself or those around him. So we are back with the problem of evil. How can Job's loss of his family be down to his ignorance? Is it just an effect of general providence as we mentioned? Is Job just collateral damage?

4. TRANSCENDING EVIL

During his comments on Job, Maimonides suggests a radical approach to the problem of evil that could even be applied to the most difficult cases. For Job's mistake, according to Maimonides, was to give too much emphasis to the material. With the ultimate intellectual perfection, however, Job attains true happiness and the realisation that 'a human being cannot be troubled in it [life] by any of all the misfortunes in question' (*Guide*, III: 23, 492–3). It is not that Job could have avoided the loss of his family if only he had been at a higher level of intellectual perfection. Rather, Job misunderstood what was truly valuable.

Job erred in the value he placed on the material things that he lost. The solution to the problem of evil is thus to transcend our material natures.

Though Maimonides does acknowledge the necessity of physical health and political stability for the ultimate goal of intellectual perfection he nonetheless concludes that if one apprehends God 'in the right way and rejoices in what he apprehends, that individual can never be afflicted with evil of any kind' (*Guide*, III: 51, 625). As Maimonides notes, Job is praised for his moral attributes, but is not called 'wise'. It is only once he understands what is truly valuable and thus understands the true value of intellectual perfection, and thus the true mechanism of providence, at least to the limits of human capacity, that he is able to transcend his physical suffering. Thus, in a sense it is our material nature that is responsible for our even posing the problem of evil. One can avoid the question altogether if one has the correct system of values in place that allows one to transcend physical suffering through the experience of eternity through intellectual contemplation. With such a worldview, the delights of the intellect can overcome any material suffering.

Gersonides does not appear to take quite such as extreme line. He does agree that 'it is apparent with a bit of reflection that true reward and punishment do not consist of these benefits and evils that we observe... [H]uman good consists of the acquisition of spiritual happiness' (*Wars*, IV: 6, 182). Thus, the realisation of what is truly valuable will allow one to 'see through' much apparent injustice, and withstand much of the apparent suffering. The perfect individual will at worst understand that the materially bound natural order, rather than God, is really responsible for that which he cannot avoid. But Gersonides does think that there simply will be unavoidable and undeserving casualties of the defective nature of matter, and the suffering through illness of an innocent child would be a classic example, though at times he seems to equivocate over whether this is simply nature, or whether there is some unknown divine justice at work.

In conclusion, we saw that for Saadia, suffering is often justified as a means to a post mortem end, and what we have discovered is that ultimately, there is a sense in which this is also the case for Maimonides and Gersonides too. Genuine knowledge, including that of the true spiritual happiness at which humans ought to aim, allows us to understand the workings of providence and either avoid or transcend the evils that might come our way. By the end of the book, Job has travelled this road to a correct understanding of divine providence together with a correct stance towards reward and punishment. But Gersonides appears to acknowledge that sometimes we will be unable to avoid certain evils that are down to matter and cannot really be justified, at least not by our rational calculations. On Maimonides' approach those evils that are unavoidable are also never really justified. But instead, they become insignificant. This again comes down to the medieval fascination with the intellect and downplaying of the animal side of our nature, both descriptively and prescriptively. From a twenty-first-century perspective, it might be more difficult to be so enamoured of the delights of the intellect as to ignore the physical and mental horrors of radical evil, though many medieval thinkers, Maimonides among them, fled terrible persecutions and were still able to offer such views. In the end though, Saadia, Maimonides and Gersonides appear to share the idea that the true reward is the key to solving the problem of evil, though they differ radically over the understanding of that reward. So, to end on a more upbeat note, in order to complete the picture we should briefly look at exactly how they construed these rewards and punishments awaiting in the next world.

5. THE AFTERLIFE

Eschatology is the name given to studies of the concepts connected to the so-called 'end of days', including such ideas as messianism and life after death. A full study of Jewish eschatology is beyond our scope, and our comments will be directed only to the details most pertinent to our discussions. But other than making for an appropriate 'end', its connection to the last two chapters, especially to the philosophical psychology that forms the background of much of that discussion, warrants this short epilogue.

Saadia's treatment of the topic, while extensive, is of less philosophical interest than those of Maimonides and Gersonides. It will, though, introduce us to some of the important terminology. According to Saadia, after we die, our soul – which is a physical substance, though far more refined than any other, including that of the heavenly spheres – works its way up (or down in the case of sinners) to a place of storage, so to speak, until 'the number of souls which His wisdom has deemed necessary to create has been fulfilled' (*Emunot*, VI: 1, 235). At that point, body and soul will be reunited for final judgement. Preceding this resurrection, however, the righteous will be resurrected earlier in this world to enjoy the messianic redemption that precedes the end of the world but inaugurates the new world – *Olam ha-ba*, or the World to Come – in which all are resurrected for the aforementioned final retribution and eternal reward is granted to the righteous. Thus we have (1) the resurrection of the dead in (2) the messianic age (brought by a personal messiah descended from the house of David), which is a prelude to the qualitatively different historical age of (3) *Olam ha-ba,* the World to Come, a phrase that incidentally only first appears in the *Mishnah* – the other two have more explicit, if limited, biblical antecedents. Each of these is discussed in detail by Saadia and subsequent writers, but from our perspective it is the last of the three – *Olam ha-ba* – that is of particular significance.

When Saadia speaks of the great reward awaiting the righteous that were chosen to suffer in this world, he has in mind both resurrection in the messianic age and eternal life in *Olam ha-ba.* Such is the nature of the reward with which those who suffer will be recompensed. None of this alleviates any of the philosophical difficulties we had with his approach to the problem of evil – but at least we now know what we're getting for our troubles. When it comes to Maimonides, however, we are on very different territory.

While for Saadia, there is single timeline along which, at a certain point, there will be a transition from this world to *Olam ha-ba,* for Maimonides this is not the case. While the messianic era remains a historical period during which the dead will be resurrected (though there is some doubt as to whether or not Maimonides truly believed in the resurrection of the dead), *Olam ha-ba* is an entirely different matter. This World to Come, according to Maimonides, exists parallel to our world as the abode of our disembodied souls that exist after the death of our mortal bodies in this world. *Olam ha-ba* for Maimonides is not something that will come into existence at an appointed historical time. It exists now, but in a parallel dimension, so to speak. And it is the immortal soul in *Olam ha-ba* that is the concept of central philosophical interest.

What is the nature of this post mortem existence in *Olam ha-ba?* As we noted in the last chapter, according to Maimonides it is through one's intellectual achievements that one gains immortality. Thus, of the different elements of the soul that we discussed at **4.1,** it is the intellect alone that survives in *Olam ha-ba.* This is explicit not only in *Guide,* III: 54, but also in Maimonides' more popular works, where he interprets the Talmudic dictum that 'in the world to come there is no eating, drinking, washing, anointing, or sexual intercourse; but the righteous sit with their crowns on their heads enjoying the radiance of the divine presence' (*bBerakhot* 17a) as meaning that

In the world to come, there is nothing corporeal, and no material substance; there are only the souls of the righteous without bodies... The phrase 'their crowns on their heads' refers to the knowledge they have acquired, and on account of which they have attained life in the world to come.

So Maimonides believes that it is through our intellect that we achieve our immortality, and presumably the greater the actualisation of the intellect the greater one's 'portion' in the world to come. This is the true reward, the appreciation of which allows us to transcend physical evil as we have seen. It is a reward, moreover, of which we can gain glimpses in this world if we are sufficiently devoted to the intellectual life. Through our intellects we can attain a hint of eternity in the here and now.

In a sense this just exacerbates the worries from the previous chapter regarding prioritising the intellect over practice. For surely, it would be argued, one's place in *Olam ha-ba* is determined by one's observance of *mitzvot*, not by the amount of philosophical demonstrations one has studied. As Hasdai Crescas noted, 'it is one of the principles of the Law and the tradition that by performance of the commandments a man attains eternal life...' (*Light*, II: VI, 1, 429). Nonetheless, this intellectualism is clearly Maimonides' view of the matter, as it is Gersonides', in a slightly different variation. And thus, much in the same way as prophecy and providence were natural achievements of man rather than direct divine dispensations, immortality turns out to be similarly defined. God does not, on this model, watch and tick off how many *mitzvot* we perform in order to grant us our place in heaven, come the time. Rather, based on the Aristotelian ideas first discussed in **4.3**, as the initially material or hylic human intellect actualises its potential, it becomes an intellect *in actu*. Both for Aristotle himself and Maimonides after him, this actualised or Acquired Intellect (the two were often distinguished by the Arabic Aristotelians but appear to be treated as one and the same by Maimonides), was the only immortal element of the human soul. Thus, one's Acquired Intellect simply *is* immortal and will survive one's bodily death. We know that the *mitzvot* contribute to this end as they are ultimately in the service of intellectual perfection. But one is not rewarded with some external reward at a divine 'prize day' for the performance of *mitzvot*. Rather, the Acquired Intellect naturally survives one's death without God having to *do* anything. That is simply how God 'set things up' in the first place. Such is the way of nature for Maimonides, and Gersonides similarly sees the intellect as the key to immortality, though the two rationalists differ in their precise understanding of the nature of and relationship between the various 'intellects' involved in human cognition. Gersonides might also have had a wider conception of the kind of knowledge that is the key to eternity, since he certainly believes that 'human perfection lies in the acquisition of knowledge of the sublunar world' (*Wars*, I: 13, 223), something that is more debateable in the case of Maimonides.

Other than the emphasis that is again being put on intellectual achievement over and above performance of *mitzvot*, this type of view is very troubling for a number of reasons. According to Crescas, all these varieties of intellectualism, 'destroy the Law and rip out the roots of the tradition', while also being 'demonstrably untenable from the point of view of philosophic speculation'[5] (*Light*, II: VI, 1, 428). Thus, among Crescas' many objections we find him arguing that this view would lead to the absurdity (at least according to Crescas), that 'he who intellectually cognizes one of the *intelligible* of the *intelligibilia* of geometry, inasmuch as they exist in the soul of the Active Intellect, will live eternally!' (*Light*, II: VI, 1, 438). As Crescas notes, on this view an evil mathematician would merit eternal reward. Although we know from our discussion of providence that both Maimonides and Gersonides believe that human beings sever any relationship with the Active Intellect when engaged in sinful acts, it seems very difficult to suppose that they cannot possibly have demonstrated any truths during their lifetime. And therefore, as Crescas notes, it would be very difficult to see how they could fail to gain a degree of immortality on their theory. Thus immortality simply seems too easy to attain, especially on Gersonides' more inclusive view of what constitutes knowledge.

In fact, Crescas skewers intellectualist views of immortality from both directions. If the sorts of truths that give us access to *Olam ha-ba* are too mundane, anyone merits reward. But limiting the type of knowledge that guarantees us eternity to something more rarefied such as our apprehension of God, as does Maimonides in many people's opinion, will not help matters. For while it might conceivably rule out evildoers, according to Maimonides' own theory of attributes immortality now becomes impossible. As Crescas notes, if we follow Maimonides' theory of negative attributes, then we cannot actually gain any true representation of God in our minds. And if that is the case then, as Crescas puts it

> the cognition will be imperfect, and, surely [the intelligibile] will not be in the intellect as it is extramentally. And so, I wish I knew how this deficient intelligibile, which does not exist so extramentally, becomes constituted as a substance! (*Light*, II: VI, 1, 438)

Effectively, Crescas' point is that if the idea we have does not actually represent the truth as it is (or 'extramentally' as it is translated above), then how can the ideas be true and actualise the human intellect? And if there is not such actualised or Acquired Intellect, there is nothing that can go on to exist independently and eternally. So on Crescas' critique, depending on the sort of knowledge that yields immortality, it either becomes virtually automatic, or altogether impossible.

Even if there were some way around this dilemma, there are greater concerns with such intellectualist models as soon as we understand the nature of what survives. We are talking here of the survival of pure intellect, devoid of any matter. But as such, how are we to 'recognise' different individual intellects? They no longer come in neat individual packages as they did when conjoined with a body. But how then can we distinguish one from the other? Or as philosophers might put it, how can we individuate them? If not by some property obvious to sense perception, perhaps we think we may be able to distinguish them through some sort of personality traits. Even if it were conceivable for us to recognise character traits at all in disembodied form, which is debateable, once we recognise that we are dealing here with pure abstract intellect, we ought to be aware that it will not have a 'personality'. If all that survives is intellect, then the elements of the human soul that might give rise to such a thing as 'character' have not survived. The very idea of individualised intellects becomes almost impossible to conceive on this model. We are left, it seems, with a pure intellect that cannot really be identified as the individual to whom it once belonged, so to speak. Indeed, it looks as if we would simply be left with one undifferentiated intellect, and buried deep in a discussion of the (faulty) proofs of the *mutakallimun* for creation, Maimonides seems to admit this:

> Now you know that regarding the things separate from matter – I mean…intellects – there can be no thought of multiplicity of any mode whatever, except that some of them are causes of the existence of others… However, what remains of Zayd is neither the cause nor the effect of what remains of Umar. Consequently, all are one in number. (*Guide*, I: 74, 221)

The idea of *personal* immortality thus seems very difficult to construct on the Maimonidean picture.

Gersonides does attempt to deal with this issue by pointing to the individualised 'packages' of knowledge that survive. My Acquired Intellect will differ from that of someone else as a result of the specific knowledge that

I have acquired. My knowledge of football might differentiate me from my wife, who is sadly deficient in such knowledge, but has greater knowledge of art history which would individuate her (though for Gersonides, neither of these would be genuine bodies of knowledge on which immortality rests). As Gersonides puts it

> one piece of knowledge can be common to Reuben and Simon yet differ in them insofar as the kind of unity differs in them; ... For when someone acquires more knowledge within a particular science, the unity of his knowledge in [his Acquired Intellect] differs from the unity of knowledge of someone who has acquired less knowledge in that science. (*Wars*, I: 13, 224)

Again, however, quite how these abstract packages of knowledge survive as individuals is a mystery. And more significantly, those with concerns for personal immortality do not seem any better off. My knowledge might survive, but I, as the subject of that knowledge, who on traditional understandings of reward and punishment ought surely to be the beneficiary in any afterlife, am not there to enjoy it. All that survives is the knowledge. It appears then, as if on the intellectualist models of Maimonides and Gersonides, quite *who* will survive might be a moot point – it is more a question of *what* will survive. And to complete the circle we have traced in this chapter, whether any of this can ultimately provide any solace to those who suffer, or even intellectual satisfaction to those seeking solutions to the problem of evil, is highly questionable. It is worth nothing in conclusion, however, that we moderns are very 'self-obsessed' in both a colloquial and philosophical sense. The philosophical importance of the self is particularly modern, arguably stemming from Descartes in the sixteenth century. Whether it *reflected*, or *affected* the general culture in which it was produced can be debated, but it certainly renders theories such as these more difficult for us to accept than they would have been to the medievals. Nonetheless one could certainly debate whether the medieval attempt to transcend the ego is any less palatable than our egocentricity.

NOTES

1   Gersonides, *The Commentary of Levi ben Gerson (Gersonides) on the Book of Job*, trans. A. Lassen (New York: Bloch Press, 1946), 3. Hereafter referred to as *CJ*.

2   Saadia Gaon, *The Book of Theodicy: Translation and Commentary on the Book of Job*, trans. L. Goodman (New Haven: Yale University Press, 1988), 382. Hereafter referred to as *BT*.
3   Robert Eisen has an interesting further suggestion – that it refers to man's weak constitution that renders him liable to illness and other physical limitations, that among other things would keep him away from sin and generally humble him. See his *The Book of Job in Medieval Jewish Philosophy* (Oxford: Oxford University Press, 2004) 243, n.19.
4   D.Z. Phillips, *The Concept of Prayer* (London: Routledge, 1965), 93.
5   All quotes from Crescas in this chapter are taken from Warren Zev Harvey, *HCC*. 'Hasdai Crescas's Critique of the Theory of the Acquired Intellect', PhD dissertation, Columbia University, 1973.

FURTHER READING

The translations of Saadia and Gersonides on Job, referred to in the footnotes, each have very helpful introductions, as does J. David Bleich, *Providence in the Philosophy of Gersonides* (New York: Yeshiva University Press, 1973).

Robert Eisen, *The Book of Job in Medieval Jewish Philosophy* (Oxford: Oxford University Press, 2004), contains excellent chapters on the thinkers we have studied that contain discussions of their views on providence and evil.

A book-length treatment of the problem in Jewish philosophy, that includes but is not limited to the medieval period, is Oliver Leaman, *Evil and Suffering in Jewish Philosophy* (Cambridge: Cambridge University Press, 1997).

An excellent collection of articles on the problem of evil in general is Marilyn McCord Adams and Robert Adams (eds), *The Problem of Evil* (Oxford: Oxford University Press, 1990), though a beginner should be warned that some of the articles are quite advanced.

For an excellent introduction to the eschatological views of our thinkers, see Arthur Hyman, *Eschatological Themes in Medieval Jewish Philosophy* (Milwaukee, WN: Marquette University Press, 2002).

Concluding Remarks

If this book has achieved its goal, then you will now have an understanding of some of the concepts and arguments that dominated medieval Jewish philosophy. You may also have built up a picture of broader trends of thought, more or less sympathetic to specific schools of philosophy, which emerged from that period. And of course, while I wouldn't hold out too much hope, if either Maimonides or Gersonides were correct, you may even have achieved a small degree of immortality. Given the discussion at the end of the previous chapter, that might not be something that we moderns will get terribly excited about. Sometimes, however, confronting our modern prejudices with those of an alternate worldview can act as a useful corrective.

This naturally leads us to the question of why we should bother studying the arguments of medieval thinkers with worldviews very different from our own, based on an outmoded scientific understanding of the world that can yield little of use to a twenty-first-century reader. There are, of course, many reasons that people study subjects that might not have *any* direct practical utility, and I am not about to launch into any generalised defence of such study here. While I find things of intrinsic and sometimes enduring philosophical interest in some of the arguments presented, the subject can stand or fall on its own without any special pleading from me, and you will have your own reasons if you have come this far. But by way of conclusion, it is worth noting the manner in which all the thinkers we have discussed approach Jewish philosophy.

Some of the rationalistic views even of highly influential figures from the post-Talmudic history of Judaism, such as Maimonides and Gersonides, could certainly give cause for concern to traditional religious believers. The engagement with philosophy does yield some highly non-standard philosophies that would continue to trouble some within various groupings of contemporary Judaism. And yet, with respect to his views on immortality for example, Gersonides insists that 'we have not assented to the view that our reason has suggested without determining its compatibility with our Torah' (*Wars*, I: 14, 226). There is probably no more fitting summary of the self-perception of all of our thinkers. Both Maimonides and Gersonides explicitly recognise that not everyone is suited to the philosophical study of Judaism, and are only concerned with 'those who are deeply perplexed by these questions and who are not satisfied with what is merely said about the secrets of existence' (*Wars*, Introductory Remarks, 94). And the reason for these perplexities and the philosophies they motivated was nothing other than the dual, yet absolute commitment to the religion of Judaism and to seeking the truth. Whether we are dealing with the views of Saadia and Judah Halevi, which converge from different directions on conclusions that might be deemed more traditional, or those of Maimonides and Gersonides, philosophy was not something that had to be left at the gates of religious piety.

Even the most dedicated rationalists among our thinkers would, however, have agreed that 'man's intellect indubitably has a limit at which it stops. There are therefore things regarding which it has become clear to man that it is impossible to apprehend them' (*Guide*, I: 31, 65). Yet at the same time

> Do not think that what we have said with regard to the insufficiency of the human intellect and its having a limit at which it stops is a statement made in order to confirm to Law. For it is something that has already been said and grasped by the philosophers without their having concern for a particular doctrine or opinion. (*Guide*, I: 31, 67)

Reason, if correctly applied, should recognise its limits without having to be slapped down by religion. Nevertheless, reason could and did force Jews to reassess their most sacred texts since 'in all things whose true reality is known through demonstration there is no tug of war and no refusal to accept a thing proven – unless indeed such refusal comes from an ignoramus...' (*Guide*, I: 31, 66). Thus, as Gersonides tells us

if reason causes us to affirm doctrines that are incompatible with the literal
sense of Scripture, we are not prohibited by the Torah to pronounce the truth
on these matters, for reason is not incompatible with the true understanding
of the Torah. The Torah is not a law that forces us to believe false ideas. (*Wars*,
Introductory Remarks, 98)

We have seen many applications of this in the course of our study,
whether regarding ascriptions of corporeality to God, the nature of God's
omniscience, or the concept of immortality.

Both a literal-minded approach to religion, and blind optimism
regarding the self-sufficiency of human reason have their limits. The
differences between some of our thinkers emerge from where they
place those limits. So, while philosophical truth could not be
contradicted by the Torah even for Judah Halevi (see *Kuzari*, I: 67,
47), in his opinion it could only ever be a preliminary stage in the
search for the ultimate truth. For Maimonides and Gersonides, in
contrast, attaining philosophical truth is the ultimate human, indeed
religious perfection.

It is the unyielding commitment to the pursuit of truth by those of
total religious commitment that remains an intriguing model to this day.
Indeed especially in this day where total commitment to a religion can
often be put at odds with any engagement with contemporary culture,
and vice versa. That the two were not mutually exclusive in medieval
times might make one suspicious of any claim that they must be today,
from whichever direction that claim is advanced. Neither religious nor
intellectual integrity need necessarily be sacrificed at the altar of the
other. One need not be forced into the principled rejection of either if it
is possible, in contrast, to find something of value in both. In
Maimonides' words again, the one who forsakes reason in order to hold
onto an absolute biblical literalism that would contradict reason brings
'loss to himself *and harm to his religion*' (*Guide*, Introduction to the First
Part, 6, emphasis added). For Jewish thinkers, leaving reason at the
synagogue door might not only be intellectually dishonest – it could be
harmful to one's religion. Maimonides therefore counsels us to 'accept
the truth from whatever source it proceeds'.[1] While the very idea that
philosophy is able to demonstrate absolute truths at all is a matter of
intense debate in this postmodern age, if the 'truth' turns out to be that
there is no absolute truth, then that will be the next challenge for Jewish
philosophy to meet.

NOTE

1   Maimonides, 'Eight Chapters', trans. Joseph I. Gorfinkle, repr. in I. Twersky
     (ed.), *A Maimonides Reader* (New York: Behrman House, 1972), 363.

Appendix:

Maimonidean Esotericism

Throughout this book we have been aware that the readings of Maimonides, while not at all idiosyncratic and finding plenty of support in the scholarship, will certainly be contradicted by someone somewhere. While the writings of all great thinkers can yield divergent interpretations when subjected to close analysis, in the case of Maimonides this is exacerbated in the extreme by his frank admission that there are contradictions in the *Guide*, some of which are intended to protect the masses from what, for them, would be troubling ideas. Given the centrality of this issue in Maimonidean scholarship, it is important to dedicate a short discussion to one example of possible Maimonidean esotericism.

The much studied case we will analyse stems from the type of seemingly innocuous comment, to which we referred in passing at **4.2**, that the careful reader will seize upon as an indication that all is not as it appears:

> The opinions of people concerning prophecy are like their opinions concerning the eternity of the world or its creation in time. I mean by this that just as the people to whose mind the existence of the deity is firmly established, have, as we set forth, three opinions concerning the eternity of the world or its creation in time, so there are also three opinions concerning prophecy. (*Guide*, II: 32, 360)

The point of departure is simple. Maimonides tells us that 'the diction of this Treatise has not been chosen at haphazard, but with great exactness and exceeding precision' (*Guide*, Instruction with Respect to this Treatise, 15). So would he take the time to state this numerical identity between opinions on creation and prophecy with such prolixity if that were really all there was to the comparison? Is there something significant in his drawing our attention to this? By comparing the opinions carefully, we might unearth something concealed beneath his exoteric presentation.

Let us then set out the opinions with their attributions:

Creation (*Guide*, II: 13):

C1 Creation *ex nihilo*: 'all who believe in the Law of *Moses our Master*'

C2 Creation out of pre-existent matter: 'all the philosophers of whom we have heard reports' and 'also the belief of Plato'

C3 Eternity: Aristotle

Prophecy (*Guide*, II: 32):

P1 Prophecy as an entirely supernatural gift: 'the multitude of those among the pagans and … some of the people professing our Law'

P2 Prophecy as a natural perfection: 'the philosophers'

P3 Prophecy as a natural perfection that can be prevented by divine intervention: 'our Law'

We know that at the exoteric level, Maimonides argues for creation *ex nihilo* (C1) and the view that prophecy is a natural perfection that God can prevent from occurring (P3). But what might a closer comparison between the opinions reveal? The question is how to draw the correspondences here, for they can be drawn in a number of ways.

We might first naturally draw comparisons on the basis of the views themselves as does Herbert Davidson. We can compare creation *ex nihilo* (C1) and prophecy as a supernatural phenomenon (P1), on the grounds that both are simply divine miracles. Yet the problem Davidson notes with this is that while C1 is identified as the opinion of those who believe in the Law of Moses, P1 with which it is equated is primarily that of the pagans, and admittedly some of those '*professing* our Law' (emphasis added). What then would this lack of correspondence indicate? We could see this as an example of a 'contradiction': Maimonides compares the views of creation to those of prophecy, but then 'contradicts' this in the execution of the comparison, which breaks down.[1] The esotericist claims that this is precisely why Maimonides points us towards the correspondence – so that we will note that it is not genuine and that hidden within this problem is the key to his real views.

Appendix

So Maimonides presents two sets of positions some chapters apart, associates the two sets of positions at *Guide*, II: 32, but then describes the positions in a manner that disrupts the correspondences between them, no doubt in the hope that inattentive readers – the masses – will simply gloss over these differences since they 'must in no way be aware of the contradiction' (*Guide*, Introduction, 17). But if this is one of Maimonides' hidden 'contradictions', what would he be hiding? We need to decide whether Maimonides intends us to accept that the opinions really do correspond or not.

Saying that the opinions genuinely correspond would lead us to try to match them up, which would leave us with a choice: either we say that 1) creation *ex nihilo* (C1) is the view of Torah and therefore the comparable supernatural view of prophecy (P1) is the genuine view of Torah contrary to Maimonides' assertion; or we say 2) (P1) is a false pagan view as stated, and thus so is the comparable (C1) – creation *ex nihilo* – contrary to Maimonides' exoteric assertion. Of the two choices, which would Maimonides have reason to hide? Surely, it is argued, he would only have reason to hide (2). Option (1) would be more than acceptable to the masses since it ascribes both creation and prophecy to miraculous divine intervention. But on option (2) Maimonides would be indicating that he actually believes that creation *ex nihilo* (C1) is a 'pagan' view like (P1), i.e. it is a view that the vulgar 'professing our Law' might accept, but is not in fact the true view of the Torah. Only this latter view would need concealing from the masses. Thus, the statement regarding the comparison, indicating to us that the three opinions ought to match, is the 'true' statement, and if so, the attributions within the positions are false. This Maimonides must conceal from the masses since it implies that despite appearances to the contrary, Maimonides did not believe in creation *ex nihilo*, and more importantly did not believe it to be the true teaching of the Torah.[2]

This is all very well, but it tells us nothing about which of the remaining views on creation Maimonides does endorse. If we continue to look at the mismatch between the theories and their attributions, however, we see that there is a structural correspondence between the genuine view on prophecy – a natural account with the possibility of divine intervention (P3) – and the Platonic view of creation according to which there is a certain natural structure of matter and God intervenes to form the world (C2). In both of these we have an admixture of naturalism and divine intervention. Yet the former is the view of 'our Law', whereas the latter is attributed to the philosophers and Plato. So yet again the positions on creation and prophecy match very well from a structural perspective, but the attributions do not. Davidson's argument here, therefore, is that Maimonides might have been trying to hide his belief in the Platonic view of creation through the device of contradiction. Again the assertion that the positions can be compared is contradicted in the breakdown of the comparison and we have a further decision to make. Either we say that 1) (C2) is the false Platonic view of creation as stated, and therefore the comparable (P3) is actually a false view of prophecy, despite Maimonides' assertion that it is the Torah view; or we say that 2) (P3) is indeed the Torah view of prophecy as Maimonides states, and thus (C2), the comparable Platonic theory of creation is similarly the view of the Torah, contrary to his explicit assertions. Again we can ask, of the two choices, which would Maimonides have reason to hide? And again, we would surely answer that he would only have reason to hide the second.

According to Davidson this conclusion is further indicated by another contradiction in Maimonides' discussion of creation. On the one hand, Maimonides defends his decision to refute the Aristotelian view and ignore the Platonic view at *Guide*, II: 13 by stating that 'there is, in our opinion, no difference between those who believe that heaven must of necessity be generated from a thing and pass away into a thing or the belief of Aristotle' (*Guide*, II: 13, 285), i.e. there is no difference between the Platonic and Aristotelian views on creation. Just twelve chapters later, however, he tells us that the Aristotelian view 'destroys the Law in its principle' while the Platonic view 'would not destroy the foundations of the Law ... [and] it would also be possible to interpret figuratively the texts in accordance with this opinion' (*Guide*, II: 25, 328), which frankly seems like all the difference in the world.

Again, we can ask which of these views Maimonides would wish to conceal. Surely the masses would be more than happy to read that Plato and Aristotle are similarly problematic. They would be less amenable to being told that the Platonic position is unproblematic. Therefore this concealed contradiction is there to indicate to the careful reader that Maimonides is actually in sympathy with the Platonic position on creation. According to Davidson then, the various 'contradictions' all concern the Platonic view, revealing that *it* is Maimonides' true belief regarding creation, rather than creation *ex nihilo*. We can note for the sake of completion that for Davidson there is a simple correspondence between the two naturalistic positions C3 and P2.

Davidson's argument is based on what he has termed narrow esotericism, according to which Maimonides does indeed contradict himself on specific issues when there is a need to conceal specifics from the masses. But on the whole, and in the absence of any such contradiction, he can be taken at his word. Others follow a more thoroughgoing esotericism, according to which Maimonides is dissimulating throughout the entire book. The system in its entirety is designed to be inoffensive at the exoteric level for the traditionalist. But buried deep beneath the exoteric layer is an entire esoteric system that undermines traditional views. This leads to further questions regarding whether or not Maimonides believed this basically Aristotelian esoteric layer to be compatible with Judaism.

To this end, many have argued that Maimonides in fact follows the Aristotelian position on creation. Thus, while Davidson argues for a [C1: P1, C2: P3, C3: P2] correspondence, with Maimonides upholding C2 and P3, Warren Zev Harvey argues for a straightforward [C1: P1, C2: P2, C3: P3] match, with Maimonides holding C3 and P3. Presumably, the point of the creation-prophecy correspondence would then be the simple numerical correspondence – that just as he accepts the third view on prophecy, he also accepts the third view on creation. A detailed examination of the basis for attributing the Aristotelian theory of eternity to Maimonides would require more analysis than we have space for here, though one can probably see how comfortably the view would fit with the majority of the views we have attributed to Maimonides in the course of this book. We can, however, give a few indications of some of the strategies used.

One can begin by weakening Maimonides' claims for creation *ex nihilo* in the manner noted above in the comparison between C1 and P1, and many also note that it is constantly referred to as 'our opinion' rather than 'my opinion'. But one can also undermine his apparent critique of Aristotle's arguments for eternity. Jonathan Malino, for example, has pointed out that the principle on which his argument against Aristotle is based is highly problematic. To remind ourselves of the principle:

> No inference can be drawn in any respect from the nature of a thing after it
> has been generated, has attained its final state, and has achieved stability in
> its most perfect state, to the state of the thing while it moved toward being
> generated. Nor can an inference be drawn from the state of the thing when it

moves toward being generated to its state before it begins to move thus. (*Guide*, II: 17, 295)

One of the many weapons in Malino's armoury is to question whether the principle actually makes sense. The problem is that it talks in temporal terms – 'after', 'before', 'while it moved toward' – but given that time is itself among the things created according to Maimonides, such temporal terms can only make sense in application to things in their final state. The very idea of 'the state of the thing when it moves toward being generated' makes no sense. Thus the principle itself cannot be stated coherently, let alone applied against Aristotle's supposed demonstrations.

Other than weakening Maimonides' claims both for C1 and against C3, there are more positive reasons for attributing C3 to Maimonides. We have already seen in chapter 1 that he bases his argument for the existence of God on the eternity of the world, though he claims this is a purely methodological matter (see **1.1**). At the same time, however, he uses it as the premise of his proof in his *Mishneh Torah* 'Laws of the Foundations of the Torah', 1: 1, as well portraying the patriarch Abraham as establishing God's existence on the basis of the eternal motion of the spheres in 'Laws of Idolatry', 1: 3. There are many more textual hints and allusions to which one can point in support of this view, summarised in Harvey's discussion.

After all of this, if one wishes to maintain that Maimonides' professed belief in creation *ex nihilo* is sincere, one could argue that the key to the correspondence lies in the attributions themselves. Thus, according to Lawrence Kaplan, the correspondence could be [C1: P3, C2: P1, C3: P2]. Creation *ex nihilo*, as the view of the Torah, corresponds to the view of our Law on prophecy. The former is miraculous, and thus the latter can contain a miraculous element of divine intervention as well. Kaplan does however allow that Maimonides might have believed in the Aristotelian view of eternity (C3), and if so, would also have believed in the purely naturalistic view of prophecy (P2). Indeed, none of the scholars mentioned here make any exalted claims for their arguments, offering them as contributions to a debate rather than with any degree of certainty, and Davidson, like Kaplan, charts an alternative route to a different conclusion.

In closing, it is important to note that these disputes over teachings that Maimonides might have concealed are not a new phenomenon. While they might appear particularly suited to various postmodern methods of dealing with texts, these esoteric readings of Maimonides have been proposed since the *Guide* first appeared. Indeed, Davidson's and Kaplan's conclusions were first suggested in the fifteenth and sixteenth centuries. Thus, Leo Strauss, the name most associated with esotericism in the modern age, was simply breathing new life into a medieval tradition. There is little doubt that over 800 years on, these disputes are no closer to a final resolution.

NOTES

1 Technically speaking there is no actual contradiction here. Maimonides simply tells us that there are three opinions on creation and three on prophecy, which is true, and entirely compatible with there being differences between the opinions. Marvin Fox has argued that Maimonides was aware that his contradictions were not technical contradictions and hence he used a different Arabic word for them, which Pines translates as 'divergences'. For brevity we will continue to use the term 'contradiction' here, but Fox's point is a good one. See Marvin Fox, *Interpreting Maimonides* (Chicago: University of Chicago Press, 1990), chapter 4.

2 Indeed, while the treatment of Maimonides in chapter 2 was offered with the aim of making some philosophically interesting points, I myself have some sympathy with this position.

FURTHER READING

For a good general discussion of Maimonidean interpretation see Part I of Marvin Fox, *Interpreting Maimonides* (Chicago: University of Chicago Press, 1990).

Two articles by Aviezer Ravitzky discuss medieval and modern esotericism concerning the *Guide*: 'Samuel Ibn Tibbon and the Esoteric Character of the *Guide of the Perplexed*', and 'The Secrets of Maimonides: Between the Thirteenth and Twentieth Centuries', which appear as chapters 7 and 8 of his *History and Faith: Studies in Jewish Philosophy* (Amsterdam: J. C. Gieben, 1996).

While Leo Strauss' views developed over time, the work that reignited the whole debate over Maimonides' esotericism was his *Persecution and the Art of Writing* (Glencoe, IL: Free Press, 1952), 38–94. See also his introduction to the Pines translation of the *Guide*: 'How to Begin to Study *The Guide of the Perplexed*'.

The solutions to the creation-prophecy puzzle discussed in this Appendix can be found in Lawrence Kaplan, 'Maimonides on the Miraculous Element in Prophecy', *Harvard Theological Review*, vol. 70, (1977), 233–56; Herbert A.

Davidson, 'Maimonides' Secret Position on Creation', in I. Twersky (ed.), *Studies in Medieval Jewish History and Literature*, vol. 1 (Cambridge, MA: Harvard University Press, 1979), 16–40; Warren Zev Harvey, 'A Third Approach to Maimonides' Cosmogony-Prophetology Puzzle', *Harvard Theological Review*, 74 (1981), 287–301; and Jonathan Malino, 'Aristotle on Eternity: Does Maimonides Have a Reply?', in S. Pines and Y. Yovel (eds), *Maimonides and Philosophy* (Dordrect: Martinus Nijhoff, 1986), 52–64.

See also Davidson's major work: *Moses Maimonides: The Man and His Works* (Oxford: Oxford University Press, 2005).

Glossary

Accident: A property that a substance could either have or not have without losing its identity as that type of substance.

Acquired Intellect: When the human intellect – initially in a state of potential for gaining knowledge and variously called the potential/material/Hylic Intellect – gains knowledge, it is actualised, and the resultant intellect is termed the Acquired Intellect.

Active Intellect: The final intellect in the chain of intellects that emanate from God. It governs the sublunar world and is the intellect with which we are somehow in contact when we gain knowledge.

Aggadah: Legends and lore in Jewish literature, though now sometimes used for all non-legal material, including philosophy and mysticism.

'Amr ilahi: Arabic term used by Judah Halevi that is difficult to translate, but a sort of 'divine principle', that denotes (among other things) that feature of certain human beings that enables them to receive prophecy.

Anthropomorphism: Attributing human form and characteristics to God.

Anthropopathism: Attributing human feelings and emotions to God.

Ash'arites: A school of *kalam* theologians, generally viewed as less rationalistic than their Mut'azilite counterparts.

Atomism: View of the universe as made up of tiny indivisible atoms that God destroys and recreates at each moment.

Cognitivism: The view that in a certain area, e.g. moral judgement, statements made are genuine knowledge claims that can thus be true or false.

Compatibilism: The view that acts can be both free and determined.

Consequentialism: The view that what makes an action right or wrong resides in the goodness (or badness) of its consequences. Contrasted with deontological theories according to which acts have intrinsic value.

Contingent: A term that, when applied to an entity, indicates that it does not have to exist. This is contrasted with a necessary existent that has to exist – it cannot possibly not exist – God being the only example. Can also be applied to truths, such that a contingent truth is one that we can conceive of as false – 'pigs do not fly' is a contingent truth – contrasted with a necessary truth, the denial of which would be self-contradictory, e.g. 'All bachelors are unmarried'.

Cosmogony: The study of the origins of the universe.

Cosmology: The study of the structure of the universe.

Creation *de novo*: Creation as a free act of God's will.

Creation *ex nihilo*: Creation out of absolute nonexistence.

Demonstration: A deductively valid argument from premises that are 'necessary', i.e. absolutely true and certain.

Determinism: The view that every event is determined. Causal determinism is the view that every event is determined by prior causes. Theological determinism is the view that events are determined by God's knowledge of them.

Dialectical argument: A deductive argument from premises that only hold 'for the most part'.

Glossary

Emanation: A process described by the Neoplatonists whereby, beginning from God, one thing produces another via an 'overflow' of its perfection, without itself being changed.

Empiricism: The view that sense experience is an important source of knowledge.

Episteme: Scientific understanding. The highest form of knowledge for Aristotle.

Epistemology: The study of the theory of knowledge.

Equivocal terms: Words that have two entirely different meanings, e.g. bank (bank of a river, or a financial institution).

Ergon: 'Function' or 'distinctive characteristic'.

Eschatology: Studies connected to the 'end of days' or end of history.

Esoteric: Concealed doctrines for the able few (in contrast to exoteric).

Essence: What makes a substance *that* substance and without which it would not be that substance, e.g. the three sides of a triangle.

Eudaimonia: Used by Aristotle as denoting the best life for man. Literally translates as happiness, but it is more appropriately understood to mean a flourishing life in this context.

Falasifa: Islamic philosophers who were contrasted to the more apologetic *kalam* theologians.

Final cause: Aristotelian concept of the 'cause' or explanation that explains something by reference to its purpose or goal, e.g. health is the final cause of jogging.

Halakhah: Jewish law.

Halitzah: The biblical levirate ritual, involving removing a shoe, whereby the brother-in-law is released from the obligation to marry the childless widow of his deceased brother.

Huqqim: 'Statutes' – used to denote commandments that appear to have no rationale that we can understand.

Hypostases: The substances produced via the process of emanation.

Imitatio dei: The imitation of God.

Incompatibilism: The view that freedom is incompatible with determinism.

Incorporeal: Something that has no body or material nature.

Ineffable: Beyond our knowledge and beyond description or characterisation, often used in relation to God.

Kalam: Islamic form of theology that began in the eighth century.

Ma'aseh Bereshit: 'The Account of the Beginning' – used to denote the opening chapters of Genesis which contain hidden teachings according to rabbinic tradition.

Ma'aseh Merkavah: 'The Account of the Chariot' – used to denote Ezekiel's vision in Ezekiel 1, and again believed to contain hidden teachings according to rabbinic tradition.

Midrash: A term that can be used for any rabbinic interpretation, but specifically used to denote certain rabbinic collections of biblical exegesis.

Mishnah: First written compilation of Oral Law, circa. 200 CE.

Mishpatim: 'Judgements' – usually used to denote commandments that can clearly be understood as rational by human beings.

Mitzvah (pl. Mitzvot): Commandments.

Mitzvot shimiyyot: Hebrew translation of Saadia's 'revealed commandments'.

Mitzvot sikhliyyot: Hebrew translation of Saadia's 'rational commandments'.

Mutakallimun: A practitioner of *kalam*.

Mut'azilites: The more 'rationalistic' school of *kalam* theologians.

Olam ha-ba: The world to come.

Ontology: The study of the basic constituents of existence – what types of thing exist.

Pesach: The Passover festival.

Predication: Attributing a property to something. Thus, in 'Fred is bald' we predicate baldness of Fred.

Privation: An absence or lack of something.

Psuche: Usually translated as soul, but more generally that which gives life to something.

Sabianism: An idolatrous sect that worshipped the stars.

Sha'atnez: A mixture of linen and wool in the same garment. The Torah forbids the wearing of such an item.

Shekhinah: Word used to denote God's immanence or 'presence'.

Syllogism: An argument comprising two premises that have a shared 'middle term', yielding a conclusion. Thus, 1) All men are mortal; 2) Socrates is a man; therefore 3) Socrates is mortal.

Ta'amei ha-mitzvot: The reasons for the commandments.

Talmud: Compilation of the Oral Law, composed of discussions based around the *Mishnah*. There is a *Babylonian Talmud* and a *Palestinian Talmud*. The former was compiled later and has become *the* Talmud.

Tanakh: The Hebrew Bible. Formed as an acronym of the three works of which it is composed: *Torah* (lit. instruction), *Nevi'im* (Prophets) and *Ketuvim* (Writings).

Theoria: Contemplation.

Torah: The five books of Moses – *Bereshit* (Genesis), *Shemot* (Exodus), *Vayikra* (Leviticus), *Bamidbar* (Numbers) and *Devarim* (Deuteronomy). Can also be used to refer to Jewish belief and practice in its entirety.

Tzara'at: Biblical term for a disease usually translated as leprosy.

Universals: General words that can be applied to (or predicated of) many things, e.g. 'red', or 'wise'.

Index

al-Farabi 14, 36, 57, 120
finite
    Power/force 70
    Time 72
    Universe 51, 70, 71
First Cause 38–40, 49, 51, 56–7, 74,
    111, 116, 117, 122, 125, 142, 160,
    162, 214, 215
First intelligible 30, 31, 35, 44,
    143, 197
First Mover 51
Fons Vitae 16
form 69, 76, 165–6, 167
    as final cause 143
    First Form 57
    of man 83, 144, 145, 189,
        193, 195, 200
Fox, Marvin 139, 153, 239n
freedom 156–8, 159, 162, 170, 171,
    173, 175–8
    and foreknowledge dilemma
        163, 164, 169, 174
freewill 101, 155, 157–8, 159–63,
    168, 172, 175–7, 212
future contingents 157–8, 167, 172–3

generation 61, 67–9
    and corruption 33–6, 39,
        47, 59
Genesis 20, 49, 74
Geonim and Geonic period 7
Gersonides 22–3, 82, 111, 158, 170,
    178, 229, 230, 231
    on causal determinism 162
    on creation 50, 60, 61, 64–5,
        66, 67, 68–9, 70–3, 74–6
    on divine attributes 94–8,
        99–100, 102
    on divine cognition 172
    on evil and suffering 206–7,
        217–20, 221–2

on future contingents
    and foreknowledge
        163–9, 173, 174, 77
    and heresy 170
    on intellect and immortality
        223–7
    metaphysics 216
    on prophecy 124

God
    of Abraham 41, 46
    as creator 31, 57, 62, 101,
        165, 166, 172
    essence 81, 90, 91, 93, 104
    the existence of 15, 27,
        28, 31, 32, 33, 41, 42, 43,
        45, 46, 49, 62, 74, 86, 206,
        238
    imitation of 191–2
    incorporeality of 38–40, 46,
        49, 51, 52, 53, 58, 80, 81,
        82, 86, 100, 117, 123
    knowledge 91, 95, 159,
        161–3, 170, 172, 174, 214,
        215
    as object of love 51
    of the philosophers 11, 132
    unity of 15, 38–40, 46,
        49, 53, 80, 81, 82, 83,
        88, 98–100, 144, 149,
        156
    volition of 57, 59
    see also divine; First Cause;
        necessary existent;
        negative attributes;
        negative theology;
        omnipotent; omniscience;
        omniscient; particulars;
        Unmoved Mover
good life 178, 180–8, 205
Greek philosophy 7, 8, 66
Guttmann, Julius 9, 46